Children of the Green

Raising Our Kids in Pagan Traditions

Children of the Green

Raising Our Kids in Pagan Traditions

Hannah E. Johnston

MOON
BOOKS

Winchester, UK
Washington, USA

First published by Moon Books, 2014

Moon Books is an imprint of John Hunt Publishing Ltd., Laurel House, Station Approach, Alresford, Hants, SO24 9JH, UK
office1@jhpbooks.net
www.johnhuntpublishing.com
www.moon-books.net

For distributor details and how to order please visit the 'Ordering' section on our website.

Text copyright: Hannah E. Johnston 2013

ISBN: 978 1 78279 374 8

A CIP catalogue record for this book is available from the British Library.

Design: Stuart Davies
www.stuartdaviesart.com

Printed and bound by CPI Group (UK) Ltd, Croydon, CR0 4YY

We operate a distinctive and ethical publishing philosophy in all areas of our business, from our global network of authors to production and worldwide distribution.

CONTENTS

Acknowledgments

Writing a book, even a small offering such as this, truly takes a village. This book was written over many years in tiny snippets here and there. A train ride to work, a 15-minute window at the park whilst the children played. It was inspired by a multitude of conversations with my family, kids, caretakers, teachers, doctors, babysitters, friends, dog walkers, witches, shop-keepers and neighbours. All mistakes are purely my own making and any moments of insight were probably fostered by some of these inspiring people.

I would like to offer my heartfelt thanks to Peg Aloi, who contributed the recipes for this book and championed it from its inception. A big thank you to those other family friends who made me a better parent and held me in the early moons of motherhood: Katie Fitch, Robin Bartlett, Kate Albers, Liz Koch, Dunja Pechstein and Heloise Saunders. To Jen and Whit Martin Wilson for Friday night sanity. Your children are a gift in my life. And deep gratitude to Jon and Valerie Grabiel Butler, who listened to my ramblings about some of the ideas here over many years, who trusted me with their children's love, and who at times loved my kids with greater insight and patience than I did. I wish every Ostara saw us rolling eggs together.

A shout out to the blossoming community of the Pagan Family Meet Up East, to the parents who offered their thoughts and insights and especially to my good friend Sam, who has always been up for another hare-brained scheme. And to Bear and Claire, my boys' Gods Parents, who cooked for me, and offered gentle editing suggestions.

And lastly, to all my family. Without you all none of this would have come to be. A special special thank you to Daniel, Summer and Boo for helping bring this into the world.

Blessed Bees... x

Introduction

Pagan, pagan, what are you seeking,
Through all the days of your long earthly tread?
Your sunrise and moonrise what chances are bringing?
And where will your travelling footsteps be led?
Extract from 'The Road', Doreen Valiente, 2000

A child is a seed of the future. If we want a vision of the planet's longevity we could look to the dreams of our children, for they embody our intentions and our aspirations. They are our desires made manifest. They are our sacred responsibility.

You may or may not be of a Pagan persuasion, but you have probably picked up this book because you are looking for an intentional way to raise a family, or to be with and work with kids. You may have a spirituality of your own making, or you may be a signed and sealed member of a particular Pagan path. Wherever you sit on this spectrum, we are all of us together in trying to work out how we are going to raise the next generation of children to have choices, and not be faced with imminent natural collapse due to our over-use of this precious world.

Many of us living in the early 20-teens are acutely aware of how the well-being of the world is becoming a daily part of our responsibility. No longer can we ignore all the signs of climate change, whatever its cause, no longer can we sit idly by whilst our most precious natural resources are the justification for war, famine and subjugation. With weather patterns changing and the rubbish mounds rising, we are faced with questions regarding our consumption needs and our waste. For many of us this call raises important social questions about the role of government, community leaders and, of course, religious faith. Some of us are moved to consider how we will be able to leave this earth for future generations.

Modern Western living with all of its screens and cellphones, champions the disposable and irreverent and too often disconnects us from the living rhythms of growth and decay that exist in the world around us. When we can have bananas at any time of the year and wear cheap clothes made by children halfway across the world, staying connected to the natural world is increasingly difficult. As popular culture requires, we are told that we need bigger, better, faster, more.

The cycles of nature, the seasons, the moon phases, the winds and the tides connect us to each other, the community and our vision for a better world. They are not disposable or replaceable. To live in closer relationship with them gives us a chance to make different choices about our lifestyle and our future. The wheel of the seasons is embedded in every aspect of a Pagan magical and celebratory life, irrespective of our different traditions. These cycles remind us that we are part of the great family of animals, and that like our brother stag and daughter frog we will share life's inevitable transformations as the sun's wheel turns. Families, the great shifting collections of kith and kin, root us in our experience of the sacred, the magical and the holy. They root us to the landscape we grow in. The family is a model organism and so many of us make or find new families in our friendship circles, our magical groups, clans and covens.

This book came about because I was looking for inspiring work on raising kids from within earth-centred spiritual traditions, something that helped me embrace this new identity as a parent and as a person who now had responsibility for two little ones. When I started to write, I had babies. I now have school-age kids. They could choose to reject it later if they wish (I joke that in order to rebel my sons will become gun-wielding, deer-hunting atheists) but I felt I was being dishonest if they didn't get to share in what was the ground of my personhood.

Maybe you feel the same about your kids. Perhaps you don't fit into any spirituality, but want a grounded sense of spirit and the divine in your family. Maybe you are interested in Paganism, but don't see how it is going to fit into your already packed family life. Perhaps you teach kids or run a preschool and want to offer something founded in nature to the kids you daily care for. Or you might be a community member who wants to include kids more fully in your celebrations and magical work. There is a place for you here, and others besides.

All of us are implicated in the raising of children, in the raising of a healthy new generation, whether or not we are parents. Think about your own childhood, about who influenced you, who challenged and championed you. Some of the most influential forces upon our childhoods lie outside our families: teachers, aunts, friends, and neighbours. When we talk about children, we are talking about everyone's future. And so we are all involved, whether we like it or not, in the caring for children as the earth's next guardians.

You may have picked up this book feeling that you would love to live a more spiritual, greener life. You can! Yet too often such intentions and desires for life are shaped and curtailed by the institutions that define where and how we live. Work, education, the law, home, family; these are the cultural institutions that we raise children within. Often these institutions do not reflect our philosophies; they may limit how we express our sacred intentions for our family or for ourselves. We negotiate due to necessity; you need to work so perhaps you put your kids in day-care, and harden yourself to make that work. You want your kids to go to a school where they will spend most of their time playing, but perversely it is a private school and will cost more than you could earn. You dream of building a 'green-home' or getting 'off-grid', but you have insufficient money for buying land, or a house, or solar panels, or even a garden. You want to adopt a child, but as an outspoken single gay witch you worry about the fight you will face. You want to live near your extended family, but they don't like your choice of life partner.

Or your choice of cats. Our visions of family require perpetual spinning. When we are alone, responsible for only ourselves we can be bold and revolutionary. When we have a family, revolutions are far riskier.

Having a family brings a whole new meaning to the word compromise, and often compromise's big burly brother, sacrifice. Rarely have we lived the reality of sacrifice as we do when we raise a family. As Pagans or fellow travellers (a term I use for those of us who don't identify as Pagan or dislike the label but share many sympathies, both philosophical and celebratory, with Pagans) we may have sacrificed incense for years, or perhaps made mythic sacrifice of bread to honour the annual cycle of the Corn Lord's death for the earth's renewal. But parenting brings us face to face with less mythic, less glorified sacrifices. We become 33rd Degree Masters of compromise. And it is not always easy.

I came to Paganism through a mystical encounter in my teens. One dull and dreary afternoon, I was 'visited' by a being that I believed was Fey, a being of light and power. At the time I was in the grip of an eating disorder. My recollection of this encounter today is as full of shimmer and light as it was then, but at the time I was convinced it was a visitation and a call to life. A series of life changes from this point (including, importantly, the recovery of my health) led me to meet some of the people who would shape the path of my adulthood and my spirituality forever. I embraced modern Paganism. My family had been 'magically' inclined so it was a small step for me conceptually. But Paganism was a place where my feminist politics and my spirit could talk to each other. For example, in most Pagan traditions, women are the embodiments of the sacred, which for a teen racked with an eating disorder was a radical concept. I cherished the knowledge that we needed no intercessor to speak to the divine. I felt that nothing was taken from me. I had to give up nothing of myself to join this path, but instead found a name for everything I had felt as a child and everything I longed for as a blossoming adult.

Motherhood, the generative force of creation, was the ultimate personification of magic. My relationship with my own mother went through a process of healing and my whole family became more involved in our local Pagan community. I immersed myself in the positive life enhancing images of the Goddess as maiden, mother and crone.

Despite being surrounded by images and stories of bounteous mothers for all my adult life, when I came to motherhood 15 years or so after coming to Paganism, my own experience seemed very different. In the very early days of parenting two sons, I found myself tackling my new role as mother and parent with intense frustration and at times deep depression. My old life felt discarded; my years as a university teacher, priestess and covener seemed surreal, at times irrelevant. All the skills I had spent my adult life gaining seemed useless in the face of the daily grind of coping with 'two under two'. My identity was shredded and I felt exhausted. The beatific sacred mothers I had given praise and made offerings to had dignity, they had poise and purpose. They seemed serene and filled with power. Maternal contentment exuded from the writings both ancient and modern in praise of the Great Mother. Where were the images of leaking, shrieking mothers, mothers who prayed to someone for a night's sleep or a moment to pee without an audience?

The old ways in which I could energise and reconnect with my life's purpose required quiet, peace and routine, all of which eluded me. I had no time, certainly no quiet, and the days dragged by, minutes expanding into hours as the rigmarole of nappy changes, walks, attempts at naps, attempts at entertainment and dilemmas regarding work vs staying home, breast-feeding versus bottle feeding consumed every aspect of me. Time took on an elastic quality and faced with the ever-present needs of an infant and a toddler, focusing on my spiritual well-being seemed both indulgent and unnecessary. Time could be better spent reading the vast array of 'how-to-be-a-better- parent' books, or going to infant swim classes, or baby sign classes, worrying whether I needed to take that infant first aid class or not. These were the new skills I needed, not tarot reading, aura feeling and dowsing, those abilities I had spent the past 20 years cultivating. Were the cards going to tell me whether or not I should look to nurse Summer for longer than a year? Should I dowse over the various infant socialisation classes to see which one would suit him the best? Perhaps I should have done, but it seemed suddenly a preposterous answer to the daily dilemmas of baby-raising. And so over many moons I felt my spirit fade; I mastered self-sacrifice like never before.

My sources of support were other new parents, and I became a researcher of new parenthood. And books. I began to eat books as I had done when I first came to Paganism, and during the period of writing my doctorate. Parenting was my new profession and I realised I was under researched. I looked to the writers from within my spiritual community, but although there are some glorious books celebrating raising children as Pagans, few seemed to address the transition into parenthood. My kids weren't at the age or stage where I could say I was 'raising Pagans' – in fact I felt ambivalent about that very notion when I first had kids. I was raised in a liberal bohemian family (more about them later) and came to the Craft as my family did – you could say we underwent a family conversion – why would my children not find their own path the same way? However, I felt the need to see what others had done to navigate this rocky rebirth, this initiation into the deepest mystery. As my own mother said, when I called her on a particularly tough day, "It is the act of parenting that is the initiation into the deepest of life's mysteries".

What I found was that by letting go, my spirituality could and did evolve to meet my changing status. In its very nature Paganism embraces change. I just had to release myself to its flow. In starting and raising a family, or working closely in support of families, many of us find our spirituality needs to evolve. For some of us, the pre-family community is no longer available or supportive. Or perhaps our lifestyle pre-pregnancy or pre-kids is not sustainable and needs to change. I recall visiting my close friend Sam when I was newly pregnant and she was in the first thrust of babyhood. I found her playing with her nine-month-old daughter on her couch amidst a terrifying array of laundry, dirty dishes and neglected cats. I looked at this woman that I had known for over a decade and who had been the most committed tech-Goth I had ever known (she married a man named Vlad for Gods' sake!) here reduced to giggles and mush, and unidentifiable stains. When I asked her what I had got myself into she looked me straight in the eye and said, "No one tells you – this changes *everything*". And I in my naïveté thought I understood what she meant. Now a few years on, I understand the profound gift she gave me that drizzly afternoon. Raising kids does change everything, and raising kids as Pagan requires us to adapt in unforeseen ways. For many of us we may have to encounter the mainstream society like never before. We may have to actively create meaningful traditions that enrich family life and ourselves. It can change the emphasis of everything.

My own journey has led me to believe that raising a family within Pagan traditions is wonderfully rewarding and challenging in equal measure. I have found that I have new depth to my spiritual perception as a consequence of my parenting. I have had to become more certain, and yet less assuming. More open to others and yet more discriminating. I have found that sharing my spirituality with the children in my life has let me see the magic in the world anew.

We live in a culture awash with 'expert' advice on raising a family. All of our parenting choices mark us as a member of one camp or another. And so many of our decisions about how we parent seem to speak our economic and social status. We are too often open to judgment from other parents and culture at large. Are we an attachment parent, or did we do cry-it-out? Is our kid the 'happiest baby on the block' or did we need Super Nanny? Tiger mother perhaps or a radical homemaker? Each of our decisions as a parent is laden with cultural burden. Grandparents are no longer the font of parenting wisdom, the wise elders (despite the fact that you turned out mostly OK), but conveyors of outdated and harmful advice. We are told to politely ignore them, and listen to TV experts and authors instead.

It begins with full force when we are pregnant. We are told that we have to eat organic food and avoid a never-ending list of food stuffs that make us wonder what pregnant women in Southern Europe/Japan/Russia/India get to eat! Pregnant women are told to rest and yet most of us work up until we are in labour. I spoke recently to a university professor who went into labour with her second baby a week before she had hoped, a week before the end of semester and so was grading finals in the labour room. Once we have finished work, we then have the territory of birth to navigate.

No one is allowed to have a simple birth these days – natural birth has become big business, medicated birth the norm. We have more methods available to enable a natural birth than ever before and yet the number of caesarean or high intervention births is worryingly increasing. Women think it is 'safe' to schedule their births like one would schedule a manicure or lunch with a friend. Fathers are told that they should be present at their children's births, and many wish to, and are a wonderful support. But for many partners this can be a terrifying, exhausting and unwelcome prospect. And unfortunately despite the expectation of sharing your birth with your partner, it is not accompanied by a societal acknowledgement of *their* need to recuperate and synthesise the experience. In all but the most enlightened Scandinavian countries, partners of new mothers have to use holiday time to be around a new child, as though the experience of supporting a labouring mother and then caring for a newborn and a new mother is a holiday. Likewise, with adopted families, the transition to family life can be demanding. Whether you are adopting a baby or an older child, time to bond and grow together is too often hampered by economic concerns. And we are expected to be back at work within six to eight weeks of a baby's arrival. In the US, babies often go to day-care at eight to 12 weeks old. Consider that. Consider that a baby has only been out of the womb for three lunar cycles. Consider that mother, full of hormones, that mother who spent ten months growing a baby, going back to work after less than a third of that time. Or a new family thrust into parenthood. Eight weeks would be a super vacation, but welcoming a new baby or child is no holiday. Even the most ardent feminists amongst us must question whether this is truly a viable, healthy and empowering expectation on women and families.

Some days it can feel that when you cross the threshold from single person or couple to a family the number of social expectations placed upon you increases manifold. It feels so loaded, and every decision has the weight of the world upon it because it will give your child 'the best start'. I have come to loathe that term – 'the best start' – as it is both meaningless and emotive. Everything seems to be sold to us on the basis of giving our kids 'the best start' and yet so little does. For many years I have worked in a variety of retail jobs, including an innovative ethical kids' store selling fair trade and organic kids' stuff. I loved this job. I loved the principles of the business. Liz the owner and I often had almost anti-business conversations stemming from our mutual loathing of marketing promoting guilt amongst parents through the 'best-start' strategy. The simple thing that enables your kid to have the best start – that's you – is so horribly undervalued. Instead we are told they need soy formula and cloth diapers. I recall one new parent who came into the shop and asked if she needed to buy special washcloths for the baby. She had read somewhere that standard washcloths were too rough for a baby's skin. Aghast I asked her if her washcloths were made from burlap, and we ended up laughing at how the pressure to consume is born from our best intentions, and a little bit of our nervousness regarding a new baby and as such makes us all a little crazy. Suffice to say she didn't buy any special baby washcloths.

Breast is best, we know that now, but we are also told that we should go back to work ASAP, so often that's you pumping milk surreptitiously in a cupboard four times a day, much to the chagrin of your colleagues. If you don't go back to work you choose to be a 'Stay at Home Mum' or SAHM and enter a different demographic for cultural pigeonholing and marketing. For 'the best start' we are told our kids need vegan shoes, they need co-sleeping, they need 100 onesies, they need a nanny. And now the giant empire of 'green' marketing has added to this machinery of guilt. Now we also need green disposable nappies or all-in-one cloth diapers that cost £200 to get started, recyclable pushchairs, organic jar food. The list is overwhelming, so we need books to help us navigate it. I understand that the economic forces require new products and new markets to keep the global economy... well, that's another agenda, but so many of these marketing campaigns play to your most basic emotional desire, to keep kids safe and well. You, healthy, happy you and your family, your community and your loved ones will give your kid the best start. All else, as they say, is window dressing.

Some days though the notion that kids' needs are simple can get hard to see amidst all the noise from commercial culture, and you may decide the only option is to opt out. You may long to buy that mythical farm/croft/piece of land and go self-sufficient, go off grid divorce the craziness that is the mainstream culture. Cut off from the main-stream – you want to become a brook, join another tributary! And I have to admit that this is still my back-door strategy. However, maybe like me, what you are attempting to do is to integrate or realise more fully the importance of changing the reality of where and how we live now.

What Paganism offers those of us who are not jumping ship (yet!) is a worldview, a community, and a set of practices and principles that *embody* on a daily basis the sacred reality of our connection to the natural world. Just as our spirituality abhors the concept of divine intercession, and relies instead on an elder communal approach to knowledge sharing, we can turn to this when we embrace the growth of our family. We can do more than tell our children that the earth is sacred, that the elements must be in balance for us all to flourish. We can show our children the simple truth of strength in diversity, not educate them about it. We can ensure that they live it and that they feel it. We can break the tyranny of religious and scientific separatism and evoke the power of synthesis. Paganism, in all its myriad forms reveals this to our children with even greater potency than it does to us as adults. In our myths, our stories and our celebrations, the rhythms of our festivals and the daily acts of family life, we can enact a revolution as significant as environmental activism, as politically necessary as boycotting the G8, and as transformative as the Civil Rights movement. We can embody the need for harmony through diversity, for our continual dependence and reliance on the elements of the world to support, nourish and inspire us. We can learn to live in connection to our place of origin, our place of living, our future lives. In order to do this we need to enchant the world anew through the key skills of magic and wonder that Pagans have refused to abandon.

This is not then a book about best child-raising techniques, or necessarily about teaching children Paganism or approaches to Pagan pedagogy, although there are elements of all three here. This book hopes to supply those of us who are parents, guardians, teachers, educators and community members with a series of ideas to help transition our spirituality from the self to the family and out to the community, like ripples in a pond. I hope that this will help us collectively work through the issues of personal and social compromise so that we come to a better understanding of what we need to strengthen and support each other if we are to feed our kids, our new mothers and fathers and thus the beautiful planet we live upon.

The central themes flowing through this book are drawn from Pagan ethics and philosophy, integrating energy/magical practices and methods in a way that I hope helps ground your everyday reality in a magical sensibility. We are all leaves on the great tree of life, and we all pull from the same source. Sometimes we simply need to know that the branch is steady, that our leaf will get the sunlight, the water, and the sustenance it needs to continue its lifecycle. And sometimes we need to know there are other leaves going through exactly what we are going through.

I have organised this book like some of those first magic books I read and loved, grounding our sense of enchantment in the elemental reality of the world. What I love about Paganism is at its core it doesn't require me to 'believe' anything – it is a spirituality that asks me to look closely at what is about me. And slowly I understand that magic is everywhere. The cornerstones around which I have focused this book are elemental. This is not designed to be another measuring stick by which to compare yourself. This is not another 'how-to-be-a-better-parent' book – we have enough voices within mainstream culture trying to assert us as a demographic or a niche. We need a Pagan voice within that like we need another hole in the ozone layer.

Pagans applaud those mavericks that do things differently – we like different. We recognise that difference and diversity are part of what will save this planet and us as a species. So use what is here if, as my friend Liz says, you are grooving on it. Think about it, meditate, take what is useful and add to it. Imagine we are in conversation with each other – perhaps we are having a play date, or a coffee morning, snatching a chat on the train on our way to work. A piece of information shared as we watch our kids at footie or ballet. Sometimes it will be a warm wholesome encouraging talk between confederates in the trenches. Sometimes it will be a fierce debate. Whether we see eye to eye, we are in this together. Heart to heart, hand to hand we are attempting to strengthen our communities, teach our charges and raise our kids with a deep reverence for nature.

To those of you hanging on, holding on to the dream of a green future where our children will be able to navigate the rocky path, I offer this book as another ingredient of the giant spell we weave together.

Chapter One

Earth

Key words: *Rhythm, Touch, Cycles, Seasons, Body, History, Heritage, Tradition, Structure, Discipline, Silence, Roots, Steady, Family, Community, Nature, Land, Substance....*

North is Earth, the Place of Power...

Earth is the heart of Pagan spiritual practice and philosophy. The most profound teachings of Pagan spirituality are founded upon our understanding and reverence for Mother Earth. This is made manifest in the celebration cycle of our ritual year, and in our conception of deity as immanent and numinous. It moves through our singular belief in the importance of an embodied spirituality, to our activism, our environmentalism, our creativity and our attempts to grow green things in our gardens and homes.

Pagans revere the body as a microcosm of the physical world in all its beauty and complexity. The physical realm is where our understanding of the divine flourishes and is home to our sources of inspiration, worthy of celebration. We start our journey into a love for the earth through our body. We carry our babies within us, in the dark womb. The ideal way to help an infant enter the world is to create a space of quiet, a space of warm security. The work of Michel Odent, doctor and natural birth pioneer expresses this so beautifully in his discussion of the best-case birth environment. Look at the animal kingdom, watch how mammals, those who are closer to nature and less influenced by fashions and sciences, have their babies. Quietly and without fear, mammals deliver their young. In the ideal birth environment, oxytocin, that wonderful 'love hormone' as Odent describes it, is released when a woman delivers a baby. In order for oxytocin to be released through the body, women need to be in the place of earth: a space of comfort, quiet, with negligible light and little distraction. Here, women can listen to the rhythm of their body bringing forth life. Odent understands that a quiet, calm and love-infused birth environment is ideal for our relationship with our children and for their entrance to the world. He suggests that how we nurture our moments of birthing define our values as a civilisation. Pagans understand that the criterion for well-being reverberates through different realms, and we understand the inter-connectivity between our actions and the world we live in. Our births are a moment of earth intensification, where the powers of earth are strong, if we allow these to guide us we birth ourselves as parents and family.

Our earliest connection and communication with our children is physical. Whether we have carried our babies in our bodies, stood witness to the growth of their being inside a woman, or whether we have been gifted a child from another woman, we show them our feelings, our hopes and expressions through our physical relationship with them. We hold our babies when they are born, nurse them, bathe them, stroke their beautiful buttery skin. As they grow we hug them after a bad day at school, or high five them after a good game. Through our touch we ask them to stay with us, and we remind them that we are here with them. Wordlessly we tell them that they are beautiful beings of substance.

As they grow we relate to their growth by altering our physical relationship with them, we allow them to move from us. As if riding an invisible tide they move in flows around us, back and forth, in ever increasing circles. We give them room to crawl, then to walk, to run and then to be outside in the garden by themselves. Their circles expand and they start to play on the other side of the park, then we allow them to walk to a friend's house across a road. Before we know it, they are borrowing the car and going hiking, and then cycling to work. With each step we show them that we trust them, that we recognise their increasing separateness from us.

And as they grow from toddler to child, from child to pre-teen, and into teenage years, we honour the changes their bodies undergo and the strength and beauty that emerges. Our physical changes are mirrored in turn by the changes we see around us, with the ageing of the land, the sun and the moon, with the shifting patterns of the cycles of the seasons we see that physical change is an inevitable and healthy part of growth. As the chant teaches us, "She changes everything she touches, and everything she touches changes." Just as we hold the land sacred, we unde stand that the stuff of our own being is a gift from the earth.

The Elements in Your Kids

Earth, air, fire, water and spirit. These are the five sacred elements that support all life in most Western Pagan traditions. Sometimes they are referred to as magical elements to distinguish them from the scientific use of the term. Earth is the magical element that rules over us in the early years of our life. Earth qualities define the strengths and challenges of this period; touch, slow and steady growth, rhythm, exploration and security. Yet despite young children being so close to this element, children of all ages require the pulse of earth in their lives, in order to establish a firm foundation for their well being as the tides of change arise. Further, at a time when we face the challenge of maintaining the earth's health, raising kids with an attitude of reverence and with knowledge of our interdependence upon the earth is crucial. Let's consider the ways in which our families can be anchored to the natural pulses of the earth.

If you are a parent or an educator of many children, you will be all too aware of how unique each little being is. Nature, nurture and everything in between means that our children come into the world with a spirit already formed, with a blueprint of some of their unique qualities, gifts, and challenges. Then they are raised and nurtured in ways that foster certain of those, and perhaps limit or ignore others. In respecting children's individual needs we can begin by considering their natural talents and tendencies. Astrology can be an immensely helpful tool here or an understanding of the alchemical humours. The elements give us a familiar framework for thinking through the complexities of natural life and human endeavours, and can be particularly useful for considering children's natures.

When I was in my teens and early twenties, I was lucky enough to have some remarkable spiritual teachers. Norfolk is awash with hidden gems. And amongst those men and women I worked with, I was able to study chirology, the art and science of Chinese hand reading, with the esteemed Johnny Fincham. In the years I studied with him, I learnt that the basis of good hand reading lies in the understanding of the elements and how, in ever-nuanced combinations, they are the flows that direct every part of our lives. From the basic shape of your hand, to the hills and troughs of the terrain of your palm, the skin, the lines that stay, the lines that shift, the lines you can change, the elements are the tools that chirologists use to read the hand's map, the map of your soul. Although I never became a hand reader, I have continued to study this fascinating skill and it has been of great interest and comfort to me in considering the particular make-up of my kids as they have grown. By considering their elemental balance I have found ways to actively change destructive patterns emerging between us, and to grow in compassion and understanding for their individual struggles.

I offer below some of the basic tenets of these five elements and their application to understanding the personality of our young folk. This is not to say that someone is purely one element – they rarely are. What you may find is that your child may have a combination of elements as their fundamental nature so what you are looking for in thinking about the application of these are your child's tendencies, patterns of behaviour, their strengths and challenges. Then your child may go through phases where another element is out of balance, or your child is struggling with an element in their life. Ideally we would have all the elements in perfect balance – and reach enlightenment!

Earth

We all begin life with Earth hands
(Johnny Fincham, *The Spellbinding Power of Palmistry* p.17)

Most children are earth-focused for the first five years of life. Life in this phase revolves around the body – sleep, food, comfort, and family. Children are still strongly connected to their parents, their need for family. All power rests with parents in their eyes. And yet, as kids grow and even during this early phase, some kids continue to show strong earth natures. Often they are solidly built, a little square and very physically present. Rambunctious and energetic, these children have stamina. They often learn to walk and toilet train without a hitch and easily establish sleep patterns. They are children of routine and habit. They may appear strong-minded and prefer the company of one or two other children who they have come to know. These children love to be outdoors, and really need to be outside come rain or shine – they are the hardiest children!

They are also kids who thrive in the countryside, rather than the city. The city can be a very stressful place to an earth child, as they hate to be rushed and crowded. They dislike big groups. They love small animals, and you may find that your home becomes filled with insects and animals of all varieties.

These are kids you can take hiking, they help put the garbage out and enjoy getting dirty. And they are excellent cooks. Their nature is patient, but when their rhythm is disrupted they may become angry and they can be explosive, which can often be bewildering as their mild manner is usually so reliable. Quiet at times and comfort seeking, they rely on external rhythm to direct their inner lives. Verbal communication is often hard for them – they express themselves through action, through their presence. They may be kids who come to language late. Expecting an earth child to tell you how they feel can often be frustrating. Instead you will see it in change in posture or energy levels.

In terms of academic achievement, they will work hard, but are rarely the high fliers, instead choosing diligence and perseverance and their own path. They find community-based work highly fulfilling, and for those who have more air in the mix, work in technology (hardware) and the sciences can prove rewarding. For those who have earth/fire natures, local politics and grass roots community organisations are valuable outlets. Get them connected early as they have a strong sense of justice and a firm moral aptitude.

Frequently an attachment object is fiercely guarded and self-comfort is a central skill for these kids to learn. Disruption, instability and uncertainty are immensely unnerving to children with earth natures. They may appear to be handling it well when in fact it may be profoundly disturbing to them. Illness is a significant manifestation of imbalance for earth kids, as they are usually so hale and hearty. When they get sick they really come down with it. When this happens, they need comfort not just medicine. Earth children need clarity, a lot of physical space; they need to be outside. Emotionally they are highly loyal – family, clan and community are intensely important to them. And of course they are also incredibly stubborn, bordering on righteous, but reliable and honest in the main.

Air

Often air children come into the world silent with eyes wide-open. They are the ones who will learn to talk before other babies and they are the most easily distractible children. Tall and thin, they are often full of nervous energy. Air kids tend to live in the realm of thought. They are good with abstracts and patterns, they will look for them and often become a little fixated with them. They will be drawn to literacy and numeracy early, but are also highly artistic by nature. Visual and musical expressions are extremely valuable outlets to air kids, and they may need a lot of time to explore these forms. For many of us, air children seem to be model kids; clever, talkative, (often attractive) but they can be emotionally distant. Non-demonstrative and fickle, they may find friendships hard to maintain, and although well liked, they often have only the emotional energy for one or two good friends. For air kids things come and go easily. Reason and objectivity are their modes of problem solving, but building empathy and compassion is a harder journey.

They often have their eye on the big picture, not the details, so can appear dreamy when in fact they are working out a complex idea. For air kids, their bodies are a source of joy and wonder and fear and anxiety, often simultaneously. They may become picky eaters, refuse medicine, and have phantom pains. They don't always sleep well and may suffer from nightmares and disrupted sleep. They strongly need rhythm and consistency in their home environment for them to feel secure and happy, as they cannot always generate such consistency from within. As they are fast learners, this allows the adults around them to ensure that they don't get locked into their head. These children dream big, dream of the world and for the world, and as such these kids have a great drive to experience new cultures, new places, new people. They do well in conventional school structures. Air/fire children are intellectually inquisitive and competitive, and will excel in languages and pattern based subjects such as maths, science and sociology. Air/earth children (an unusual and complicated mixture) may appear to be like water children at first in their dreamy uncommunicative nature. These children can be quite hidden and secretive. Draw them out by exploring history with them through expressive means – re-enactment societies like Living History, traditional music and folk dance are good. Air kids, with their big picture perspective, are also strongly motivated by righting the world's wrongs, and often feel worldly injustice more keenly that they experience emotion in their personal relationships. These are children who need a big cause to fight for.

Fire

Fire is the prevalent quality in Western culture, so many of our children will strongly display these traits. Fire kids are generally energetic, outgoing and gregarious. Quick on their feet and quick in their moods and tempers, they are kids who are always on the go. And yet, fire children in their purest form are highly creative in their approach to the world. These kids love to sing and dance. They are theatrical by nature and may appear to be the centre of any group. They are naturally charismatic, but not always benign in their leadership skills! These kids are often emotionally fierce and can be described as an emotional roller-coaster. Yet they are fantastic people kids – they love people, they love parties, they may love competitive sport because they thrive on both competition and the energy of crowds (what kinds of sport will depend on what other elements are present.)

These kids are also strongly influenced by mainstream culture, and may find it hard to be an outsider. If you are an unconventional adult, you may have to work hard to give these kids enough of a rich culture to allow them to thrive. Fire kids are strongly motivated by goals – whether it's a star chart for good behaviour, or a hill to summit, a play performance or a football game, they thrive on attainment. When results do not come quickly they can be tempestuous; as Johnny Fincham writes "impatience is a key failing" (*The Spellbinding Power of Palmistry*, p. 20).

These kids use action, not words or presence to work through things and often perceive themselves only in terms of how well they are achieving. This means that a fire child's confidence, their sense of self is often strongly connected to their outward abilities. They need goals, but they can be crushed by them. This can be particularly difficult for young adults, who are in a fire phase of their lives, and for whom self-esteem is too often focused on externals such as fashion, friends and academic achievement.

Fire kids are also the risk takers; there is in them a love of danger. For fire/earth kids long-term goals and adventures are really valuable ways of tempering their drive – saving money to go on a long trip, or building a complex Lego city, or playing a game of chess over a series of weeks are all ways to engage these kids. These are also the kids who love outside sports such as rugby and hockey that are good in all weathers, and don't mind a bit of mud! Fire kids want to succeed and they realise that this means taking chances. These are the kids we worry about when they get to teen years because they can be thrill seekers. This isn't your fault, nor is it theirs, but needs to be channelled into pursuits and activities that respond to this need.

Water

Water children are often pale and physically are soft – their skin is soft, their joints flexible and their body reflects how they are feeling. Water children are interested in relationships above all. They are by nature intuitive and highly emotional in all aspects of their lives, which can be difficult for adults around them, as they may seem to possess the most irrational, flighty and inconsistent nature. Yet these children are strongly empathic, they find ways of understanding people that as adults we should value. They are natural bridge builders between people, which makes them valuable friends. Relationships are intensely important and water children seem to do their best when they work co-operatively.

What moves these kids, and what motivates them also, are things that speak to or of the depth of human experience. Art, healing, the realm of the spiritual and devotional come naturally to water children, but in many other ways these kids seem to lack attention and direction. Unfortunately children with water talents are rarely prized in Western culture – we have no monks who will come to our village and choose the most devotional children for training, we have no apprenticeships that start in childhood for the healing arts. Many of our institutions fail these children. They appear to be dreamers and although well liked by adults and children, they can be frustrating as they seek pleasure, beauty and play above regimens, homework and obligation. They can become self-indulgent if not given other ways to express their water nature, and their empathy can tip over into hypochondria, overindulgence, and depression. Water children strongly need a purpose and they need things to take care of. These children should always have pets, or work at an animal sanctuary or a zoo. They are motivated by causes that seek to resolve pain and conflict as they loathe these elements in their own lives. They can become remarkably passionate and willing to sacrifice all their time and energy to organisations that seek to protect and shelter the vulnerable.

These children are the least physically robust and, as such, their health can be used as a barometer for their emotional well-being. Like air kids, water kids need the rhythms of home to be constant and consistent. They also strongly respond to a consistent emotional life at home. Water/fire kids will love to play – acting and musical theatre, for example, can be super. They are also the most sport minded of the water blends, and may love swimming, yoga and softer martial arts such as aikido or budo can be excellent strength and stamina builders.

Kids may have a dominant element with combinations of other elements at times in their lives, or pertaining to different parts of their lives. You may have an air child who is a fiercely competitive swimmer, or an earth child who cries at the emotive content of pop songs. But this frame can be useful in approaching children's more bewildering behaviour.

For example, a five-year-old fire/air kid will find an air meditation and visualisation a real challenge, but will love dressing up as a bird, and be specific as air kids will need to know the *kind* of bird, in order to 'be the bird'. A fire/water kid will love playing psychic projection games with you, and keeping a tally of who is getting the most answers right! An eight-year-old earth/fire kid would hate to dress up as anything, but would love to hike with you to find nests, or rare heather. She would also be excellent at gathering objects for an air altar. He would love to go horse riding with you, or cross-country running, and enjoy using his body in feats of endurance, with just a smidgen of competition.

An eleven-year-old water child will need a lot of grounding and centering exercises, and will love to learn to dowse, but would find going for a hike a tiresome pursuit. If you tell her she needs to dowse to find ley or energy lines you may have a chance of having her co-operation. Older water children may appear remote or very emotional. They are likely to become Emo kids, and have a propensity for changing their identity and their looks with great frequency – don't be alarmed if they are a punk one month and then preppy the next. This is a way for them to find their place. You will be rewarded if you frame this as a strength of theirs.

A sixteen-year-old air child will be fascinated with technology, but may spend far too much time on a computer, locked in a bedroom. You may need to find ways of unplugging them and getting them to join in and stay in the present. Board games, card games (especially those that involve money) and a regular family debate night are ways of ensuring he remains connected to family life.

Thinking about these elemental dispositions can help inform your understanding of your children's energy. For a child who has extreme sensitivities, for example, a child who perhaps senses otherworldly presences, suffers great flights of fancy and terrible moods, you may recognise that they are strongly water and need to be tempered with earth, for grounding and security

Grounding – Staying Connected to Earth

Whatever the elemental balance and make-up of our children, one of the key techniques we can use to show our kids how to stay calm and focused is to teach them to ground. We now use this term so frequently that it has almost lost its meaning, but to ground means to connect yourself to the earth, literally and energetically. To bring our attention to the ground in order to stop, take stock, breathe. This is such a wonderful thing to do with kids of all ages, so simple so beneficial and a great means to get them to connect to their surroundings and to their feelings. You can combine this with breath meditation, with visualisations and, with practise, you will find that kids begin to do it for themselves. Now I watch Summer, my eldest boy, stop and put his hands over his heart, take three deep breaths and ground himself to the earth when he feels overwrought or has too much pent-up fizzy energy. I have included two grounding exercises below. The first is a simple exercise that you can adapt to use with small toddlers and kids, and the second which involves visualisation to help both ground and revive, is great for older kids (and adults too of course).

Exercise: Simple Grounding For All Ages

Stop. Take a breath. Close your eyes if you like. Bring your attention to your feet. Feel all four corners of your feet connecting to the earth. You are standing still, strong and firm. Your feet are on the earth. The earth is turning and you are part of her.

Exercise: Grounding and Energising For Kids 5+

Stamp your feet on the ground, feel where your feet touch the earth. Breathe into your feet, and imagine that, like a tree, your feet grow roots, pushing down into the ground. You find a source of water, flowing under the ground. Let your roots dip into the water and pull it up, suck that water through your roots, through your tendrils up into your feet, and now up your legs, your tummy, your chest, your head, it feels so good, makes you feel warm, and sparkly, and that sparkling underground water fills you, and then drips from your branches, down you arms out of the top of your head, back down to the earth....

Seasonal Cycles: The Sabbats

The celebrations in most Pagan calendars are in essence celebrations of the changing seasons, and the consequent changes in our human, plant and animal communities. We join in the dance between the earth and the heavens as we move through the summer and winter solstices, the spring and autumn equinoxes and the minor sabbats: known by various names but most commonly as Imbolc, Beltane, Lammas and Samhain. Each Pagan tradition has its own mythic cycle that accompanies these festivals, and many celebrate the transitional points of the seasons at differing point. There are some wonderful resources available to those of you wanting to understand the history of these festivals, the folklore that surrounds them and the various ways in which they are practiced today. (I have listed these in the Further Reading section at the end of this book.)

I want to focus on the themes and stories that accompany the major eight sabbats of the general Pagan festival cycle, and I hope to encourage you to find ways to build upon your family's festivities to create your own traditions.

Whether you celebrate as a family, a community group or a school, you will need a few simple ingredients, both actual and spiritual.

- Space – sacred space is created by cleansing, casting, consecration and invoking the elements, the Gods and Goddesses, ancestors etc.

- Statement of purpose and intent.
- Energy raising/ritual play – this can be done through creative dance, song and chant, a re-enactment or ritual play.
- Thanksgiving – an opportunity to reflect on what has been given and to remember that which we need to give back.
- Devocation – opening the circle.

In all of our seasonal festivities, the integral relationship between our world and the sun and the heavens are honoured. The solstices and equinoctal festivals are defined by the precise moment of the sun's movement in relation to the earth. The major sabbats are not defined by astronomical and astrological movements, but by the tipping point in the seasonal balance. These festivals mark the dynamic of light and heat, the lack of one the abundance of another and the balancing points between the forces of light and dark are literal. As Cait Johnson and Maura Shaw so eloquently describe in *Celebrating the Great Mothers: A Handbook of Earth Honoring Activities for Parents and Children*:

There is something deeply satisfying about those cycles, a promise of rebirth and renewal whilst honouring the processes of death and decay. By consciously aligning ourselves with the pattern, we honour our own process – and we make a deep and powerful connection with our planet. It becomes a kind of sacred trust to share that connection with our children. (pg. 12)

For young children you can explain and define the celebration of these festivals simply. This is the point where the sun is at its peak – it is the longest day – this is the point of balance between day and night. Some of the definitions found here and in Pagan literature may seem to go against what in broader culture are detailed as the beginning of seasons. Midsummer for example, that some Pagans call Litha, is often referred to as the beginning of summer. This confusion stems in part from a misinterpretation of the festival's energy. It seems that the peak moments – the moments of celebrating a release and renewal of seasonal energy – have been transformed into transitional moments. This seasonal cycle was at least in large part formed in relationship with the European weather and seasonal changes, and thus some of the grand sabbats can be adapted. However, those great cross-quarter days – midsummer, midwinter and the two equinoxes – cannot be moved, they astronomically represent a tangible relationship between earth and the heavens. In terms of common sense it seems illogical to begin summer when the sun is waning. OK, enough of the pedant. Let's consider these festivals:

Midwinter – Yule – Winter Solstice – December 20-24th

This is the longest night, and the shortest day. This is the point where the sun moves into the sign of Capricorn. The battle between light and dark is personified in the mythic battle between the Oak King and the Holly King. Each of these Kings rule half the year. Now the King of the declining or waning year, the Holly King, makes way for the King of growth and light, the Oak King. Their battle is blessed by the Goddess, who is queen of the land. In the world around us, all has turned to bare branch and bone, animals hibernate, bulbs and seeds are deep in the earth. Mother Earth is dreaming the land anew as she nurtures bulbs and tubers, and watch as everything in the land becomes bare. Most importantly at this festival we celebrate the promise of the light's return, the sun, on the longest night and the shortest day. The miracle of the heavenly sun is cause for celebration and we light candles, exchange gifts, feast and burn the Yule log in honour of the celestial light's return.

Imbolc – Early February

This sabbat celebrates the first stirrings of new life to the land.

Imbolc honours the sprouting of the first spring flowers, which in Western Europe include croci, hazel catkins, snowdrops, early daffodils and primroses, and we begin to hear more birdsong as nest building season begins. Importantly, this festival marks the birth of new lambs, one of the earliest signs of life returning. At Imbolc we see that the burgeoning force of spring is not far away now. This festival marks the beginning of the spring tides, in its glimpses of snowdrops and frogspawn. This is a good time for cleansing the house, to blow away the cobwebs of winter, and welcome in the possibility of spring. This festival honours the Goddess Brigid, a Goddess from Ireland revered for her smithcraft, poetry and Awen – inspiration or fire in the head. From Brigid comes the life spark of the land. Gather with your friends and family, write poetry, forge new ideas for the coming season, sing and dance together.

Spring/Vernal Equinox – Ostara – March 20-24th

A point of balance, when dark gives way to light and the daylight grows. Literally the centre of the sun's plane is in the same plane as the equator – sun and earth, day and night are about equal in measure. Here the sun moves into the sign of Aries, the first sign of the zodiac, ruled by Mars, and is a time of great energy and renewed action. This is the festival of spring proper, sacred to the Saxon Goddess Eostra. Now we breathe in tune with the life returning. We see buds and green shoots and can begin to plant our gardens as Mother Earth is telling us she is ready to bring forth new life. We bless, paint and eat eggs as a reminder of the generative force of the land as the light and warmth returns. We go on egg hunts. The symbiotic relationship between the return of life and the return of light and heat is honoured at this festival.

Beltane – May Day – Early May

A time when the veil between the worlds is thin, the first of May heralds the transition from spring to summer, as buds turn to blossom and a robust love of life is felt running through the land. It is told that the great Sidhe, the spirits of our land, ride at this time, blessing all as summer is promised. This is an intensely joyful magical time, and often great works of magic are performed. In keeping with the lusty bursting forth of the season, Beltane festivities are marked by their joyous, rowdy and active dancing, cavorting and any celebration where love and pleasure are paramount. In some areas, a maiden is chosen as the Queen of the May to represent the early summer's beauty. This is the only day where May blossom, hawthorn, is allowed into a home and often gifts are left out for the nature spirits we live amongst, the wee folk, in thanks and offering.

Midsummer – Litha – Summer Solstice – June 20-24th

This festival marks the peak of the sun's might. At midsummer we see the sun at its highest point, and at its strongest. This is the true summer celebration, where roses bloom and bees buzz around. The Kings of the land, Holly and Oak, meet once more to mark the earth's movement from light to dark. The Oak King relinquishes his crown to the King of the waning year, the Holly. The Goddess gives blessing as queen, mother and partner. At the peak of the sun's power we acknowledge its inevitable decline, and whilst we celebrate the wonders of flowering and greening in the world around us, we know that from this point on the days will shorten towards equinox and that the harvest is not far away. We see now what needs to be done to ensure a good harvest and we ask for the perfect combination of warmth and rain to ensure our projects, and our landscape, flourish. From Beltane through to this period of the summer time, garden fairies, spirits and genius loci are honoured as we see the life in the world around us is dressed in green.

Lammas – Early August

This is the start of the harvest season, and you can mark it as the day the combine harvesters come out, or when you first see the fields around you shorn of their crop. This is summer's last hurrah and the beginning of the grain and honey harvest. If the crop is ready and the weather has been good then the early wheat will be gathered in. John Barleycorn gives himself in sacrifice to the land in return for a good harvest and the promise of harvests to come. The Goddess is abundant and we feast in her praise. Long hot days are hoped for, and certainly in Britain too much rain at this point can be troublesome for the later harvests. Now is the time for thanksgiving, the baking of bread and the acknowledgment of the earth's bounty in crop and grain.

Autumn Equinox – Mabon – Sept 20-24th
This equinox, the Autumn Equinox marks the turn of light to dark, as from this point on the dark will grow and the light diminish as the earth looks towards the winter coming. The land is once more in balance with the sun. This is the peak of the harvest season where the fruits and nuts are gathered in, by us and our animal allies, and we look ahead towards colder days. Often considered the fruit harvest, now is the time to begin making cider, wassailing the orchards to bless and thank them for their fruit. The earth seems to exhale as the trees begin to turn golden, and this festival honours the trees' harvest. Revel in their beauty as they give us air and food.

Samhain – Halloween – Early November
Often celebrated as the Pagan New Year, Samhain, or Halloween, is the final harvest, the blood harvest, when traditionally all the cattle were brought in from the pasture. This festival marks the beginning of winter, when the earth beings to dream again. We grow root vegetables, warm and snug in her muddy embrace. Like its mirror at Beltane, this is a time when the veil between the worlds is thin, so we honour the spirits of the land, our beloved dead and our ancestors. We look back now, to the year we have

had and assess the year's trials and joys. A time for reflection, this is a festival of solemnity where we revel in the darkness in and around us. We build altars to our beloved dead, we acknowledge the unseen forces at play in our lives, and we give ourselves time to mourn and grieve for losses counted and people missed.

Knowing Place – Biomes and Homes

Whatever shape the mythic cycle of the year takes for you, what is so profoundly beautiful about Pagan celebrations is their anchoring to the rhythms of the biome. In celebrating the turn of the year, we acknowledge our connection to place, to the actual place and to the spirit of place, the genius loci.

For those of us displaced, cut off from our cultural and ancestral home, forging new communities away from our place of origin or our extended network of kith and kin, celebrating the sabbat festivals is a way of connecting to our personal and cultural history and looking ahead to rooting ourselves in a new home. In this way then, we seek to celebrate the cyclical pulse of the year through connecting to our habitat. Look around, and see what signs of change and transition are apparent. A change in the breeze, birds migrating, new flowers blooming. When we are rooted in a place long associated with our family there can be intense comfort in revering and recognising these signs. What such a connection requires, rather than a pedantic obsession with celebrating the festivals on the right days, is that we use these festivals to acknowledge where we are and how our environment impacts us – so we need to be outside every day, observing what is happening around us. For kids, this is exceptionally important. If we hope to instil in them an awareness of the changing tides of the year then outside play is vital. As practitioners of magic know, you cannot bend and shape the world, you cannot work with energy of any kind, unless you know that world, unless you have experienced it in all its colours.

Think about where you live, its climate, its habitats, its

landscape. It is unique, it is dynamic. Do you live by water, or by mountains? Do you live somewhere where the seasons are subtle shifts in rain and heat, or where the drama of weather is an ongoing source of neighbourly conversation? By exploring, listening and opening ourselves to the landscape we live in we expand our ability to be connected to our world.

For my first 30 years I lived in one small provincial city in East Anglia, a rich agricultural landscape once home to the brave horse tribe, the Iceni. My parents were knowledgeable about local history and geography. My papa, much to the chagrin of my teenage self, would spend most weekends brass rubbing at all the old churches, or walking the coastal tracks, the strange mounds and common lands. My mother, who had extremely green thumbs, took us to wherever there was water – the sea, lakes, tiny rivulets that passed through common land. As kids my siblings and I got to experience the landscape we lived in through the lens of our parents' interests. And despite our moaning disinterest at the time, I now consider these elements crucial to my love of landscape today. Now I know what intentions my parents had, deliberately trudging us through forests and architecture that we didn't necessarily enjoy – that we often complained about, but which they loved.

I grew to know the distinct energies of local spaces, both in terms of the flora and fauna, and as I grew older I was able to articulate the feelings that I sensed in certain places. The Norfolk coastline, for example, is an immanently powerful place for magics of manifestation and communication – the low horizon, the easterly facing shore. And then the coppices are perfect for celebrations and festivities.

In my late teens I took it upon myself to be the guardian of a local park, a park I had grown to love but which was sorely neglected by the local inhabitants. It was part football field, part dog park, and part drug user haven. It certainly wasn't an enchanted garden! Yet just below the gate was a little old coppice, complete with the original enclosure hawthorn bushes that were hundreds of years old. This park space, obviously used for various nefarious purposes, had very conflicting energies. And as a teenager I loved to sit there in the dark, amidst all the wild vibrations of those old hawthorns. It was shabby, yet over many years I worked in this park both individually and with my siblings and friends. We held small seasonal rites there with my very young brothers, making sun wheels and rolling eggs, and then I would swing on the swings in the dark, visualising my life and manifesting my dreams. I did cleansings of the space at dark moon and at Samhain, to try to rid it of the negativity held lightly on the surface through neglect and abuse. And on weekends I would take rubbish bags and litter pick. This was an extremely meaningful role for me. I did some of my most potent magic in this place, and honed my awareness through listening to the messages it gave me.

One night I went as I had done hundreds of times before – it was only a five-minute walk from my home – it was during the last phase of my undergraduate degree and I wanted to meditate on the completion of a creative project that seemed gargantuan in the light of day. I arrived at the park and duly asked the genius loci to protect and guide me in my working. I blessed the grass and the flora and went and sat on the swings. After about ten minutes, a strange, cold feeling surrounded me, and I had the overwhelming urge to leave. The air got tight (always a sign of magic), my skin began to crawl and for the first time in many years in that place I began to feel scared. Then I saw a man approaching from the other side of the park. There was nothing in his gait or his approach that would have warned me had this spirit of the place not given such a distinct warning sign. I simply got off the swing and left the park by a small side entrance, and then ran home. The next day I returned with an offering and a gift to the spirit of the place for keeping me safe.

The relationship I developed with this particular place was

defining for me, and I urge those of you with teens and older kids to encourage a custodial relationship with a place near to your home. Preferably this would be somewhere safe, and with trees, flora and fauna. It could be down the bottom of the garden, or the wild edge of a school playing field. Help frame this as a place where they can develop a magical connection, where they can take on the mantel of guardian, and allow your kids to feel responsibility to a place without defining how this should happen. For me, my guardianship came as a progression from my fascination with local flora – I took great delight in the weeds of my neighbourhood, and learning what they could tell me about the area I lived in, its composition, its land strengths. At this time, I could walk a two-mile radius of my home and name every wild growing tree, flower and shrub and fungi that I found. In order to do this, you have to be rooted in a place, to feel connected in a space.

Living halfway across the world in Boston, USA, in an unfamiliar landscape I worked arduously to recreate a similar relationship. My kids and I learned together, and I never left home without identification books and an eye to the ground. Trees looked different, the mammals more exotic, the birds louder. Seven years in and I was still barely scratching the surface of this foreign place. It was a biome rich with fungi, with birds, and so my attention was given to learning and appreciating the strength of both of these kingdoms. I remember one spring evening when my friend and I ate supper on the front porch, three floors up, and listened to the robins sing across the trees. We watched the orioles, grackles and cardinals so rarely spotted in England and yet so commonplace here. Here we welcomed the red breast robin as harbinger of spring – which once seemed so discordant with me, as in Britain robins are winter's emissary. Now it has become a sign of the unique nature of this landscape. And today I tell my kids both of these meanings, the reason why robins are spring bringers in New

England and winter birds in Old England, so they are cognisant of the diversity that our beautiful green earth holds and the importance of knowing where you are upon her.

To allow our kids to develop their own relationship with place and perhaps become a guardian to a local park or green patch, we need to give them time and space so that the spirits can speak to them. Allowing that invisible rope between you to extend can be hard, especially today when we are all too aware of the stranger dangers and threats that our kids face. Add that to the overscheduling many of us feel inclined to do with our kids and the increasing use of cars time... And yet, in reality without developing a relationship with outside spaces beyond the reach of our 'helicopter parenting' our kids rarely get to try out their prickle sense, their instincts. Some spaces are certainly unsafe at particular times of the day, but let us consider how we can allow our kids, over the age of eight perhaps, a little more freedom in their locale. Author and activist Richard Louv has brought our attention back to the significance of nature play and how its removal from our lives causes Nature Deficit Disorder. His rallying cry confirms what many Pagans feel. Experiencing the energy of a place can often be found first in the kind of place that grows from it. Will they create a game of high drama and conflict, or will they build a wall with rubble? Will they run wildly or simply straggle bored and whining. Is it a space that facilitates quiet or loud play? These responses may tell you and your kid that today is not a good day to play, or it may reveal to you some deeper energetic experience, some character of the place itself.

Kids have quite different responses to places, as they literally see them differently. Whereas adults may like open, light places, kids often look for dark overgrown edges to play in, they offer greater fodder to the imagination, they feel different. Lawn, grass and wide open spaces give children little to work with imaginatively, yet abandoned lots, well that's a different matter. My boys loved the abandoned, rusting, frankly probably dangerous bear cages in Boston's Franklin Park, a beautiful part of the Emerald Necklace. This park is used in various ways, many of them somewhat insalubrious, and yet my boys loved the spooky and derelict part of this park, complete with rusted cages, a snake pit and caged trees (which I assume was to stop the bears from climbing out). Here they scampered about being animals, bad guys, ghosts, ghost catchers, snake hunters. They happily spent time playing in this abandoned place, in a way in which they couldn't when we were in the tamed order of other parts of the Emerald Necklace or the nearby Arnold Arboretum.

So much play today is 'educational' and 'directed' in nature; we chaperone our kids through activities designed to 'help them play'. Play is constructed as enriching by its content and supposed outcome (I will talk more about this in Chapter Three). As a culture we forget that play (which is the basis of magic) is instinctive, intuitive and above all relational. We need to allow our kids a relationship with *where* they are playing for play to really teach our kids. Let them direct the where and what of play and we allow them to authentically inhabit the magic of a place, and we let our kids to experience what it, not us, has to say.

So your lesson, should you choose to accept it, is to let you kids dawdle home and play in the woods. Push the limits of your comfort zone, by letting them out on their bikes without you hovering, and allow them to experience the world without you always framing the experience for them.

Rhythm, the Pulse of Life

Pagan spirituality is founded on the centrality of rhythm. Our festival cycle reveres the rhythm of the earth; our rites of passage, our creative work and our magical endeavours all aim to attune to the rhythms around and within us. Unsurprisingly then, rhythm can be a great teacher when raising a family and being in relationship with kids.

Our earliest sense of home is the dark warm place of the

mother's womb, and a defining feature of this place of beginning is the heartbeat. The heartbeat is a constant pulse in utero and is the source of comfort, the first rhythm we come to feel and move to. We put a baby to the breast or a bottle, and we keep them close to us, to our chest, our heartbeat. We pat them rhythmically to sleep, we rock a sick child as we hold them to the invisible pulse of our heart. This heartbeat can provide us with a defining pattern and model for well-being in the early years, for rhythm is at the root of wellness.

When my eldest son was a newborn he wouldn't stop shrieking. He seemed to find being in the world an exceptionally difficult experience. Some said it was reflux, others gas, others a soul issue. However, when he was three weeks old, my mother came to stay and performed some kind of 'mother magic' as she held him firmly in the crook of her arm, across her body with his head near her heart and patted him on the back firmly and rhythmically. I watched as within moments his little body relaxed and he let go, surrendering to the rhythm that had held him for the ten moons he had been growing inside mwe.

When we look for comfort and intimacy as adults we often revert to the rhythm of the heartbeat. With a new lover we sleep close, our head on their chest, so we can attune ourselves to their energy and hear the beat of their heart. For Pagans, this source of rhythm is reflected not only in our relationships, but it acts as a reminder of our heritage. Through our own heartbeat we recognise the voice of our ancestors. The blood in our veins is the blood from those who stand behind us, mother, father, grandparents, and beyond. The beat of our heart is the testimony to our rich heritage. As we chant to honour our beloved dead at the festival of Samhain, "It's the blood of the ancients that flows through our veins, and the forms pass, but the circle of life remains."

Many of us also acknowledge the power of the heartbeat by drumming. Drumming is a path to power, a means of both energy raising and communicating with the divine. Drumming is an expression of earth, and many of us are compelled to drum. Drumming is an excellent form of expression for babies, and many kids are unconsciously drawn to drumming, using household objects, pots, pans, spoons to make the most fundamental (and loud!) sounds after speech. They are instinctively aware of the power of externalising the rhythm found in their body. Rhythm also facilitates dance and movement, connecting us to ourselves and others

Pagans attempt to come into daily alignment with the rhythms both within and outside us. For many, the reverence of the natural rhythm of the earth, the stars and the moon is the most profound body of teachings within our spirituality. The earth has a cyclical rhythm, as do the moon and stars. This places us in a rhythm that far exceeds those of our own bodies. Yet when we begin to live in harmony with our body's rhythms, we bring our lives into closer alignment with the natural ebbs and flows of the world, and we can begin to see the patterns that define our lives. Children have a natural understanding of the importance of rhythm, and we can cultivate this within our home and neighbourhood.

In the spring, when the sap is rising, we plant – it is the best time to work with the rhythm of the land, and so we also begin new projects, we consider coming out of our winter hibernation. We make new friends, take up new opportunities. In the summer, when all the world is in bloom and the sun is at its peak, we are outside a lot. We go to the beach, we socialise and we nourish and feed those projects begun in the spring. And in the autumn we harvest the results, and consider with gratitude the sun's wealth. And we prepare for the winter. Our celebratory cycle, which is practiced by the large majority of Pagans, follows the tides of the year in this way, perhaps revering different festivals. The rhythmic nature of this flow ensures that we are constantly brought into alignment with the tides of the earth and the dance between the earth and the sun and the celestial bodies. When we work within the rhythm of the year, we also allow ourselves to live in mindful awareness of what is going on around us and how such energies and flows are found in the nature of our own lives.

Rhythm is at the root of the Pagan celebration calendar, the Wheel of the Year. What is so central to this festival calendar is not necessarily its accompanying mythic drama, which offers beautiful and powerful stories to understand the transition from season to season. The cycle of this calendar allows us to understand the passing of time in a particular way. It enables us a conception of time as rhythm, that extends in circles ahead of us and behind us. It connects us to our past and helps us think into the future.

Children of all ages respond to rhythm over chaos and above rigidity and routine. From when they are small we can help our children learn the power of rhythm by acknowledging the rhythm of the day, the season, the year, and of course, by creating rhythms in our family life.

I was a parent who needed routine right from the beginning. My family was grown in an entirely new soil, as we had emigrated just months before my eldest son decided to arrive. Without a support network of family and friends, I relied on the routine of a day to carry me through the trials and tribulations of those early months. Every day became an exercise in routine, and I now think that the rigidity with which I organised our day was a consequence of my own anxiety and a way of structuring my life at home with a little one in a foreign place. However, I have found that with a little loosening, now there is an intuitive rhythm to our family's life. This is not rocket science, and anyone who talks to their parents or grandparents before consulting an 'expert on childhood' will find that this is a very old-fashioned approach to raising children. Rhythm creates security and comfort. So, even if it goes against the rebellious free spirit in you, consider this a gift to your child, to bring them into alignment with the rhythm of the day.

With a newborn baby your daily rhythm may go something like this:

- Wake up, nurse/feed the baby.
- Get dressed and washed, and go out and water the plants.
- Go for a walk, go to see a friend, place the baby in a pram out in the garden to watch the birds and listen to the trees. This may be a perfect time for a morning nap.
- Snack time – yours and baby's.
- Read books.
- Lunch.
- Nap time, as the day begins to wane…
- Wake up, another snack.
- Play! Dance, sing, make music, do a project, lay the baby on a rug and do tummy time…
- Tea time.
- Bath time.
- Read stories.
- Bed, sleep, at last.

Now with older kids, I find there are elements of this early routine that haven't changed. Bedtime routines, or after-dinner routines, are particularly important, as they prepare us for sleep, allow us to wind down, and get our minds and bodies ready for dreaming. They are often also the hardest and worst pockets of the day. For working families, this is often when one or more parent will return home, and for families with school age kids, this can be a time when tempers are frayed as everyone is tired, there's last-minute homework to do. We resort to bribery for them and wine and TV for us! Building up a rhythm can alleviate a lot of stress at this time. To begin with you may clock watch in order to get a sense of how the rhythm works with the tides of your family's needs, but soon you will find there is a natural flow to it. Allow this to be a time when your kids know that quiet play is expected, whilst you make dinner; or when Mama has to have cave time before joining the family.

Consistency is key to establishing a fruitful rhythm. For example, we know we must brush our teeth twice a day if our teeth are to be healthy. Likewise, to be sure that our children are emotionally secure and happy we create a rhythm that moves from day to day. If we aren't able to be with them every day then we find babysitters, daycarers or friends that can carry the rhythm from our home to the other spaces of care. There are periods when your family rhythm will change depending on the age of your kids, their needs and your lifestyle. School, if you choose it, carries its own pulse so your home rhythm will inevitably have to incorporate that. But some things can be constant for you all. Every day we bless the morning, and we bless the evening meal. We light the candle on the altar before bed, and every season we celebrate the sacred festivals. These consistencies quickly become family rhythms and are probably the elements of your own family history that you have the clearest recollections of. For me it was painting eggs, carving out pumpkins and the wonders of birthday parties, which were always extravagant, imaginative times.

Start by acknowledging the existing rhythm of your family and let your rhythm blossom from the things you love. If you practice yoga every morning, don't stop. Perhaps you could let this be the time for everyone to do quiet play, or reading, or homework, or you could include your kids or your baby. You may have to slow or syncopate your own rhythm to fit with those needs of your children, so you may only be able to do 15 minutes of yoga rather than an hour, but this is the wonderful element of parenting around rhythm, it has many shades, many different kinds of rhythms.

Rhythm, unlike rigid routine, is dynamic. Just as some years spring comes late, or the winter lasts forever, the seasons still change, the rhythm continues. So look for the points in your day, your week, your month where there are already consistent activities, and consider where you would like to build a firm rhythm. In this way too we can see when a child is at a point of change and growth. When your charge bucks against a rhythm, they are telling you that they are ready to find a new rhythm. If they don't settle to sleep easily, or don't go down to nap, or fall asleep over dinner, they are communicating to you a disharmony within them, and asking you to adapt your rhythm to acknowledge the change they are going through. And at times, they are asking you to make that rhythm firmer, to give them boundaries and asking for the security of what is known. The magic comes in knowing which it is.

Just as we find with our heartbeat, when our rhythm becomes irregular, too fast or too slow we start to suffer. Children who have had a life of chaos often attempt to introduce certainty through repetition, another form of rhythm. This instinct I believe is in part a consequence of them looking for a source of rhythm and security. Yet instead of it manifesting in a structured and healthy way they may develop strange ticks or habits. I am sure you have seen this before. They may need to brush their teeth 100 times or to put their shoes on in a particular way. Or they may start to scream a lot and develop frustration or anger issues.

Such obsessions are an inversion of rhythmical action, and compulsions such as these can often be cries for security and a foundational rhythm. Children can also demonstrate their pain by a complete removal from the basic rhythms of the body. Bedwetting, night waking, daydreaming and over forgetfulness are ways in which a child can demonstrate the need for consistent physical rhythm in their lives. This awareness can be especially helpful if you are parenting or working with children who have gone through periods of intense change – adoption,

illness, house move, and divorce. Reinforcing a simple foundational home rhythm allows them to let go of extraneous anxiety
and focus on making the necessary emotional and physical
adjustment, secure in the knowledge that they will be rested, fed,
and warmly cared for.

If you feel that a child you know or a child of yours is demonstrating the need for deeper rhythm there are many ways in
which you can help. Firstly, bring them back to the heartbeat.
Lots of affection, hugs, patting, and then, if you are able,
encourage or ensure a consistent physical routine around eating
and sleeping. Three meals, naptime, a good amount of sleep. Find
a way of marking the beginning and ending of the day, bringing
your child into the day consciously and releasing the day's end.
This could be as simple as a morning blessing or prayer, or
setting an intention at the breakfast table and discussing the
happiest and most challenging part of the day at the day's end.
Eating, sleeping and playing – these are earth's domain and they
are the benchmarks of rhythm within all of us.

What you establish through promoting rhythm with children
and especially those in distress is how to self-care. You are
showing them that to be happy and comforted you need consistency. Just as a child needs to know clear expectations from you
and those people around them, they need to know that when
those expectations are met there are clear rewards and consistent
comforts. I remember hearing a wonderful story on NPR one
afternoon – a This American Life programme entitled 'Love is a
Battlefield', about a couple that had adopted a child from a
Romanian orphanage (originally aired 9/15/2006). This child was
about seven when they bought him home and he had never been
touched and had no speech or communication. His profound
neglect had left him with an inability to attach to anyone or
anything. After time, his adopted family taught him to speak and
fostered expressive communication. With language he was able
to realise what had happened to him, what had been lost and he

was dangerously aggressive in response. These brave and stalwart parents found that the only way to reach him was to help him regress, to learn to attach and bond through returning him to a state that was akin to a mother/baby state. Holding therapy and attachment therapy helped this child. They described spending vast amounts of time taking him back to a womblike place, dark, warm, rocking him, patting him, staring deep into his eyes and holding him safe and contained until his rage had worn itself out and they were able to come to words again. In listening to these astoundingly courageous parents, I marvelled at their ability to know what he needed. He needed to be a babe again, and to have the foundational rhythm of his infancy replicated.

Rhythm confers predictability, which in children under the age of five and again around aged nine and then during the teen years is particularly significant. When so much change is happening internally, emotionally and physically at this time, outward predictability can be lifesaving and can ensure at least periods of serenity. Creating a predictable rhythm means children can anticipate expectations, they can have a sense of how a day, or an occasion is going to go. Predictability also allows the fostering of trust – I know that after one beat of the heart, another will occur and another and another. So your toddler or teenager will know that family dinner is important because everyone gets to say how their day is and what is going on for them. They are listened to without comment or judgment. You can negotiate the expectations of the day based on your knowledge of every family member's rhythm. If your teenager comes home from school exhausted, don't make them sit and do their homework immediately. Encourage them to rest and eat something. Find a way of physically making contact, a reassuring hug or a pat on the back can be a simple reminder to them to settle into their body.

If the rhythm of your family is stuck and is no longer working then consider where it needs to change. When my kids dropped their naps, this was one of the hardest changes in rhythm I have ever had to face. I realised that I was maintaining an old rhythm not because it was healthy for them, but because I needed the quiet time. So we changed to having quiet playtime in their room instead of nap. This allowed them to stay awake and the rhythm of the day to quieten and slow. This also allowed me some down time to do household chores. If your child is going through a particularly challenging period, defiant, angry or depressed, consider if your rhythm needs changing or if there has been a disruption to your existing rhythm. Are they going through a growth spurt, are they finding it hard to hear their body's rhythm? Have the rhythms of your home changed? Is there a change in the emotional terrain of your home?

In establishing a sense of rhythm for our kids in the actions and pulse of our household, we also embed important rhythms for self-knowledge. We show them how to pay attention to rhythms in their own body – to know when they are tired, hungry, irritable, and emotional. Look for connections with your kids; see if there is a daily, weekly or seasonal rhythm that helps them to make sense of what their body is telling them. Such investigations and the encouragement of self-knowledge also helps develop personal responsibility early on – they promote self-regulation.

My kids went through an odd phase when they were both around three, of forgetting their body's signal for hunger. Every morning at about 7 o'clock, after they had been playing quietly in their room together for a good hour, my eldest boy Summer would rush and tell me that he felt sick. I tried to explain that this is because they were hungry and just needed breakfast. To his disbelief I made breakfast and invited both of them to eat it. After the questions and panic about what would happen if he were sick, my eldest ate, forgot all about the sick feeling and went about playing. Day after day this happened, until one day he was

able to interject in the pattern. *"I feel sick!!! I'm gonna be sick!...*
Oh, mum – I think I need breakfast". This was a great parenting
moment for me, where my boy had realised that his body was
giving him a signal and he had learnt to listen to it and act on it
without anxiety or fear.

Today my eldest still forgets his body's signals, especially if
he has been ill or is overly anxious. He has to remember how his
body works, and we do this through connecting him again and
again to his body's rhythmic needs. I ask him questions – are
your hands and feet cold? When did you last eat? This way I try
to promote his recognition of his body's needs. It also helps as a
reminder to me that I must model this in my own life. Building
rhythm and comfort for your kids also enables you to value it in
your own life.

On Home and Hearth – Building Altars

Altars and shrines are a part of almost every religious tradition.
They are a consecrated place to honour a deity, to make sacrifice
or to give offerings to the Gods. An altar is the place where we
can talk with the divine, we make communion, and we give
thanks. A shrine is a sacred place dedicated to a God/dess where
you may leave offerings and place pleas. Today, altars in Pagan
traditions have moved beyond the remit of sacrificial offerings
and are used as a site for divine honouring, a place of prayer and
meditation, as well as a means of reflecting the changing rhythm
of the ritual year.

Altars are at their very best a doorway to the divine. Unlike
those beautiful altars found in other faith traditions that are so
often statically positioned in a building, Pagans build altars in a
variety of places and spaces. We also look for altars in nature.
Altars may be built for the purpose of a specific ritual, in
reverence of a sacred site or they can become the focal point of a
home, as a place of meditation and a means of worshipping
family or household Gods.

Household altars or shrines, as established in the ancient civil-isations of Egypt, Greece and Rome are of particular importance to many Pagans. These are often placed in the heart of the house or in a northern facing space. In most Western Pagan ritual practice, we place the altar in the North of the magical circle. As Wiccan author Vivianne Crowley writes in *Wicca: The Old Religion in the New Age*, "Having the altar in the North/South axis is also important in that it aligns the circle with the Earth's magnetic currents." (p.99) There are also times when in ritual we place an altar in the centre of the circle, to make it easy to dance around and allow all gathered to sit and use the altar as the focal point. The centre is considered the place of Spirit. We can place the household altar in the northern most corner of a home, or a garden, or perhaps in the central room, the place where we spend the most time.

If you haven't already established a household altar or shrine then find a place where everyone can see, touch and respond to the changes in your home and the seasons. The building or trans-forming of the family altar can be a family event – and keeps it constantly in your mind and the minds of your kids. When you are walking home from school or tidying a room, set them tasks of items to find or pick up. Some elements may always remain – photographs of beloved dead, Goddess figures, a plant, stones and shells, those objects that define your relation to the elements, and your family. The altar can become the spiritual powerhouse of your home and family life. In a school or community group environment this could be called a nature table and be a place where kids can bring in found objects and contemplate the seasons. Wherever you build one, an altar grounds your spiritual practice in a simple and homely way and allows you to express the rhythm of life. It can also act as an invitation to friends and family.

My friend Peggy regularly visits and always brings something delicious she has baked and a small object for the family altar.

This could be an acorn from a tree on her street, or a tchotchke she picked up at a yard sale. She is then connected to the hub of our household and our family's spirituality. When she is sick my boys instinctively go to the altar and find the something she has left there and can say a few words of blessing for her. Or they can be reminded of her by playing gently with whatever she brought for us. Other friends are inspired to start their own family altars by being in the presence of yours and realising it as a living, generative way of honouring the seasons or elements.

You can create projects for objects to go onto the altar, paint a bowl for water, a feather fan for wafting incense. Make some incense to burn or paint a picture to represent the festival. Make representatives, dolls or poppets, for friends who are sick, or for each of your family members. I often like to put growing things on the altar, as those flowers and plants have a special energy once transplanted to a garden. It can also be a place of offering and invocation. Here we give thanks for the recovery of a sick family member, or for a successful piano recital or for a bountiful garden.

Building an altar together can be the perfect place to teach children how *to keep silent*, one of the central teachings of the earth element in Wiccan traditions. In the simplest sense altars contain a peaceful quality. I enjoy watching boisterous kids become still and quiet when they are beside an altar. They intrinsically know it is a place of sacredness. It is more than a nature table, more than the sum of its parts.

Stillness and quiet are qualities rarely esteemed in today's ever busy, talk heavy culture. When was the last time you were able to sit in quiet stillness with your own thoughts uninterrupted? For kids such time and space is particularly hard, with the bombardment of media hardware and content that persistently maintains the urge for moving and talking. For young kids, just getting them to stay in one place for a minute can be a challenge! Our children encounter more visual and aural stimulation on a daily basis than they can possibly process. It strikes me that the symptoms of ADHD and ADD and other sensory perception disorders are quite rational responses of the brain trying to cope with the volume of 'information' thrown at it. For children with such challenges, the blessings that earth shares are of particular importance, and here an altar can be a meaningful tool. Reduce stimulation, promote stillness and quiet and you facilitate a rhythmic life. These can be valuable teachings for everyone who works or lives with kids and can help on the pathway to well-being. A fun way of embedding the cyclical nature of a month's passing is to take regular family time for reflection at your altar.

Turn off all screens, all phones and all noise-making devises. Take time to teach just 30 seconds of quiet before the altar on a weekly or daily basis. Before bed, or soon after waking are good points in the day to build in altar time. It doesn't have to be for any particular purpose. Just allow yourselves to take a moment to observe. Perhaps a silent question will be formed, or a hope for the day. In fostering small moments of everyday silence we give our kids a great gift, of being able to listen to their inner voice and the heartbeat of the world.

Earth Care

Pagans often define themselves as people who generally consider the world to be an animate entity and we try to spend as much time as possible attuning to her, giving and receiving energy and attempting to restore the balance that mankind has skewed. This has never been so crucial. As the human population hits 7 billion, we strain the resources of beautiful Gaia. We live in a time of great global uncertainty. Whether through natural cycles of the earth's change or whether as a direct result of mankind's actions, or a combination of the two, we are all aware that through over population and consumption, the earth's well-being is threatened. Despite her inexhaustible resilience, teaching our children about our reliance on Mother Earth is fundamental to our survival. Pagans are obligated to take this to heart. By seeing all of nature's creations as an intricate part of the whole, and that together this great buzzing mass of the world is sacred, we have a responsibility both spiritual and practical in nature to do our part to ensure its healing and its continuation. We must learn to tread gently.

There are some old-fashioned (well, let's just say these were ideas pioneered in schools in the UK when I was a kid) exercises that can promote healing for the earth. We need such approaches to become as natural to them as the self-care techniques we teach kids – so we say wash your hands, brush your teeth and conserve the water before you leave. Here then are some basic points of earth care to start your thinking process with the kids you know:

Conserve, Conserve, Conserve
I first heard this sung by a mum at a playgroup as she taught her two-year-old to turn off the water after washing her hands. Simple yet so effective. Use this when switching off lights, turning off water, saving food for the rabbit. Whatever it is, if you sing this little mnemonic you will quickly find your kids doing it – well, as long as they are under seven, over that they will think you have lost the plot.

Reduce, Reuse, Recycle, Respect
The four Rs are a literal interpretation of the means to tread gently. Reduce our consumption; reduce the unnecessary waste of energy. You could say that this is a model of streamlining output. Reuse – can you use that old T-shirt as a duster? Can your rubbish become precious in another's hands? In the natural world everything has multiple functions, and goes through stages so that even in death it brings nourishment, shelter or use to another life form. Consider whether your rubbish can be transformed into something new. And if it cannot be reused, then

recycle.

We all have our big blue bins in my city and feel good when they are overflowing, that is until we realise that much of this waste does not get recycled, or perhaps travels halfway across the world to be so. We need to ensure that every child knows where waste goes. Tell them that there are whole cities built on our waste, because our waste gets sent to developing countries. When we weigh the energy costs of recycling commercially it doesn't always give us the warm feeling we hoped it would. If you show children the results of such waste disposal, unencumbered by the lackadaisical attitudes we adults have developed, they will see through to the heart of the matter and before you know it will have organised their school and their friends to campaign for local recycling! However, there are some simple ways of recycling. Firstly, for clothes, toys and household objects, donate them. Compost everything – get worms! Use our animal allies. Keep scrap-eating animals – chickens, goats and, of course, rabbits. Rabbits are wonderful when properly kept, as both pets and as allies in recycling. They will eat so many of your scraps and they require less space than a goat.

Be conscious of packaging – try to buy goods that have little packaging, or compostable packaging. It's worth those extra pennies. Importantly, cook only what you need and encourage kids to finish their food – tell them what happens to discarded food. By blessing meals we help kids connect to what they eat, and show respect for the food before them, and then they may be less inclined to waste it. In our home we bless the food by acknowledging the communities that have brought it to our table, the elements of earth, air, fire and water, but most specifically farmers, the factory workers, packers, supermarket or delivery people. If you eat meat (itself a moral and spiritual questions you may have raised) then a blessing can be said to the animal for giving its life for the meal. Trust me, whether the blessing is long or short, kids (over five) waste less when they acknowledge what has gone into bringing a meal before them.

Respect becomes a natural extension of these approaches. These actions demonstrate our respect for the earth, for ourselves, and for each other. Respect is a crucial Pagan ethic – respect for self, for others and for the planet. By reducing consumption, reusing and recycling we are literally embodying our respect for the earth.

As You Sow, So Shall You Reap

All things are connected. Teaching and modelling conservation, whether this is helping a four-year-old turn off a running tap whilst they are brushing their teeth or allowing your teenager to hang out at the local park, as long as they have an old plastic bag to do some litter clearing whilst they are there, demonstrates the connection between our relationship with the world and our relationships with each other. It also builds self-respect. To conserve something means to keep, to protect, to work *with*. Conserving is different to preserving. It is dynamic. Preservation attempts to keep something as it is, or as it was, resisting change, and maintaining the status quo. Conservation means working to protect something that is valued. Conservation is the perfect model of care as it fosters an approach based on stewardship and guardianship. Encourage your kids to be modern day knights, healers and witches. All these roles were created to help conserve the well-being of a place.

These are the building blocks to understanding karma, or the law of eternal return. By karma, I refer to the ancient belief that as all things are connected through their relationship here on earth, we meet all things with respect and consideration. In doing so we hope that such respect will be reflected back to us, and the balance of the world maintained. Many people misinterpret karma as a 'tit for tat' understanding of the world, as if to say, "If I do something bad, something bad will happen to me". In our daily lives we often consider this notion of karma and rail against it. Justice, we proclaim was not served. Or upon hearing what we deem as an unpunished crime we assure ourselves that 'natural law' will fill in the gaps.

Boo, my youngest at age five saw the world entirely in these terms: "If Julian hits me, then I hit him back". A five-year-old, as you may know, has the uncanny ability to be judge, jury and executioner. If we turn this around and say, "I understand that Julian hurt you, but does hitting him fix your pain?" we question nature of consequences. Essentially what we attempt to foster is the law of consequences, which suggests that for every action there is a reaction, and that we have the capacity to choose that action, and thus choose some of the consequences, for ourselves and others. If we successfully do this then we have established an ethical and moral framework for them to test.

Karma is a map to move through the world, enabling us to see the consequences of our actions before they bear fruit. As such, karma is a means of understanding the future, as powerful and insightful as any tarot reading or crystal ball can be. Thus for many Pagans, with our love of threes (and our backdoor adoration of old occultists!), when we discuss karma we refer to the law of threefold return – whatever you do comes back to you threefold. As adults, we understand that this is a safety measure to ensure that we fully consider both our magical and mundane actions. This is not to quash our ability to make decisions, but to help us maintain an awareness of the interconnectivity of the world, and perhaps to help us think about the ways our own actions may ripple beyond our immediate sphere.

I often think about this law when I think about our old car, silver fin. Dan (my husband) and I love beautiful things, we are both strongly earth people, but we also have a compulsion to give our belongings to people when they need them. I am constantly cataloguing our belongings, and when we get to what I consider overload I give them away. I enjoy the feeling of lightness it brings me, and the frisson it creates between Dan and I as he tries to guess what I will get rid of next!

With two boys constantly growing we gave our outgrown clothes to our good friends Val and Jon as their son was a wee bit smaller than ours. One of the most wonderful models of the threefold return came when we realised we needed a car, and these same friends gifted their old car to us. A strong friendship and all those months of ensuring their son had our boys' outgrown clothes were recognised in one extraordinary act of kindness and generosity. Such a model of threefold return may not always be your reality, but to show our kids that what you do comes back to you is an excellent way of inspiring them. Thus recycling, conservation and respecting take on deeper levels of meaning. Recycling becomes a spiritual act, conservation a duty of care, and an attitude of respect a modus operandi for relating to people places and all beings. And in cultivating these qualities we encourage the Goddess to smile upon us.

Self-Care is World Care

To be able to take care of the world, we must first learn how to care for ourselves. Our basic job as parents and as educators is to keep our kids alive until they become capable of caring for themselves. We do them a disservice when we do everything for them, because we interfere with their capacity to self-care. The educational pioneer Maria Montessori based her approach to education around the notion of self-care, and the importance it has for healthy self-esteem and self-knowledge. With small kids, we encourage them to wash themselves, make their beds, and put their own shoes on, even though it would be quicker and easier if we did it for them. We allow them to do it, because it builds self-respect and autonomy. These become visible signs of growth and maturity. Although I am a firm advocate for play-based childhood, children thrive when given work that is real. Self-worth comes from doing valued work as well as being told that we are loved and being lavished with affection and warmth.

As part of self-care, giving kids chores become a crucial means of demonstrating our trust in their capabilities. Just as play is essential to children, for it affords children rich opportunities to problem solve, imagine, project, manipulate and evolve, so too does work. Often children's play involves the taking on of roles and responsibilities. To my mind play and responsibility go hand in hand when we are raising kids to be able to confidently care for themselves, others and the planet.

Today so much is done to and for our kids that the simplest of tasks can become a battleground – taking the rubbish out, tidying the bedroom, laying a table are valued by a whole community and are important life skills to learn. But unless we value them and remain consistent in our approach to them, our kids will not see them as a sign of self-care. To teach a child, they must be motivated and be allowed to approach a skill of his or her own volition and see how the task/skill fulfils a greater purpose. So, the key here is starting them young! Allow them to strive but keep their work age appropriate. Model doing it yourself. It is hard to teach a kid to clean when you hire a cleaner. When we ask children to undertake self-care and household work, we can reward them. You could offer star charts, or simply give praise, tell them how it lightens your load, and that these are the things that make family life easy and amiable. This way we acknowledge the meaningful contribution they make to family life.

Age Appropriate Household Work

Three years: Carry items to the table, tidy toys away, dusting and sweeping!

Four years: Begin to help cook, wash face and clean teeth with supervision, independently get dressed/undressed.

Five years: Make their own bed, put dirty laundry in basket, feed pets.

Six years: Help do dishes, unpack groceries and lay the table.

Seven years: Vacuum, help choose weekly menu.
Eight years: Put away laundry, sweep yard, clean the car.
Nine years: Make their own lunch box, pack school bag.
Ten years: Clean the bathroom, prepare breakfast table.
Eleven years: Walk the dog, buy groceries locally.
Twelve years: Cook at least one evening meal a week.
Thirteen years: Tidy the bedroom! Run errands.

Not only do we foster self-care and thus self-respect in the work we allow our children to do, but also in our expectations of their behaviour. It has become the norm to associate creative children with a laissez-faire attitude towards cultural customs. For my family, part of the job of allowing kids to be kids, is to recognise that we are adults and it is our job to help them get along in the world. One of the simplest and yet least valued aspects of this is manners. For Pagans who value connection to the earth, to the land and to community, manners are a way in which we extend respect to all our relations. I discuss manners under self-care because I believe that etiquette and manners are the behaviours through which we demonstrate respect for others and ourselves. It is also a sure way to help kids get along in the world. Now, I know you may argue that manners are essentially codes of social control put in place to detail your social status and standing. But conservative though it may sound, I also think that manners are an integral part of showing respect. I want to propose an updating of manners and think that instead of manners as modes of social control and signifiers of status, that we consider them as offerings or honourings.

To say good morning to neighbours, whether they are strangers to us or not, helps to cast the world as a place full of friends and it oils the wheels of our travels. By asking politely people will be well disposed towards us. By being quick to apologise, we show a willingness to accept responsibility, we show that mistakes are easily made and remedied. In our home we have a saying, "Manners make the world go round." I truly believe that by raising sons who are mannerly I am bestowing upon them a great gift, as politeness can make a difficult situation easier.

Looking people in the eye, removing sunglasses, shaking hands when you meet someone, are all means by which we show ourselves to be people of substance, that we are confident, even if we don't feel it. This can be very useful for children and young adults. Such small behaviours are reliable passports in the world. These pleasantries are signs of a considerate, generous spirit. Manners are also an expression of kindness between strangers. They are easy to learn, easy to offer and make a huge difference. Children who have good manners, even in the simplest ways, are esteemed by the community around them. Let me reassure you though, this is not the same as compliance. I am not advocating that our kids are robots. To know when and how to speak with our elders is a sign of respect cherished in every tribal society. Kids are allowed to be individuals. Yet manners are increasingly undervalued in our society.

Consider the role manners play in your home, your school, your community, and how they could improve all your lives. Holding the door for someone (irrespective of age or gender), learning to eat quietly and without too much mess, offering someone our seat on the train or the bus, asking someone if they are OK, all of these small moments of honouring embed us in our community.

The first home my family lived in was in a largely Hispanic community. My then precocious two-year-old learned various basic greetings in Spanish so he could talk to neighbours and say thank you to the employee at the local bodega. Every time he did, the friendly owner would give him a lollipop – this was all the motivation he needed. Very quickly he began to realise that basic pleasantries, good mornings and goodbyes, were simple passports to good times, treats and praise. He says, "Good

Morning Mr Mestre!" to our elderly Cuban neighbour every day and so gets to pet his dog and chat. And because of this, I know that our neighbour knows my boys and watches out for them, for their belongings and our home.

For kids of the social networking generation, such verbal pleasantries are often dropped in favour of the exchange of information. In a culture of speed typing and texting, language use is often reduced to the bare necessities. Despite this language reduction having worrying Orwellian undertones, I also worry that our kids' face-to-face interactions may be suffering as a consequence. Simple daily signs of care and concern, pleasantries and manners place us in good relationship with our friends, family, our neighbours and strangers, and begin to build the bond of neighbourhood. When my kids started school I was astonished and they were dismayed to find that their calls of "good morning" were met with stony stares or ignored. I have continued to explain to my kids that they should persevere. This model of engagement can extend beyond your immediate sphere and as kids get older polite exchanges, good manners, help us extend our network – to local shop owners, dog walkers, bus drivers and beyond.

There are times of course when our kids will put out such excellent honourings only to be met with scorn, indifference or grumpiness. These are also valuable experiences for our kids to encounter. Adults also have bad days, we behave badly, and such occasions allow our kids to fine-tune their instincts. Could you tell he was going to respond like that? In such a time when our children's engagement with 'outsiders' is fraught with fears of abduction, showing our kids how to trust their instincts is part of being streetwise, of knowing when it's good to be bright and cheery and when it's worth crossing the street.

Expressions of care are not restricted to our human neighbours. We can expend such honourings to all our neighbours from the mineral, animal and plant kingdoms. We daily greet the willow tree that dwarfs our neighbours' houses, the birds on our porch, our neighbourhood animals. Maybe when kids are older they will be less inclined to verbalise this, but watch and you may find they casually touch trees in greeting as they pass.

A final word on self-care and world care should be about survivalism and safety. Many earth-path folk do not live in the backwaters, but nonetheless, instilling preparedness and some basic survival techniques is always good to know and as sensible as teaching your kids the foundations of first aid. Knowing the basics of staying safe is invaluable. Think of the number of times your toddler wonders off when you are in a shop, or loves to run and hide when you are playing in the park, or when you have broken down in the middle of nowhere.

The **S.T.O.P.** acronym (preparethinksurvive.com) is a great place to start teaching survival safety. I have also found it is just as useful in an urban environment as it is for surviving in the wilderness. My boys and I have played related games at parks and playgrounds, building dens from found materials, looking at the weather and seeing what wild food is growing.

- STOP AND SIT. If you are lost, stop. Don't go walking around. Stay where you are. Take a breath. It is easier for someone to find you if you are stationary.
- THINK. Make a list of your options, what you have and what you are going to need? Do you have a working cellphone or torch? Batteries? Do you have a map?
- OBSERVE. Look around and see what is going on, what does your immediate surrounding have? Listen – what can you hear? Is there shelter? Is there material for fire/warmth? What poses a risk and what is useful?
- PLAN. Once you have done the previous three you are clear headed and will be better able to create a plan of action and execute it.

In any form of safety and survival preparedness there are crucial needs: physical safety (shelter/warmth), nourishment (water/food) and navigation and signalling. Teach your children to stop, look and listen if they are lost. Let them know where the flashlights and batteries are kept in case of a power outage. Show them how to read a compass and to dowse for water and you have already begun basic survivalism! Water is the most important survival item, so make sure your kids always go out with their own water bottle. Can they recognise berries that are edible and do you know which wild herbs (otherwise known as weeds) can be eaten? You can weave in this knowledge when you are on a nature walk, or in conversations about 'what if...?' around the table.

If your kids find themselves lost in any space knowing how to signal for help is crucial, whether using a mirror or smoke if they are in a wild place, spelling out SOS in rocks, or if it's with a phone or running around, yelling like a crazy person in the city! Lindsay at outsidemom.com has some other great pointers for kids surviving in the wilderness.

However, in the UK, you are unlikely to be attacked by venomous snakes or coyotes. Instead, charging bulls can pose a threat! If you have ever wandered into a field with cows you are probably aware of how large they are. A hilarious discussion ensued one day as I walked through a field with my boys and we discussed what we would do if a bull charged at us. Despite my kids' protestations that a good bash on the behind with a stick would send it off, when I told them that a face off was more likely, and that yelling and throwing a backpack or something to distract a charging bull is the only viable option, they fell about laughing.

The likelihood of such an event is small, however, family life constantly gives rise to minor safety issues. As my mum used to say – sometimes parenting is like constantly putting out fires. Giving kids tools to handle the minor emergencies that plague every family (house fires, car accident, thunderstorm blackout) can be as simple as putting a list of your In Case of Emergency (ICE) numbers on the fridge, or having a special bag beneath the sink with batteries, torches, water purification tablets, matches and candles. Safety techniques for dealing with minor accidents and emergencies to larger problems requiring family disaster preparedness plans can be found at www.rospa.com, www.redcross.org.uk or www.ready.gov.make-a-plan.

The Importance of Growing Things

Growing and tending green things is good for everyone, big and small. For us all, growing things keeps us connected to the rhythms of nature. It is also a fantastic stress reducer and brings abundance, well-being and nourishment into our lives. I was lucky that I grew up in a family where my mother's love affair with her tiny back yard garden was prominent. When I became a teenager I used to find the amount of time she spent out there totally baffling. What a waste, I would think. The roses she adored and spent all her money on (she would happily spend more money on plants than anything else) would bloom, fade and die. Her morning stroll around the garden could take two hours, which for a space of 18 feet square was pretty impressive. Her garden was full of life – birds built nests in inopportune places, frogs found old tins full of water and turned them into pools teeming with life, and the neighbourhood cats... the less said about them the better.

Then I became interested in herbal lore and the whole thing about gardening made sense. I learnt about the lore and power of herbs and flowers, and although our points of interest were different I joined in some of her passion for gardening. She helped me as I developed an intimate relationship with Artemisia (mugwort), and every day we would work the garden, weeding, planning, talking, meditating, reading in this tiny enchanted space. I loved showing the neighbourhood kids the herbs and my young siblings became excellent at recognising herbs and flowers. And of course they loved the ability to find bugs hidden everywhere.

Not a lover of indoor plants or houseplants, all our green things were outside, but cut flowers, herbs to cook with or make incense from, brought them inside on a daily basis.

Today I share a community garden and I am an avid pot porch gardener. I don't have the space or ability to grow the array of poisonous plants that so fascinated me as a younger adult, and I am not a naturally green-fingered person. I am no gardening expert, I am most certainly average and amateur, but I love the process of putting something in earth and watching it grow. This is the most basic form of magic. It is also the most democratic – as pretty much anyone can grow things, irrespective of age, financial status, or location. Something will grow. Not always what you want, or where you want, but it will. If you live in an urban jungle you have to work harder, but I have friends who guerrilla garden, turning tiny spaces of exposed soil on inner city sidewalks into miniature fairy gardens. There is always space, however small, to grow green things.

Kids of all ages and abilities respond to working a garden. For younger kids it is simply the opportunity to see what can grow and their interest may pulse in and out. But where you can, grow a range of plants – vegetables, herbs, flowers, to eat, use medicinally or just to look beautiful. Allow small children a small pot or patch for themselves. For older kids and teens the capacity to include them is only limited by your imagination. Grow veggies, and then make a farm stand, or sell them in your front yard. Grow flowers and practice flower arranging, or magical posy making.

Teach kids about the magical history of plants and you open the door to another world for them. Learn about weeds and wild flowers, about foraging and you give them life and survival skills that older kids and teens will enjoy. If you are an educator, this can be interwoven in every aspect of your day – build a garden, go on nature trails in your neighbourhood, plant bulbs in the autumn, and allow each child to grow an edible plant – tomatoes are easy, or lettuce.

Allow plants to cover your classroom and you will find that it creates quite a distinct vibe. I once looked after a neighbour's plants whilst she travelled. She loved her houseplants more than most of us love our animals and you couldn't see the walls for them. There were literally hundreds of plants in all sizes in her small apartment. And the place had a very distinct aura – calming but invigorating. My sons would come with me to water the plants and said her apartment smelt really clean, and I think his was due to the quality of the air.

Gardening and growing green things can be as exciting as you want it to be – but however you approach it, whether through survivalism, permaculture, simple pot herb growing, the lessons gardening offers us are the same. The cultivation of plants means we have to get our hands dirty, it is work and it takes time and effort, planning and thought. Collecting and storing seeds and bulbs. Picking, harvesting and conserving. Considering the right time for every action in the garden. It also brings into sharp focus the cycle life, death and rebirth. Think about perennials, every year, with the right climate, the right surroundings and tendings they return to life after lying dormant all winter.

Such a model for rebirth is a clear, tangible model of our belief in an afterlife.

For kids of all temperaments growing things can give great peace. For those who need quiet and to learn to be alone, gardening can be beautiful, or you can construct ambitious community or school gardens. Whichever form our growing takes, gardening places us in our bodies, and within a community of growing, rotting, and dying living things. It is also the creation of a place excellent for magic. Wassail your garden plot around Yule, give thanks in harvest time and bless the earth in spring, and you are setting sacred foundations for the growing of things. If you are fortunate enough to have a long-term garden space, you can design it to be able to mirror the sacred symbols of our spirituality – a spiral herb garden, a vegetable plot based around the elemental correspondences of the vegetables or crop cycles that reflect the dance between sun and cold, summer's king and winter's king. Teach your kids about companion planting and show them how, just like us, plants thrive when they are with those they love!

You can also make fairy houses and honour the unseen companions in every garden. My kids left a patch of long grass in our front yard for ages much to the consternation of our landlord, so the little folk in the garden had somewhere to play. Gardens can facilitate the magical mind like few other domesticated places.

Growing food to eat is a profound and enriching experience. If you don't already do it, I urge you to start. Kids of all ages and stages really groove to this – to picking veggies in their garden and eating them. And there are endless ways in which you can organise this, from potted herbs in your kitchen, to full-scale raised beds in your garden, or buying an orchard (a personal dream of mine). Whether grown, found, foraged or five-fingered (scrumping) getting food to eat that does not come from a supermarket shelf but from the land you live in is intuitively right – we know somehow, deep within us, that it is better for us. You also get to see what fruit and veggies really look like – that they come in all shapes and sizes and are not uniform as supermarkets would have us believe. Gleaning organisations, like Gleaning Network UK (http://www.feeding5k.org/gleaning.php) are helping to redistribute thousands of unwanted veggies that are laid to waste every year because they don't conform to supermarkets cosmetic standards. Let's help limit our food waste by supporting them and by being happy to have spots on our apples.

Generally, eating food more locally grown is better for everyone although, sadly, it is often more costly. As a family you may have to weigh this up. Growing your own food requires one set of costs, buying locally grown food or organic another. This could be a great project to set your older kid, to weigh up the advantages and disadvantages of buying local food. What we can be sure of, though, is that when kids get to see, feel and experience food grown, with all its precariousness, they will appreciate the earth as the bringer of nourishment in more than simply name.

Delicious Dishes made from Foraged Plants by Peg Aloi

Cream of Nettle Soup

Nettles are chockfull of nutrients, an excellent way to revive the body after winter sluggishness. You will want to pick young nettles, no taller than a foot, for this soup.

Nettles sting! So wear thick gloves when picking them, and keep them in a basket or paper sack. Wash them very well, as they can be gritty; if possible find a source well away from the roadside. Blanching or washing in hot water briefly will kill the stinging fibres. Then, strip the leaves from their stems. If you're very sensitive to nettles, wear gloves during this process. You can prepare this soup as you would any cream soup made with greens.

You will need:
115 g butter
Salt and pepper
1 onion, chopped
1-2 cloves garlic
1 carrot
1 medium potato
4-5 handfuls of nettle leaves

Splash of milk
Sour cream or yogurt for garnish

Melt two tablespoons butter in a saucepan and sauté one coarsely chopped onion. Add one or two cloves of garlic, one sliced carrot, and one medium potato; cut into chunks (leave the skin on for added fibre and nutrients). Cover with two inches of water, and then cook with lid on over medium heat until the vegetables are soft. Add the nettle leaves and heat until bright green and wilted. Pour nettles and veggie mixture into a blender and puree until smooth. Return to pan, and add some low-fat milk, stirring in until it's the texture and thickness you want. Salt and pepper to taste. Serve immediately with a dollop of sour cream or yogurt.

What Kids Can Help With
Because this is mostly made on the stove, smaller children won't be able to do much. They can put the spoonful of sour cream or yogurt on the soup before serving or, with supervision, measure water or milk for pouring, sprinkle salt and pepper, or help put carrots or potato chunks into pot.

Dandelion Green Quiche
Dandelions are another abundant spring green, full of healthy goodness. The chlorophyll in greens helps tone and cleanse the blood and digestive organs, and helps eliminate bad breath or body odour. The nutrients in dandelions provide important vitamins and minerals including iron. Pick dandelion greens before the flowers go to fluff stage, and make sure they are far away from the road or anywhere pesticides are sprayed. Rinse the greens well and cut the white part near the root off. Chop well and use in salads, or make this yummy quiche for a main dish.

You will need:
115g butter
472g flour (white and whole wheat)
Salt and pepper
1 onion, chopped
Dandelion greens
Cheese (Cheddar, Swiss or fontina)
Cottage cheese (optional)
4 eggs
500mls milk

You can use a store-bought crust, or make your own. Use 115g of butter, add the flour (you can mix whole wheat and white), plus some salt and pepper. Cut the butter into small chunks, and use a fork or pastry cutter to blend with the flour (add more flour if needed until mixture is crumbly; it's also helpful to use your hands). When it has a dry crumbly texture and the butter is blended, make a well in the centre and add in some cold water (slowly, mixing with your finger in a circular motion) to make the dough stick. It if gets too sticky you can add a bit more flour. Press into a glass or metal pie or quiche pan with your fingers, pressing up sides and trying for even thickness, about an eighth inch thick. Bake the crust at 350/180 degrees for about ten minutes; remove from oven. You can brush it with egg white if you like. Let cool while you make the sauté.

Sauté a chopped onion in butter or olive oil in a heavy cast-iron pan. Add the dandelion greens and some salt and pepper to taste, sauté until wilted and bright green. You may add other herbs if you like, but the dandelion greens are very flavoursome on their own. Layer some cubed or grated cheese over the partially baked crust. This will form a layer to prevent the crust from becoming soggy and add great flavour. Use a semi-hard cheese like Cheddar, Swiss or fontina. You may then add some cottage cheese over the other cheese if you wish, for a nice light texture. Layer the vegetables over the cheese.

Then beat 4-5 eggs (room temperature) with 500mls of milk (depending on size of your pan; if you use some cottage cheese you may use fewer eggs and less milk) together to make the custard. Pour over the top.

You may then sprinkle pepper on top, or freshly grated nutmeg, or a bit more grated cheese. Bake it at 350/180 until the middle is firm and doesn't 'jiggle', which should take 40-45 minutes. Cool before cutting and serving.

What Kids Can Help With

Kids can help pick and wash dandelion greens. They can help make the crust, with clean hands, once it is mostly mixed, and help press it into the pan. They can put the grated cheese in the crust, scoop cottage cheese on the grated cheese with a spoon, and beat the eggs with a fork or small whisk in the bowl. Enjoy!

Body Awareness

Pagans believe that the body is sacred. The stuff of flesh is a divine reflection of universal matter. We are made of stardust. In the Drawing Down the Moon ritual, one of the most sacred mystery rituals in the Wiccan tradition, the priestess manifests as the Goddess and reminds all present,

You shall be free from slavery, and as a sign that you be free you shall be naked in your rites. Ye shall sing, feast, dance, make music and love, all in my presence, for mine is the ecstasy of the spirit and mine also is joy on earth.

This beautiful passage by poet and witch Doreen Valiente exactly expresses the concept of the body as a sacred expression of the divine. Through loving our flesh we celebrate the generative forces of the universe.

From when a child is newborn, their experience of their new world comes from feeling the limits of their own body. Allowing your children – of all ages – to explore and express their joyful body is a gift. Of course you are thinking, this is the bit we were waiting for, now comes the bit on nudity. Children are not adults engaged in Wiccan mystery rituals. That is not the place for them. Instead, I'm speaking here of the way in which we can foster self-love through learning the strength and beauty of our body. I strongly believe that for kids to know themselves, they have to be able to experience their bodies. Shame, fear and prudishness have no place around small children. But knowing how to do this in age and place appropriate ways can be difficult.

Adults have become hypersensitive to the issue of child nudity due in large part to the media attention given to cases of child abuse and child pornography. Both of these frightening and dreadful abuses of power over children have made the question of children's bodies problematic. I wish we lived in a simpler time when my five-year-old could run round a sprinkler park naked as he wishes. However, our problem with children's nakedness comes from our own fears – is someone looking? Does someone have inappropriate feelings towards my child? Is this appropriate for a child this age? We are plagued with these questions and it is terribly sad.

Simultaneously, though, we work to make our children appear more and more adult-like in the clothes they wear and the toys and accoutrements they have. On a societal level we cannot make our minds up – adults who prey on children are irredeemable, yet parents who dress their kids in low cut jeans and bikinis are not vilified. We are fearful that any image of children's nakedness may provoke inappropriate responses, and so we outlaw artists' renditions of children showing their naked beauty and innocence. All images of children carry the burden of sexual anxiety it seems. As is the case with various "sexting" crimes of late, rather than dealing with why young women would want to send such pictures of themselves, we make them both the victim and the perpetrator of a crime that could label them a sex offender. This kind of skewed thinking demonstrates our confusion around the sexuality of children and the knee jerk fears for children's innocence. The true cost is that children are more body conscious than ever before.

In addition to the issues of child sexualisation, the obesity epidemic has created a discourse of shame and fear-mongering regarding children's weight. Children's relationship with their body is constantly scrutinised in such a way as to distort their impetus for self-care. I am not denying that child obesity exists, but the climate of fear surrounding it in mainstream media and our health services and schools has furthered a culture of body comparison. Do we need more of this? How can we navigate these issues and help foster our kids' unencumbered attitude towards their unique body, whatever its size and shape?

When I watched my kids play naked mud games in the garden, I envied their lack of self-consciousness and, for this reason alone, I advocate naked play for our little kids. There is a point where our kids will become aware of their nakedness, where naked becomes nude. But, by allowing our kids to be naked and to experience simple sensual pleasures – the air across their skin, the sun on their bodies or as we found recently, the rain on their little naked dancing selves – we let them get to experience their bodies joyously engaged in the world while they can.

Over the age of six (and earlier in some cultures) nakedness beyond the home becomes complex, but there are some small ways we can allow our kids to continue to have naked time. Around the house, bath times, allowing our kids to sleep naked, encourage them to see strength and beauty in their bodies. If we can cultivate an atmosphere of relaxed and mindful appreciation of skin we may also stem the tide of body consciousness that ravages so many of our young folk.

For those of us who work with organisations, schools and festivals, the issue of children's nakedness or modest attire, and the issues of safeguarding, will undoubtedly have to be considered. How we tackle this is crucial to the message we send our community and the wider culture about how Pagans view the body as sacred.

From the moment our children are born we mark their body in culture. We clothe them, we may even pierce their ears, or cut their skin, gender them with colours and symbols – pink for girls these days (although 100 years ago pink was a boy's colour) and they then begin their lives with a set of expectations placed on them. They are rewarded for eating well, using the potty, and later for being clean, sporty, pretty.

So often the terms we use to praise our kids are those that somehow reward their body's behaviour, that if they perform well then they are working well. Whether consciously or not, values regarding the body are inherent in our forms of praise and shame. Our culture indoctrinates our children into thinking about their bodies as a part of them rather than thinking about themselves as bodies of flesh, skin, feeling and thought. Contemporary Western culture primarily values our body by placing a culture of reward and punishment around the body. We grow up with three modes of body awareness:

- FEAR: youthfulness, weight, proximity to others, touching, nakedness, fitness, appropriate behaviour.
- COMPETITION: sport, action, strength, comparison, fashion, athleticism.
- ALLURE: attention, beauty, prettiness, reward, youth.

How can we encourage our kids to experience themselves outside these modalities? Especially for older kids and young adults, finding ways to praise and value the body that does not fit into these categories is hard. How can we value the diversity of our kids without comparison, shame, or narcissism? Being in our body, learning that there is no separation between self and skin is crucial to an understanding of embodied spirituality.

When we say to our loved ones, our coveners, or our children, "Thou art Goddess," we literally mean that each person is a living embodiment of the divine universal spark. Our bodies are not vessels for the spirit, they are not the fleshy stuff within which the divine inhabits as we might inhabit a house. Instead Pagans understand that our flesh is sacred, is in itself spiritual. When we begin to really feel this inside our bodies, we may as adults come to realise how far away from that understanding we have drifted.

For women, we may experience moments of this when we are pregnant or giving birth. We may also experience it when we make love. I have heard that at moments of intense physical exertion, athletes and yoginis alike experience themselves as physically connected to the divine. But often this is a fleeting moment of understanding. Yet children can show us how to truly be in our bodies, especially babies and small children. We can stem the tide, and let our kids experience themselves in various ways, as fairies and fire engines, in pink and in blue. And if we can safeguard this experience of embodiment for them, we may help hold onto the sense of self that is not a head on a stick, but a complete being. We are beings of flesh, of physical rhythms and desires and these uniquely reflect the beauty of the universe.

To feel well in our body, to feel healthy, alive, invigorated, connected, requires us to actively exert ourselves. Many children naturally do this, running everywhere. Others are slower to find a way of being in their body through activity. Some children are born with heightened sensitivities, such as my oldest boy, Summer, who feels every breeze, every clothing tag and every temperature change. He is our home's own barometer; as the pressure changes he gets a nosebleed. Boo, my little lad, is the opposite, hardy and physical, mastering physical skills and taking great delight in his body's ability to *do*. It can be useful to return to an elemental understanding of your kids to work out how to keep them positively connected to their body.

Whatever inclination your kid has, to be able to positively channel their physical energy is a great way to help them to maintain their sense of their body as sacred and beautiful. I'm not saying send them off to ballet and gymnastics as soon as you can, although these can be great. Encouraging their body in motion helps them find and test their limits, stay fit and healthy and delight in their body's abilities. Too many Pagans have not taken care of their physical health, but have instead focused on their etheric and psychic skills. We need people with those skills in our community, but ideally we would have them with us as long as they could be so they can pass on those skills, and physical well-being is one way to ensure our longevity.

Here are some ideas of matching the elemental types of your kids to various physical activities:

Water

For kids with heightened sensitivities, try the following activities. Yoga, non-competitive gymnastics, country dancing are good options and do lots of improvisational dance at home. Although you would think swimming and other water sports would be good for water kids, often they get too cold and self-conscious. However, they often would really benefit from time spent in water. Try hot tubs, lots of sprinklers or bath play. For water/fire kids try all forms of dance, they love that imaginative and graceful element of dance with the focus on performance and role-playing.

Earth

The best physical activities for earth kids will be work-based, so let them help you lift things, move things, and do lots of walking in all weathers. They are hardy kids. Games that are competitive are good for earth types although they aren't always too bothered by the winning and the dirtier the better so try out rugby and hockey. Earth/fire kids might enjoy more competitive and community driven outdoor games.

Air

These kids are the kids that find physical activity harder – they would rather be reading or working out a maths problem. For you this will be a question of framing. Set a problem; can you climb to the top of the climbing wall only moving diagonally? Games such as tennis, cricket, or human chess would be good choices. Air/fire combinations will enjoy gymnastics or fencing, combining the tactical flair with dance and form.

Fire

Competitive sports and athletics are good choices for fire kids, where they can be pushed by their peers. For fire kids, it can be important to build confidence in their individual skills, build on personal targets rather than through comparison, which they will keenly feel. For this reason I often recommend martial arts to strongly fire kids. With its focus on discipline and form, this can be a great way to channel their energy!

In Waldorf education, circus arts are highly valued for the role they can play in building physical skills, gross motor skills, but unlike so many structured 'sports' they promote co-operative work, they are play-centric and fun. I know this was true for my younger sister; she lived in circus arts during her pre-pubescent and early teen years, and now, as I watch her as an adult, the ease she has with her body I am sure is a consequence of navigating this difficult transition with a focus on skill, play and activity. And you should see her on a unicycle! Circus skills are fantastic for all kids of all ages and all physical skills, and allow kids to be expressive and creative in their exercise.

Pagans have a wealth of earth-based exercises that we rarely consider as essential to our well-being. However, singing, drumming and dancing are all key means to being physically engaged and all Pagan traditions venerate these energy-raising skills. Drumming, singing and dancing are skills that live at the heart of Pagan spiritual practice, as they are community building and magic weaving. They also require us to be truly within our body. They teach us that raising energy and expending energy requires a level of body awareness that often goes deeper than our everyday awareness. These expressions require us to be in tune (sometimes literally) with our environment, others and ourselves.

The capacity to sing, dance and drum is also universal – it is another wonderful democracy of the body that means that most people are able to do at least one of these. They are hard-wired into us, and allow us to make relationships with the world we live in. They are also wonderful tools to help us work with children as, whether solo or in groups, they allow us to connect with children across cultures, ages and abilities.

We can sing to our kids, to help them sleep, or to teach them stories, as discussed in the last chapter, or we can teach them chants to raise energy, or rid themselves of bad feelings. Likewise, we drum with our toddlers to help them develop their gross motor skills, and later to help them learn about patterns, rhythm, matching. And through dancing we allow our children to express themselves beyond words. Dance and drumming are ways in which we embody rhythm, and children are naturally born with this. Lest we believe those things we may have been told as kids, "You can't dance," or, "Please just mouth the words," I am telling you now you were sold a lie. All children, irrespective of ability, culture or ethnicity were born with the urge and mostly the desire to sing, to move, to dance. Dancing can be an amazing way of getting kids back in their body. If you have a dreamy air kid who seems clumsy or spacey, have daily dance parties or send them to a dance class and watch them blossom.

Soapbox alert – I am a strong believer in teaching children folk or traditional dance. If we expose our young to the dances of our own cultural backgrounds, or the place in which we live, we help them connect to their bodies and the body of their heritage, their family and place. I did country dancing as a kid in first and middle school between the ages of six to 11 years. It was part of the now almost defunct Music and Movement curriculum we had and we loved it (we called it "pants and vest" as you did it in your underwear – would a school even allow this today?) It was always at the end of the school day and included some circle dance, some partner dance and some wallying about. Girls and boys had to hold hands. The music was loud. It was a totally joyous part of the school day, although none of us admitted it.

Now as an adult I have a deep love and appreciation for dance. What I love about folk and circle dance is its inclusivity and the stories that accompany the dances. In circle dance, we learn basic steps and importantly learn how to move together. Whether we do it right or wrong is not really important, as long as the circle keeps moving. But there is skill in circle dance too, and grace and beauty. You can do it anywhere with nothing but your voice for music, you can do it spontaneously; you can teach it to all kinds of people of all ages. A spiral dance, a traditional dance used in ritual to raise energy, can also be a wonderful dance to teach children, as it allows them to greet each other, and see the power of eternal return. Spiral through your home anticlockwise to get rid of bad vibes, or bad dreams, circle dance in a park and see how everyone at first watches then wants to join in (details of these are given later in Chapter Five).

Dancing is a part of our festival cycle. The Maypole, that wonderful symbol of summer's arrival, is erected at Beltane, and danced around, with ribbons to bless the fecund earth, to ripen and enrich the soil. This beautiful custom, which we still use as a means of ensuring the earth fertility, was traditionally danced around a living tree whose roots trunk and branches span the

CHILDREN OF THE GREEN

different worlds. However, all too often I have been to great gatherings of Pagans and found that no one knows how to dance a Maypole, it becomes a free-for-all – which although fun for some, is not what a Maypole is about.

In dancing a maypole we wrap the ribbon around the pole, we embellish it, with the juicy maiden energy, and we make the pole beautiful, with the ribbons detailing wonderful patterns. There is the Grand Chain, Jacob's Ladder, the Pyramid and the Spider's Web weave. All these wonderful weaves make different patterns, when danced with the perfect number of eight to 20 dancers. If you are an educator, or a community leader, these can be wonderful to teach in the lead-up to a May Day celebration. And if other kids or adults want to dance freely, allow them to do so, but please, let's keep the traditions of the Maypole weaves alive.

Song, dance and drum are free, they are ever available, come rain or shine and they are rich with stories, history and heritage. They maintain our kids' connection to their own body and to the land, and to the relationships they have with others. They don't need words, and yet they are expressive ways we can communicate our feelings.

Feeding Ourselves

The earth is the element that brings us nourishment, feeds us, comforts us, and gives us energy through the universal exchange between plants, animals and humans. This is such a vast subject and one of such importance that I could write a book on this alone. Feeding our family, and teaching our children to nourish themselves healthily, is critical to supporting their growth and development. We know this, we see it and we feel it instinctively. Healthy eating is a way of honouring the Gods. What we eat comes from the earth, and so by eating well we have an opportunity to commune with the divine. What we eat and how we eat are of upmost importance in the fostering of a whole spiritual and magical life.

Our culture's relationship with food at every level of production, distribution and consumption has become an economy of waste and over abundance, of boom and bust. Food is delivered to us by trucks, from all over the world. And even food grown locally is often shipped to central markets to then be driven back to the place of origin. I remember my mum talking to a local greengrocer in England about this – how frustrating he found it to have to drive 200 miles to buy food that was grown down the road. Common sense tells us that this is wrong. And then we are used to eating foods out of season – of having straw-berries in December, pumpkin soup in the spring, potatoes all year round. Meat is entirely divorced from the living animal it was, as it is packaged in ways that disconnect us from the living being that gave its life for us.

The green food culture around fair trade and organic produce has made great headway in questioning our cultural attitude towards our food, how it is grown, and where. GMO protesters have also brought our food growing practices into sharp relief as we begin to realise the impact upon the whole environment, from insect life to human health, when we interfere with the systems of pollination and plant life. We are questioning who brings the food to our tables.

For many earth path folk, the issues surrounding eating locally grown produce and organic food are economic and logis-tical as much as they are ethical. Organic food is more expensive and if you are shopping for a family it requires considerable resources to shop exclusively organic. And then, just because it is organic, does that ensure a guilt-free, earth-loving relationship with food? Unfortunately not. The problem then becomes consumer overload, which can lead so many of us to a place of 'organic-guilt'. We would love to eat local veg but how many times a week can you feed a kid kohlrabi when they will only eat fish fingers? When we work or live with kids, we realise how we are bombarded with intense food marketing campaigns. The continual marketing of children's food products, complete with this week's TV or film character, can make supermarket shopping a nightmare. Going to a large supermarket can often feel like you are running the gauntlet between the devil and the deep blue sea. Children are targeted in supermarkets by the placement of items on a shelf, the colours and the packaging design. As my friend Val says – they don't put the broccoli on the bottom shelf with a picture of a cartoon character on it! Given the amount of visual stimuli that surrounds food, and our culture's mixed messages about food and eating (*Mmmm*, I'm not loving it…) it is no wonder that many children develop complex and infuriating fads around food, or in the worst cases develop phobias and disorders around eating.

Pagans generally love food. We love eating! It is a source of pleasure, a central part of our celebrations and an expression of our hedonistic relationship with worldly abundance. Cooking, baking and, of course, feasting are skills highly prized within our communities, and our esbats and sabbats often involve the making of great meals as a means of honouring the Gods. Yet many of us, despite our love of food, suffer poor nutrition and health as a consequence of over indulging or placing too little emphasis on the body's health, instead focusing on the spiritual and psychic sides of ourselves. When we consider this in light of a family, we can begin to see that in placing our kids in good relationship with their appetite we may have to look at our own.

Hunger is an incredibly powerful feeling. To put this simply, I believe that faddy eating in a three-year-old and a problematic relationship with eating in a 13-year-old are motivated by emotional and spiritual needs. We may think that difficulties with eating are attention based – a cry for help, a powerful way of drawing attention whilst not having to own our need for it. And whilst there is a truth in this, I think these imbalances are a consequence of feeling overwhelmed by other needs to such an extent that there is little room for a consideration of food.

For a three-year-old, eating may be getting in the way of mastering a new skill or exerting independence. For older kids, food may feel weighty; it may ground us, when what we want is to remain in a dream space that hunger allows. I watch my children spend entire days eating like sparrows and I cluck and squawk around them, worrying that they are not eating enough, only to find that they will eventually hear their hunger and eat. Babies and small children do not deliberately starve themselves, they may experience hunger in varying ways, they may have difficulty recognising hunger, but they will not use food pathologically like an older child can. Place good food in front of them and they will eat – at least some of it. Older children and teens, however, well that's quite a different kettle of fish.

My own teen experience has led me to believe that older kids and teens who develop complex issues with eating, body image and food, are striving for a new spiritual perspective, and that control over the intake of food is akin to control over the body in an attempt to create a different mindset. Many spiritual traditions use fasting or minimal meals as an aid to meditation. Consider the medieval anchoresses, bricked up, living on air and water and the occasional piece of food and allowing their bodies to become detached from their spirit in order to communicate with spirit. Somewhere in us we know that the feeling we get when we deny ourselves food, or control the intake and expulsion of food from our body is a means to entering a new reality.

Pagans have other means of doing this that are less deleterious on the body. If you have a teen or kid who is having these complex issues with their body and food, consider what other ways they might be able to achieve the state of lightness, of bliss, of cold comfort.

Having survived anorexia and been a part of various organisations that help to re-educate young people after disrupting their body's relationship with food, I have come up with ten simple, easy to follow ideas for helping establish a loving relationship with our bodies, our appetites and food:

1. Model. If we have a healthy relationship with food, and eat well, children will see this and mirror it in their own relationship with eating. If you are constantly worrying about your food intake, you teach your children the language of anxiety around food. If you are very controlled around food, likewise. If you over indulge and have little self-control around eating, so will your kids.

2. Grow your own food and if you can't then visit farms, community gardens, and a slaughterhouse. See where your food comes from, read the labels. In this way we begin to become involved in what food production is, we become conscious eaters. Find the food that grows locally – scrumping, blackberrying etc. Eat seasonally and connect your meals to the rhythms of the earth in your land.

3. Cook. Now I don't enjoy cooking, it's not something I am particularly good at or enjoy, but my kids need to see me do it – not unpack prepared food, but at least try to make meals in an anxiety free way. And one of the best ways to do this is to get them involved. Food preparation is one way in which we help our kids take responsibility for their food and connect them to their appetite. My husband has the most natural, healthy and pleasurable relationship to his appetites of anyone I know. He describes himself as a chubby kid, because he loved to eat. But his wise mother taught him how to prepare and cook food at a very early age. So when, aged eight, he came home from school with the urge to snack, she told him to prepare something 'proper'. He credits her ability to anchor his hunger to making his own food with his love of cooking and eating today and of course he is as fit as a fiddle

as a consequence!

4. Bake. There is an alchemy to baking. Baking requires a precision, it teaches us to follow directions and we get to define the portions. So this way you can have a limited supply of yummy things in your house – cookies, breads, cakes.

5. Prepare the table. Lay the breakfast or dinner table together and eat together. Simple and yet hard to do in this busy world. With two working parents and kids at different schools this may be a real stretch, but it is worth it. Eating together, preparing a meal table, serving a meal and learning about how to make conversation over a meal are all ways in which we can connect positive emotional experiences to the act of eating. Some families prefer to eat in silence. This can also be a very warming experience. As long as a family table has love, eating becomes nourishing on many levels. This can be a challenge for small children – it may feel like you are eating at the zoo, but the investment of time will pay great dividends for the future.

6. Be mindful of what you put on your plate. Apply mindful awareness to what you eat and where it came from. Whether you are a meat eater, a vegetarian or a vegan, make mindful eating a part of your relationship with food. Mindfulness can also apply to manners and good table manners add a ritual element to meal times that can be greatly comforting.

7. Bless every meal you eat. This can be a simple prayer of thanks or a complex and involved blessing, but by making a meal sacred we connect to the substance of our food and the journey it took to reach us. Here is one my kids often improvise around: *"We give thanks to all who brought this meal to our table, to the farmers who farmed the vegetables, who grew the*

wheat for our pasta, to those working in factories who work hard to package it, to the chicken who gave its life for our body's growth, Brad who baked the bread, the nice people at City Feed who sold it to us and dad who cooked it – Blessed Be."

8. Avoid using food as a reward or a punishment. Although there are times when we use food, especially sweet yummies, as bribes (yes, even the most spiritually minded of us do this, to tempt a kid onto a potty or to try a new pair of shoes on) remove the notion of food as an emotional tool. Instead, emphasise that, "it's good to try," but take the emotional pressure off. Make portions small, introduce new foods regularly and allow your kids to develop likes and dislikes.

9. Hydrate! Water is sacred. One of the biggest causes of mood shifts in our kids can be easily remedied by hydration. Most of us as adults don't drink enough water and school, with its rigorous schedule, rarely gives kids time to keep themselves hydrated. Hydrated kids are happy kids – alert and connected. Show your kids a love of drinking water. Water is the stuff of life, we need it to keep our bodies and our spirits refreshed and renewed. So water and milk, with a glass of juice a day, is the perfect way to hydrate your kids.

10. Eat regularly. Eating is another cycle, and we love cycles, so make sure that your kids' eating cycle ensures that they don't go for hours and hours without food. High protein snacks, like dried fruits, nuts and seeds and boiled eggs are perfect for quick energy boosts. Keep sugar minimal but present – allowing a little sweetness to keep kids happy but make sure it's only once a day.

Food is energy, energy is will and will makes magic. Without a healthy and sustainable relationship with food we cannot connect to our appetite, without appetite it is hard to feel what our body needs, and wants. By eating and shitting we embody the lifecycle, we attune ourselves everyday through this simple animal act to the natural process of converting matter to energy. That energy then allows us to fulfil our life's potential. Without food we exist in the realm of faery, where all is illusion. Like the great tales of the Sidhe where no mortal may eat the food, if we do not nourish ourselves properly we exit the seen world. When we become adults, we can begin to relax this relationship – we may use fasting as a means of loosening our hold, our thread to the world. Some shamanic and magical work requires this, but in order to do this we have to have a well-nourished connection with our body. We cannot undergo such arduous work until we have learnt what it means to be grounded in our body, to be fully in the world. For many of us, myself included, simply learning to live in living relationship with my body and my appetites is a life's work.

As I write this I can hear a nest full of baby starlings, all squawking to their busy parents who are flying about the street looking for food to feed them. Like so many young they noisily let their parents know their need, and remind their beleaguered parents that it is their job to provide a safe, secure nest and to feed them until they are old enough to do it for themselves. All of us guarding our young, human or starling, share the basic responsibility for nourishing our young.

On Life and Death

To me all things shall proceed and unto me shall all things return
Doreen Valiente, The Charge of the Goddess

On approaching the topic of death and its role in the cycle of life, my instinct was to open the rich and illuminating work of Sogyal Rinpoche, *The Tibetan Books of Living and Dying*, looking for a section that might guide my entry to writing about death. I open at a subsection entitled "Doubts on the Path" – a perfect piece of bibliomancy if ever there was one!

Whilst reading his analysis of the prevalence of doubt and its relative, cynicism, I was struck by how riddled our culture and our spiritual traditions are with the language of doubt. We doubt ourselves and rely on experts to tell us how best to experience life changes. We replace our own unknowing with others' opinions. When we come to the question of death, we may face the biggest doubts of our spirituality, we reach the limits of our known understanding. We create beautiful and poetic myths to help us navigate the passages of life, but for many of us, these beautiful stories offer comfort but not meaning to the inevitable end of life.

Instead of turning to 'experts', perhaps there is another way to find comfort in approaching the greatest of life's mysteries. For myself I am moved by Rinpoche's assertion of "noble doubt" – I do not doubt the teachings of reincarnation, of the ever-evolving cycle of life, but I doubt my capacity to fully comprehend its meaning, and I turn my attention towards gaining a deeper understanding through observation, reflection and ritual. Noble doubt allows us to sit with the knowledge that you don't know exactly what happens after death. If we use nature as our key, we see that everything that dies has another use – it becomes food or shelter or makes space for new growth. Nothing is ever wasted, even in death. Likewise when my kids ask me, "Are we going to die?" I assert, "Yes, yes you are, you will return to Mother Earth, but not yet."

As Pagans our approach to death is at once practical and poetic. Life begets life, and death is an inevitable part of the cycle of life. How we help children make sense of this great mystery is in the first element a reflection of the sacred and serious nature of the question. Children, in their first realisation of death, are often veered towards other topics – we are not ready to tell them about the nature of death. And yet, consider how much easier it would be if the topic were dealt with gently and easily from babyhood so that by the time we were teenagers we had come to an understanding that death is a part of our process here on earth. Mother Earth is of course our greatest mentor here for she can show us the reality of life after death. Show children a fallen tree in a forest, hollowed out by the insects, where creatures and fungi take nourishment and make a home. In rotting down, the tree returns valuable nutrients to the soil that will then allow new life to emerge. With its fall, its life spark is transformed, evolving into many new things. It becomes a part of a web of energy through the garden or forest. And yet we can still grieve the particular loss of that tree, unique in its shape, its location. We cannot afford to deny grief, or loss or death as in doing so we cut ourselves off from our capacity to understand life, fertility and the true value of things.

As witch and activist Starhawk writes in *The Pagan Book of Living and Dying*:

Acceptance of death as part of the cycle of life has both personal and social implications. Imagine if we truly understood that decay is the matrix of fertility, if we designed our products with that truth in mind, as nature does, if everything we manufactured were recyclable or could in its breakdown feed something else. Our landfills would be empty and our true collective wealth would increase. Our cemeteries might become orchards. We might view our own aging with less fear and distaste and greet death with sadness, certainly but without terror. (pg.5)

Our children have the capacity to be rooted in the reality of the lifecycle from infancy, and an honest, open and forthright approach to discussing birth and death is our wisest path. We can use language that disregards fear (just as when we are talking to our kids about going to the dentist, irrespective of our own hatred or fear of dentists) and ensure our answers are appropriate to the age and stage of the child.

We do not want to shatter innocence – very much the opposite – so we don't need to explain the intricate biology of death, just as we might restrain our explanation of sexual intercourse to a preschooler to help them understand where their baby brother comes from. But neither do we need elaborate stories about storks or shining stars that fall from heaven. If we root our responses in the natural world, we allow our child to experience the numinous nature of the Goddess firsthand. All things are born of a generative body, the body of a mother, the earth. They come to being from a seed, an egg. Whether blown by the wind, or placed in a syringe by a doctor, some force compels them to meet, to grow and be sustained. And that same force defines when it is time for that spirit, that life to depart. For some families, looking to nature to model the need for life and death is enough, but for some, for whom the myths, legends and tales of the Gods are of central import, these mythologies can provide deeply resonant tools for explaining the laws of eternal return to our kids.

The cycles of eternal return are found in the oldest stories of the world, and offer entrancing poetic myths to help us understand the cycles of life and death. Their inextricable connection can be traced back to the 'mute' cultures of the Minoan period and culture. Through exquisite objects and visual representations, the myth of the descent and ascent of the Goddess (which many of us know through the later Greek myth cycles of Demeter and Persephone), we see the descent and rising of the Goddess, or perhaps her priestess, with flowers, corn and barley. The linking of the Goddess to the land's fertility can be found in mythic cycles from all over the world: Inanna and Geshtinanna in Sumerian myth, Isis and Osiris in Egyptian, Cerridwen and Bran in Celtic myth. The myths and lesser stories of our culture give us tools to help our children come to an understanding of how nature's cycle is connected to our own mortal coil. The Summerland, the place beyond the veil as many Pagans refer to it, is the place beyond death where the spirit goes to await its next incarnation. But always we return – Mother Earth recycles everything. At Samhain we honour those who have passed the threshold of death and travelled to the Summerland, who have left us and returned to the earth. In my home we build an altar to our beloved dead with photographs of ancestors, pets, friends now gone, and intone this prayer and then the names of all those we remember:

> "Beloved Mighty Dead, We honour you this Samhain. We remember what you gave to this world, your love the pattern of your unique being, your struggle and perseverance. We cherish the gift of life you carried and how in your death, your spark is returned and renewed once more. We see you in the drops of rain, we hear you in the robin's song, in the thunder clap. We know you in the smile of a friend and the cry of a child. Our blood is your blood, our breath was once your breath. And so we remember you, always with us, the circle of life remains."

Death may be the last known transition in our life, but we go through many transitions that mark the passage from one phase to another – many mini deaths if you like. By recognising these transitions, these points of release and growth in the lives of children, we embed the knowledge in our children that we are constantly changing; and that with growth comes death, with death comes change and with change comes new growth. We recognise the seasons of our lives, if we wish to live attuned with nature. In doing so we embody the gift of each moment and the strengths of every phase of our life. We learn to cherish the moments we have and when to let go. The following list offers some transitions that you may enjoy celebrating in your child's life, and in doing so demonstrate the world's capacity for eternal return. These are the beginnings and ends of each phase.

- The first 100 days – Baby blessing ceremony to welcome the new child and family to the community.
- Leaving toddlerhood – about age three with the giving up of a pacifier or final nappy.
- Age seven the start of childhood – formal education begins (whatever shape this may take).
- Age ten – reaching double figures.
- Maturity/menstruation rite.
- Embracing adulthood – fleeing the nest.

By recognising the passage of time and growth we embrace change, demonstrating that this is a healthy, life-enriching part of our evolution as human beings. These transition points also allow us to mark important areas of difference – they can allow us to celebrate our gender identity, our sexuality, our growth of skills and knowledge. Despite the contentious nature of some of these ideas, gender being perhaps one of the most troublesome at present, marking such transitions gives us a time to consider the power and joy of a given phase – to acknowledge its challenges and reflect on the strength of the period – something so crucial in a generally secular society.

A New Baby Blessing

You can expand or adapt this to include a naming ceremony if you wish but the purpose of this blessing is to welcome a new infant into the family.

You need:
A blanket
Salt
Water

The sun
The air
A gift of your choice

In the first moon phase that your new baby has been with you, wrap her/him in a special blanket and stand outside in the light of the morning sun. You can choose to have just your immediate family or just you and the babe, or a whole party of people.

Holding your baby, turn to the North and sprinkle the baby's feet with salt.

Say: *"Little one, you are a creature of earth, a being from the Mother. We welcome you to this family. We are glad you have come to us. May your journey be blessed with strength and deep wisdom."*

Turn to the East and breathe down upon the baby gently, a little whistling breath.

Say: *"Little one, you are a creature of air, a gift from the sky. We welcome you to this family. We are pleased you have come to us. May your voice be heard and your hopes find purchase."*

Turn to the South, and hold the baby under the sun's rays.

Say: *"Little one, you are a creature of fire, a gift from the sun. We welcome you to this family. We are so happy you have come to us. May you feel our love and affection for you like a warm blanket always around your shoulders."*

Turn to the West and sprinkle the baby's head with water.

Say: *"Little one, you are a creature of water, a gift from the womb of the Mother. We welcome you to this family. We are delighted you have come to us. May you feel your kin and kith always aiding and supporting you, may you always know where you are in the order of things."*

All attendants are invited to kiss or touch the blanket that wraps the baby, bestowing their blessings upon the wee one. Finally, if you wish, you can call down the blessing of the baby's ancestors and any Goddesses or Gods you have an affinity with.

Say: *"I ask all the mothers and fathers, the sister and brothers who stand behind me, tracing our blood line back through the history of our families. May you bring all good wisdom and knowledge to this little one, first and newest in your line.*

"Ancient ones, great Mother and Father from whom all things proceed and unto whom all things shall return, smile upon this babe as s/he starts her/his journey. Bless their footsteps, their voice, their passion and their dreams. May s/he walk always in your beauty. So mote it be."

At this point give your gift to the baby, and present it in words, in spite of the babe's lack of understanding. This is a formal presentation, and in its formality it has gravitas. Then give thanks to the earth, the air, the fire and the water, your ancestors and the Goddess and Gods for their continual blessings. Go inside, feed the baby and yourself and any guests.

I am a big believer in birthday traditions. In my family home, birthdays rather than Yuletide were the times of abundant celebration, with a day dedicated to that individual as they said goodbye to one year and looked toward the next. Gifts were given, more extravagant and personal than those given at Yule, and it was a day where the birthday child got to do something special. We had birthday tea – the expectation being that every family member would to be present to eat cake, sing, light candles, and talk about the year just gone, our achievements and blunders!

In large families this can be complicated, but whether it is making a birthday tablecloth which is used every year to cover the supper table, or having a special candle holder with the appropriate number of candles, or incanting a blessing that is said only at this time, building in small traditions allows us to recognise the unique year that that child has had.

Gifts and elaborately themed parties are all good and I have had and made a fair few of them, but they are not necessary. Gift giving is often considered part of engaging in reciprocal relationship and highly prized within Pagan community. To act generously, yet not unnecessarily extravagantly, is considered a sign of a generous and giving spirit. Yet the nature of giving should be thoughtful, not motivated by money or showing off. Within Pagan communities gift giving is important as a means of marking special occasions, but the gift is less important than the act of giving, so handmade gifts and regifting are welcomed.

There are of course times when our children need special attention or energy to help them navigate a challenging period of growth. Many small children find home transitions particularly hard, especially those that disrupt the 'grounding' of their lives.

The "I change" moments are those changes that are to do with the child's natural physical growth, and are often accompanied by some form of illness or physical disruption in normal patterns of earth – eating and sleeping. At these times we can help a kid through by honouring the transition and solidifying the rhythms of the day and the place.

"We are changing" are family transition moments, which can be the hardest on us all to navigate. This can be a divorce, the introduction of a new sibling, disablement or illness in the family, or even the death of a close friend or family member. The loss of a pet can also be a huge wrench on kids. Such transitions can be marked by re-establishing home rhythms and making an altar as a living expression of this change, to be maintained by the whole family. Likewise, "we change" moments often require outsider help – draw one or two people closer to your family for extra support and love.

"My world is changing" periods are transitions where a child is realising their place in the world and that their place is shifting. This can be as pragmatic as a long holiday away, a house move, emigration, or a year spent studying abroad. Or such moments can be subtle psychological shifts, such as a realisation of global environmental or justice issues, which shape a child's growing perception of planetary flows.

For these points of change, we can look to the elements – we can help bring our kids' awareness to the points of connectivity and sameness between phases. So, for managing the transition of a house move, consider and reinforce what and who will be constant. Also bring attention to the elements that are constant across place and time and allow these to be the building blocks for creative enterprise – make a mural to release the old and welcome the new. For those psychological shifts in awareness and perception, encourage action and creative responses to these changes.

Life brings us all into contact with struggle, whether by pain, fear, grief, rage, decrepitude or death. A denial of these elements of life is an imbalance, and stands in the path of us truly appreciating the moments of contentment, happiness and well-being. As Pagan author Amber K. writes:

> [...] our faith and our parenting would be incomplete if we focused only on the beautiful and positive side of life. The Wiccan religion does not draw a line down the middle of the universe and label one half "good" and the other "evil", nor seek to become part of a mythical cosmic battle between the forces of light and darkness.[...] We are creatures of both light and darkness and must come to terms with that fact.
> (Anne Carson, ed. *Spiritual Parenting in the New Age*. pg. 28)

Change and struggle are natural parts of the lifecycle and without them we wouldn't have the necessary skills to grow into realised and grounded people. As parents, mentors and community members, we work to model our young folks' healthy and authentic responses to these moments.

I was recently at an acquaintance's house, a kind neighbour who is also a Brit abroad and who agreed to sign and fill in a passport form for my eldest boy. I don't know this woman well but she is sweet natured and kindly, and obviously enjoying early motherhood. Her daughter asleep in a sling, she kindly let me into her home and filled in the form whilst we chatted. She disclosed quite by chance that her mother had just died after a short but painful battle with breast cancer. I am sure you will understand my feelings then at this moment of her disclosure – "I don't know this woman well, I don't want to pry, maybe she doesn't want to talk, I don't want to make her cry…" the dialogue in my head went on. And for a moment I was going to say my condolences and move on.

Then I caught myself. This woman may be me one day, it may be my children. What would I want at such a moment? I looked in her eyes and said how very sad I was for her and asked if she was able to talk about it. I watched her visibly relax as she opened up about her mother's painful battle, and her sense of displacement as a consequence. She said she had told so few people because she didn't want to make them feel bad. This made me feel doubly sad. We labour through so much pain and struggle alone in today's world, as our obvious sources of support are uncoupled from our family and our geography. Grief is such a long and lonely road, and yet one we all travel at some time. Surely these moments above all are those we should share, we should reach out and find ways to help.

We can model such responses for our kids and teach them that such times are an inevitable part of life. If friends are in distress we can create healing spaces for them in ritual and prayer, and we can pragmatically help – take food, check in daily, offer to help clean – all the things we would do at times of great celebration such as the birth of a new baby, are needed with even greater strength at times of pain and grief.

When children encounter tragedy and trauma, on a large or a small scale, they may see themselves as the centre of that change, believing that they are in some way its cause. If this is not their experience then they may feel entirely powerless, such an experience of grief can be the first time a little person has realised that their actions are powerless in the face of certain events. Whether a family is facing divorce, illness, hospitalisation, death or strife, it is imperative that the children involved are allowed to express their feelings and reassured with words, actions and behaviours. We can guide them towards knowledge that this change is one that they must navigate, but that it is not their fault, and that they can truly help themselves through it. By sheltering them, or denying them knowledge about a situation, we may do them a disservice. What they can imagine may be far more frightening to them than the knowledge of what is actually changing around them. If we can let our children see the truth of a situation, we show our kids that you can experience pain and still be OK.

For older kids who 'know' what is changing and logically know it's not their fault, reassurance and comfort are still high priorities. Many older children need the affection and simple physical comfort we more easily give a smaller child. A teenager won't always ask for hugs, you have to be the one to reach out and embrace them. There are some extremely useful energy-based forms of medicine that can support the other work you may be doing at this time – homeopathy, cranio-sacral therapy, massage, Bach Flower Remedies and reiki can be gentle healing aids and I encourage you to find a practitioner of these arts that you and your family can work with. There are also several focusing techniques that enable us to create supportive and emotionally warm spaces for children undergoing dramatic or painful transitions:

- Play: Kids need time to work out their feelings and responses and play is one of the best healers. For Pagan parents hoping to instil a magical understanding of the universe, play is the first means of exploring the limits of the known universe. Make-believe is essential medicine for a child undergoing difficulties. Let them read more, dress up more, act out, play outside a lot – anything that helps them nurture their own innate coping strategies. Less structured activities woven through a consistent daily rhythm is key here. Whether you witness their play as symbolic, literal or simply expressive, make play as important as good sleep and nutrition at these times. For older children, such times can be perfect doorways to learning a new skill. For kids aged seven to ten, helping them become industrious can be another way of working through pain – dexterous hand-eye skills such as knitting, beading, weeding, and spinning can bring their mind to pinpoint focus, which can be a useful way of 'zoning out' whilst also making something of value.

- Pets: I knew a little girl called Artemis. Artemis was two when her father left. Although she was so sweet and sunny in nature, the pain of him leaving caused her to undergo a period of temporary mutism. She couldn't express her grief with words so she shut them out completely. In her wisdom her mother decided that she needed the love of another nonverbal small being to identify with and care for, a little soul who would repay attention with love and devotion. And she brought home a tiny ginger kitten called Buttons. Slowly, through this little kitten, she began to emerge and express herself once more. At first she began talking to Buttons, and then to her family with the kitten and finally she returned to speech. This anecdote illuminates how pets can be intensely valuable allies in coping with transition or stress, and we are wise to include them in our strategies for helping kids navigate difficult times.

- Ritual: This can be as elaborate or as simple as the time, space and occasion requires, but ritual here can mean two things. Firstly, doing something with regularity, so that it becomes second nature. In times of transitions, rituals can be great sources of comfort. If mum always closed the curtains this way, then even if mum is no longer there to do it, make sure the curtains are closed just so. Likewise, now can be a time to start little rituals – a small moment of holding hands before the school day and thanking the world, the taking of homeopathic remedies, walking the same way home from school. Allow some of the normal anchoring rituals and rhythms of your life to remain constant. Secondly, allow rituals to come from this time, as a means of marking and honouring these painful changes and include your kids actively in the execution of this ritual. Encourage them to do these with people outside the family too – now is a time when you may find kids needing external help, and be thankful that they have additional sources of comfort and support.

Pagans feel, indeed know, that all things are connected. The spirit of life that binds us together through joy and pain does not necessarily have a plan for us as individuals, but all change, whether small or dramatic, makes a space for new growth. Sometimes to see this we need the love and support of those around us. To give this to our kids, whether as parents, teachers, mentors or community members, we need the nourishment and support of all our relations to remind us that when all else is gone, in simply being alive we have the gift of connection with all living things.

Earth Activities

Go mushrooming	Learn about magnetism – magnet play
Make salt dough wreaths	Plant a garden
Make a compost bin	Bake bread
Learn to give a hand massage	Crystal recognition
Fold napkins	Practice grounding exercises
Learn to draw pentacles	Knitting, quilting and sewing

Bless salt

Make a charm bag for wealth

Make your own yoghurt

Camp in the garden

Build a fairy house and make a fairy tea party

Make your family tree – genealogy

Treasure hunt

Visit local historical sites

Chapter Two

Air

I remember, I remember
Where I was used to swing,
And thought the air must rush as fresh
To swallows on the wing;
My spirit flew in feathers then
That is so heavy now,
The summer pools could hardly cool
The fever on my brow.

I remember, I remember
The fir-trees dark and high;
I used to think their slender tops
Were close against the sky:
It was a childish ignorance,
But now 'tis little joy
To know I'm farther off from Heaven
Than when I was a boy.
Extract from 'I Remember, I Remember' by Thomas Hood.

Keywords: *Swift, Fly, Air, Cloud, Breeze, Flutter, Wings, Feather, Motion, Movement, Birds, Light, Transparent, Omnipresent, Unseen, Thought, Words, Messages, Singing, Voice, Connection...*

East is Air, the Rising Sun...

When my youngest child Boo turned four he wanted a rainforest birthday party. We decorated the house with green crepe paper. We made a Blue Morpho butterfly birthday cake. Boo was a monkey and sometimes a crowned eagle. His birthday is in the heart of winter, but he is a hardy kid, so we had to get outside.

We played Tiger Tag and broke a tiger piñata, but despite the kids' love of candy, the most exciting part of this party was when each child took a green helium filled balloon into the garden. We were going to release them into the sky.

The excitement was palpable. Grammy, aged five, an industrious and sincere kid (a classic earth/air combo!) was jumping with joy, desperate to go first. We were sending wishes to the rainforest on the back of the balloons.

"I wish the rainforest many trees!" Grammy shouted and let go of the balloon.

And every child squealed as the balloon lifted into the air.

"I wish the forest never gets cut down by giant bulldozers!" Boo yelled and we watch as his floated into the air. The energy got fizzy as the kids hopped about in the cold, watching the last of the sunlight glisten on the balloons.

"They are going South!" cried Sophia, hair whipping in the wind. "They are going to the jungle, they really are!"

Carlito, Boo's best friend, overcome with excitement, whispered his wish to the balloon before letting it go. Each child spoke a wish and let the air take it, and it was a magic moment. There we were, in a backyard in Boston, sending balloon wishes through the cold wind to the rainforest. For a moment the world contracted and we were in sacred relationship with the spirits of air.

Air connects us to all other animate living beings. Trees make breathable air for us. Through the cycle of photosynthesis, ingesting, cleansing and expulsion, breath is the exchange of life force between the animal and the plant kingdoms. The trees of our earth give us this daily gift and allow our species to flourish. This air that surrounds our planet as an invisible skin carries sound, enabling basic communication between us. We create the symbolic forms of this communication, just as birds, monkeys, and all other land dwellers do.

Thus the two most fundamental gifts of air are revealed to us. Firstly, air is the element associated with the power of communication in all its forms. And, secondly, air is the element of connectivity. Communication and connectivity are intimately joined – communication facilitates connection, connection is forged through communication. It is the relationship between plants and creatures that air facilitates – it shows us in the simplest of ways how our species' ability to listen, respond and act is imperative if we are to remain connected to the earth's sources of nourishment and inspiration.

This sacred relationship shows our children and us that we are all in complex and continuous connection with the entire world, and in fact that our well-being is dependent upon it. The trees of the Amazon basin are essential to our health and well-being as we play on the playground in our Boston neighbourhood.

Fostering Mindfulness

For small children we can embody the gifts of air most simply through developing mindfulness, sometimes called awareness. Air rules all acts of communication: speech, song, dance all move air; they require the laws of gravity and space to cross from one place to another, from one ear to another. When our kids are babies, we can begin to develop this acknowledgement of air's rulership over the forces of communication and connection by simply allowing air to move around, across them, and of course by talking and singing to them, and with them. Lay an infant on a blanket beneath a tree and watch them begin the journey into fascination and wonder as they see the lines of connection and companionship between us with unclouded eyes.

Air shows us the importance of listening, of watching. Communication is only enabled if there is a speaker and a listener. A relationship only thrives if there is a mutual connection. Air facilitates one of our greatest gifts, yet one that our busy urban modern lives give the least time for. Mindful awareness, as many Buddhists call it, is the art of cultivating stillness and space within us, and in doing so we give room for the universe to rush in, for the voice of the Gods to be heard above the clamour of our thoughts. When we are pregnant or caring for a newborn, our lives seem to become an entire experience of mindful awareness.

Parents at this point often describe the day in the minutia of moments. Each coo of the beloved infant, every kick of the unborn babe is noted for its miraculousness. We become keenly aware of our bodies, of our environment. We may be highly emotional, volatile, as we attempt to juggle the expectations of our daily lives with the new reality we are embracing. And with our contemplation and wonder at the movements and sounds our babies bring, it is amazing how much energy this constant vigilance takes! Like anyone who has practiced meditation for a long time, mindful awareness of a small being requires a lot of energy.

Those of you reading this who are in the thick of late pregnancy or newborn-hood, I applaud you (as does every other parent further along this path!) – you are a walking example of sleep-deprived mindful awareness. The focus and intensity that this period demands of us is rarely matched later in our lives. My first son was born in early May. I remember the quality of the dust in the sunlight in one particular patch of my living room, as I spent many, many hours there, staring at my new baby with the intensity, anxiety and wonder that I had never mustered in 15 years of meditation and visualisation practice.

My new mum friend Robin and I would have daily, sometimes hourly, telephone conversations as we tried to work out the things our babies were telling us. Her baby wouldn't nurse, my baby wouldn't sleep. How many times had she burped today, how many times had he cried to the point of exhaustion? Whenever any new thing happened we would need to touch base with each other and swap notes, reflect on our findings from other new mums, our own mothers, hearsay, and book advice. It was like a series of rigorous dream analyses. In any other circumstance it would be considered the most exhaustive spiritual training ever undergone.

This kind of mindfulness often wanes as we gain confidence, as we move further away from the moment-by-moment wonder of a new life. Yet mindfulness, bringing one's self fully present in every moment, is a key skill in developing calmness and awareness. In her wonderful book *Buddhism for Mothers*, Sarah Napthali discusses the benefits of cultivating mindfulness. She says for us adults and for our children they are immeasurable. In the practice of mindfulness, or wakeful awareness, we literally pause and focus our attention inwards to notice what we are experiencing, where we are in the world at that particular moment. Pause right now. Take a breath. Close your eyes. Mentally feel the edges of your body. What can you feel on your skin? What can you hear close to you? What can you hear outside? How does your body feel? Take another breath. Thank the air...

With small children and all their joyful noise and needs, mindful awareness for us can be a meditation practice that is integrated into the routine of our most mundane daily chores. We can do this whilst washing up, folding laundry, grading papers, walking to the shops, walking in the night with an infant who won't sleep. Although it may be impossible to do all the time, you can use these moments as nourishment for your spirit and your magical self.

The daily grind of raising small children can often bring us face to face with our own mental limits. Frustration, boredom, anger, resentment, entrapment can be part of the list of emotions we experience all too frequently along with joy, wonder, astonishment, amazement, and love. And this is not the only time we will experience this heady combination of feelings – many parents say that this is mirrored in equal parts when our kids reach their teen years, where exclusion, loss, uncertainty and bewilderment can be added to the list.

With such fierce emotions at play, daily mindful awareness exercises enable us to pause, to take stock of where we are and to change the direction of our inner dialogue or redirect our feelings. Such exercises help us maintain our centre; they help us stay sane in the heart of the whirlwind that is part of starting a family. This also helps in another way – we show those around us and, most importantly, our kids, how to pause, how to take a 'time out', we start to model for them how to transform their feelings, and how to control their mental energy.

Fostering mindful awareness in kids can be as simple as asking them to pause before the day or saying a prayer or blessing at meal times. I advocate positive time-outs as, if framed appropriately, this is exactly a promotion of mindful awareness. Use time to go within and consider how this could have happened differently, or how it makes you feel. Or simply sit and breathe to calm yourself. Allow kids time in quiet.

Exercise: Mindful Awareness for All Ages

(You can turn this into a game; a surprise stop or you can build this into a classroom activity or a family practice.)

Take a breath – stand or sit still. Pause. Think of nothing in particular, but make no sound, allow your eyes to become unfocussed, allow your body to relax. Feel where you are, still, whilst the world turns and spins or her axis. Allow the world to speak to you. Be in peace. Bring your attention back to your breath. This breath made for you by the trees around us, and the trees thousands of miles away. Breath in and out... always come back to your breath.

Monkey See Monkey Do

Modelling, otherwise known as Observational Learning, is how a large proportion of the animal kingdom goes about educating its young. Drawn from the work of Albert Bandura (1977), social learning theories propose that kids, in fact everyone, learns through being attentive to the behaviour of others. Despite the bad press such a model of communication gets, there is wisdom in this method. Let's be clear – this is not imitation. This is not your kid mimicking you although they may do that plenty (have you ever seen a kid play at house, or school? It's hilarious and luckily we know that they often elaborately fabricate parts of their play).

Small children learn through observation and listening, they watch what we do, when we get it wrong and they learn how to be in the world from those who are around them. Modelling is a central way in which we can show our children meaningful methods of connecting with the sacred. Authenticity, clarity and openness are the ways in which young kids, toddlers and babies, approach and understand *our* experience of what we consider sacred, and are encouraged to find their own ways. What we model to them is that honouring the sacred is important. So we pick up litter, we don't let the tap run continually, we recycle and compost, we bless the bees when they arrive in the spring. We can use mindful awareness in the simplest of our household tasks, and in the moments of rushing.

Modelling as a way of teaching requires your authentic behaviour. If you want to teach your kids to be good to the earth then you have to lead the way. Modelling our spiritual or magical practice is often harder, as many of us have little time or have a very personalised practice. I recall in the early days of parenting, trying to do a full moon ritual. Summer must have been about four months old and I was determined to honour and give thanks to the bountiful Goddess of the moon who had guided me through pregnancy and birth. I set the space, which was hard in our small apartment, harder still in an apartment suddenly festooned with baby equipment. And I cast the circle. And inevitably in the middle of circle casting my baby awoke; "*I cast this circle, I draw this round, may here be a place where peace...* shit... that's the baby... shit... OK where was I, oh yes, *here is a place where...* oh... OK Dan's gone to get him... good. He sounds quieter. So, yes, *may here be a place.*" You get the idea.

The entire ritual I felt really between the worlds – worried that he needed to nurse, anxious that he would start to wail any minute and concerned that my husband was exhausted and I was being selfish. Suffice to say, it wasn't a particularly satisfying ritual, although I felt I needed to do it. Now I have come to the happy realisation that the kind of magical and spiritual work I do with my kids looks very different to that I would do alone or with a group or coven. The important thing is that I do it, and that they see me do it, that they see it is valued and it is authentic.

A close friend of mine, Heloise, who is a mum to three wonderful kids and a very wise young woman, expressed this perfectly when I phoned her one particularly tough afternoon. We were talking about those moments where the ideals of raising our kids meet with the realities. She began that day with a list of wonderful spiritual explorations, a day of dreaming, of finding gnomes in tree trunks, of making offerings to the place, of mending dad's bike, a day of mindful action and awareness in the house and gardens where they live. Instead they ended with a day of shouting, tantrums, sibling squabbling and broken crockery. This resonated with me at home with a baby, trying to work out whether I should cut the grape in half or not and whether I was allowed two glasses of wine whilst I was nursing. Every decision seemed laden.

She reminded me, as we licked our wounded spirits: "Your kids recognise your striving – they see it and their soul thanks you for it."

I think on that day both of us would have liked the kids to thank us for it, but this form of modelling, even when it all goes wrong, is worth doing. We don't have to show them this through pious observations or necessarily through showing them rituals or teaching them meditation (although these are all worthy spiritual practices), but by allowing them to witness our striving for spiritual connection in our everyday. We model the integration between our spiritual life and our role as their parent; whether that is allowing them to witness us breathing, grounding our energy, and closing our eyes in the moment before we lose our temper. This allows us to bring ourselves to a better place to deal with the situation. Whether this is being able to put a screaming baby in the crib, take a moment to ground and tell them we love them and we are just in the other room. Or whether we spend all day setting up material for painting Eostra eggs, only to have our kids half-heartedly paint one and abandon them in favour of playing with their trucks again. It may not be the spiritual practice of our unencumbered selves, but it is deep and valuable work.

Modelling our spirituality doesn't demand perfection or absolutism or even certainty on your part. It demands a vigilant openness and creativity to model for your children what you value and consider sacred.

If we want them to understand that all life is connected, that their body is sacred as it is part of the great whole web of the world, we have to reflect that attitude in the way we treat ourselves, and our attitude towards other people and our neighbourhood. Words and teachings fall on fallow soil in children's deepest self unless they are nourished with living examples. If you tell a child that trees are sacred and yet you spend no time with trees, your words are empty. If you tell a child not to kill animals or not rip up plants because they are living beings, but then you squash spiders because you fear them, you may need an explanation. Even babies witness these inconsistencies, and as for kids, well as you may already know, they live for such parental discrepancies! So what does a Pagan approach to mindful awareness look like? What can we do to model magical ways for our young that are meaningful? Here are some of the ways to navigate the early years:

- Start from the beginning; nurse your children, wear them and spend as much time with your infant as you can. Not necessarily because you are a devotee of attachment parenting, but through this kind of action you communicate to your child that they are precious, beloved and worthy of your time and effort, and you also allow yourself to take time, and lay firm foundations for a relationship that will define both your lives.
- Teach your infant and toddler to pay attention to their body. Developing sensual awareness can start really young and is an excellent self-care skill for babies, toddlers and small children. Within appropriate limits for the age of the child, allow them to experience the full range of sensations – warmth, cold, comfort, discomfort. I spent hours with my newborns lying on a sheepskin wafting coloured scarves over their bodies, they loved the sensation of it, and the excitement, and it was one of the first examples of play we had together. Baby massage, bath times, all allow babies a range of feelings. Many Pagan parents try EC, or elimination communication, where though watching and waiting they are able to catch the signals their baby gives them and use a toilet rather than ever having to use nappies/diapers. This is physical communication par excellence, but will not match every parent's life demands.
- Surround them with beauty. We can all do this, whether we have kids or not. Plant small gardens with flowers, wear colourful clothing, speak to the kids and babies you meet. Communicate with them through the place you live in. If you are around small babies a lot get outdoors with them, grow plants, and use natural materials in the gear

that they will be using every day. Ensure the toys they play with are made of natural materials and allow them to wear clothes from natural materials. They don't have to be new. Think about how much you appreciate the grain of wood on your kitchen table, the feel of silk, the colours on your walls. Your children are just as discerning, and these are simple ways in which we begin to show them what we are striving for.

- Congratulate moments of quiet and stillness. This is a challenge for us all. When children under the age of seven manage to achieve stillness and silence it is worthy of praise, if only for 30 seconds. For older kids and teens often the challenge is to promote and praise 'unproductive' time. Not time spent texting on the bed, but perhaps curled up with a book or looking out of the window. Don't force kids into meditation, but instead encourage moments where they can be idle. Read books every day, many of them if you can, listen to the radio, or to story CDs, allow reverie and dream time. Boo and I often used to simply sit in the play structure in our back garden. It was small and cramped for me but he loved making a den in there, and when we were all settled with blankets cushions and apple slices we'd listen to the birds. We'd put our "listening ears on" and I'd watch him suck his thumb and listen and watch as the birds flew about. I watched him seamlessly move from everyday reality to that wonderful place of light trance, of reverie where he was listening to nothing but birds. This lasted all of a minute – he was only three – but it is still a wonderful experience for us both and one which always ends with a hug!

- Breathe properly. Baby's breath, as we all should, to our belly, allowing the ebb and flow of our body with our breath. As we get older we lose the natural element of breathing. I wonder what age a girl becomes self-conscious of her belly and learns to shallow breathe? Consider when you began to shallow breath, and how different you feel when you allow you body to be fully infused with breath. If we bring our kids' attention to the breath whenever we can, we give them a chance to be energised, to feel clear and bright, – run, swim, skate, dance, meditate, or simply place your hand on the little tummy and tell them to breathe into your hand. This mindfulness is the necessary foundation for showing the power of grounding, centering and energy work more generally. And from these techniques great magic is made possible.

Imagine you were taught some of these most basic techniques as a child, so that as an adult they were obvious and second nature, as embedded in your body as needing to go pee or feeling hungry. What would you have done, or be doing differently if you could, at will, focus on your breath, clear your mind when you faced a shocking or painful experience? With such a mind, magical thinking becomes not only possible but is the only sort of thinking you wish to do!

Fostering Fascination

Learning to work magic is mostly a process of learning to think-in-things, to experience concretely as well as to think abstractly. All of us begin life as young children thinking concretely, but this ability, instead of being developed and refined as we grow is devalued in our culture in favor of abstract reasoning.
Starhawk, *Dreaming the Dark* (p. 27)

Our mind is a mysterious and wondrous thing. It is capable of feats of imagination, invention, and creativity that we rarely fully comprehend. We know too, from medical research and mystical exploration, that the mind is an integral part of our body's other systems; the web of health is woven between body and our mind. If we are stressed, we can develop headaches, if we are perpetually denying grief or anger we may develop digestive problems.

The wondrous work of Ayurvedic and Chinese medicine, in fact the majority of the world's health systems, recognise the relationship between mind and body and treat it thus. And yet so much of our time we deny this connection. When we are around children we often see the connection between mind and body awareness most keenly. Somehow we know, just instinctually, when our kids are about to get sick, or are sad and exhausted. We catch the little signs. When we look at them like this and recognise their body's signals to us, we are thinking concretely, sensually. We may be rationally assessing the information – she hasn't eaten much today, her sleep was fitful, she has an exam tomorrow, his best friend just left on holiday – and yet what we are often doing, without knowing, is thinking-in to them. We are using sensual communication; we are witnessing it and acting on it. We are using our instinct – another word for what Starhawk refers to as "concrete thinking" and it is not random, it is not supernatural, it is the ability we have to bring our whole selves to something, to think with our skin and our nerves as much as with our rational mind.

Fascination exercises are those that build concrete thinking, which itself is founded on principles of immanence, integrity and responsibility. They also foster independent action, self-knowledge and care. Such exercises found here and throughout this book, can be used as you would a cookery book, as ideas for things to do and make with the kids you are with.

Gaining sensitivity is a skill we can all work on. Using some of the ideas and techniques for concrete thinking and the ability to think-in things is a wonderful consequence of growing sensitivity. To give you an example, a few years ago, my family and I took a trip to Shenandoah, a wonderful National Park in North

Carolina. Living in the city sprawl I wanted my boys to have the balance of urban to natural environments as commonplace. So with this grand intention we decided that we would take a short hike, all together, everyday. On the first day we set off on a mile round trip – the one-year-old in a back carrier, the three-year-old walking and the adults hauling enough snacks to feed the entire forest.

And, of course, despite the lovely surroundings, on the outward hike my boys grizzled the entire way – they were tired, hungry and needed the toilet every ten yards. My dreams of a 'nature walk' were shattered. Then about halfway round Summer found a stang. This stang was about five feet high and came from an alder tree. A rather unbecoming stick to my eyes, but this stick transformed our hike homeward as it became stag horns, a broom, an airplane, and a fairy wand. He wasn't playing with the stick; this wasn't a game, but the most basic of magics. We did not interrupt him, or frame the use of the stang in any way. We offered no comment, instruction or guidance on how to use the stick. We were just grateful it had turned a potentially ugly hike back into quite a different experience. I came to see on this hike that he was thinking-in to it, *fascinated* by it and recognising qualities I could not see. He was changing himself to work with the stick. At once he was a stag, then a fairy, then he was an airplane. He and the stang were shape-shifting, communicating, playing together in a way that reflected something in him and the space we were in.

We see it when our kids hug trees; when you find their pockets full of stones, or when they can't sleep because they are star gazing. Fascination compels them, it offers another way of being. To fascinate is to charm, to enthral and to captivate. In the moments of fascination our attention moves from the everyday reality to feeling a deeper reality. In magic we call this process by many names, we may call it shape-shifting, vision-questing or sacred play. Fundamentally, this is simple magic at its most unencumbered. And those objects or places that are especially compelling we may say are charmed or fairy touched.

In fostering fascination the world becomes imbued with enchantment, and small children are excellent at it. If we let them, every day is an exercise in fascination. When we are fascinated by something we instinctually move in positive relationship with it. Just as the stang changed its purpose in Summer's hands, when we facilitate fascination or think-in things we watch our children's creativity flourish and witness their capacity for invention. We are also fostering the concept that we are in continual relationship with the world around us. This is not because they are being asked, what does it do? How does it work? Instead, in allowing the process of fascination to unfold, those questions and their responses arise naturally from the unmediated communication between place, object and person.

Fascination is a form of concentration. We tend to think about concentration as something that requires work, it's hard, and needs a furrowed brow or chewing on the top of a pencil. This idea of concentration is synonymous with studiousness. What concentration truly means, however, is the capacity to bring our whole attention to something. In Buddhism, Samadhi, or right concentration, is a path to gaining spiritual enlightenment. In scientific terms it is the intensity of a substance, or the amount of something in one place. We can think about fascination in a magical sense as concentration paired with longing.

As we get older it can become hard to hold onto this level of awareness, to keep up our capacity for thinking-in things, for fascination. With the introduction of abstractions, fascination is often replaced with linear thinking. And for many children and young adults who do retain this ability they may be ridiculed or at worst 'diagnosed'. How can we encourage concrete thinking, how can we create space for our older children to think-in things and retain that other form of knowing about the world?

For parents, teachers and caregivers, holding back on introducing abstractions to kids is hard – we are given alphabet flash cards when our babies are born, and baby videos that promise to teach our children to read by the time they are two. The compulsion as a culture towards literacy and numeracy in early childhood has overtaken our ability to allow children abstract-free time. The drive for early literacy came from a desire to ensure that all children, irrespective of familial circumstances, disadvantage and economic status have the resources necessary to read and write by the time they are in grade school, or first school. This means by the time they are six or seven – not by the time they are three.

Yet all too often we are led to believe that by the time our child is three they should know their ABCs and be able to count to 20. It can be hard in the face of group parental pressure to go against the grain here – to not buy ABC books, to not show your kid Sesame Street every day (a prime purveyor of early literacy and numeracy information packaged as entertainment). Such parental behaviour may have you marked as extreme or weird or Waldorf parents. It takes courage to say to other parents, "We are not introducing letters, or numbers until Jonnie is older, but we are encouraging our child to hug trees, pick up dead insects and learn cloud busting."

You may find that your invitations to play dates dwindle! However, various globally esteemed educational methods, including that of Maria Montessori, John Holt and Rudolf Steiner, based on research and a love of children's fascination, show that introducing abstractions later in your child's development does not limit their academic capacity or their life skills. A child who reads at three has no intellectual head start on a child who reads at seven. However, a child who is full of stories and play and has the freedom to dream has a great head start. As Albert Einstein famously said, "If you want your children to be intelligent, read them fairy tales. If you want them to be more intelligent, read them more fairy tales."

For those of us who live in urban spaces, the entrance into literacy and numeracy also means that our children become increasingly aware of the mass media, and may require early media awareness intervention on your part. Look at the billboards, the text-based information around you every day and consider the impact that may have on your child. Surely a few more months of innocence from marketing, charitable organisations and businesses is no bad thing.

The difficulties of holding out on introducing abstractions and categorisations is that your child may feel, especially around the age of five, that they are somehow behind their peers. In school and even preschool and kindergarten, children are all too often taught in ways that encourage comparison, if not competition. You may have to inform teachers, childcare providers and family members that you have been limiting your child's introduction to abstractions for a while. If you are a childhood educator then you may be already coming up against these issues and have ways of working around them. Children are all too good at realising when they are different. If you think this is becoming an issue with a child you are working with, or you feel your child is ready for abstract learning, here are some embodied tactics that may help:

Counting

Count in concrete terms. Count your fingers, or count petals on a flower, count the number of whiskers on your cat's face and practise multiplication by using trees. I have used trees and rocks as the basis of introducing abstractions and categorisations. Trees are our best teachers. Look at the shapes in a tree, what patterns do the leaves grow in. Which is bigger, which is smaller? What percentage of leaves fall from the tree on a daily basis? Talk about deciduous or evergreens, or you can talk about the family of trees in your garden, the community of trees in your neighbourhood. Before you tell them the type of tree, perhaps allow your child to think-in to it, to tell you what the tree is, whether it has a name, a tree spirit or fairy within it.

Mushrooms can also be extraordinary teachers of sensual numeracy as they grow in groups, in differing sizes, yet are all connected, to each other and to other life forms such as trees and plants. And of course anything that is potentially hazardous is all the more exciting to learn about! A few years ago I was with Summer and his best friend Sophia, it was my homeschool day and we were doing a neighbourhood nature trail. We had begun to gently introduce the alphabet, one letter at a time. This day's letter was P, which is naturally hilarious to a scatological five-year-old. We were walking and the neighbourhood was full of fungi. It was a warm wet October and they were everywhere, but we stumbled upon a whole area of amazing spotted yellow mushrooms and using our identification sheet, we found that they were Panther Mushrooms so of course P was for Poisonous Panther Mushrooms. We came home and drew them and studied them under magnifying glasses, then (they) ran around being panthers. This was concrete thinking at its best. From this day on we watched as the panther mushrooms' village grew, we looked at their habitat, their beautiful colouring, their cycle of growth and decay until finally in January there was not a trace of them left. Led by the kids, we connected early forms of counting to our physical neighbourhood, and their knowledge became applicable.

You know how many oak trees live on your street, how many red cars drive down your road, what time of day the birds sing the loudest at. Rather than learning the physical shapes and abstract notions of dots on a page this is concrete thinking, knowledge that is rooted in your place and that they will be able to use.

Such an approach ignores the somewhat linear perception of 'subjects' that have deemed numeracy and literacy to be separate yet connected skills. There are few educationalists that dare to contradict the monolith of academic subjects, the notion of disciplines, the idea that when we learn it must be in defined, boundaried terms. We learn maths in a maths class, stories in a literature class and acting in drama. However, in so many ways outside the school environment we learn in far less rigidly demarcated ways. And what of those disciplines that are no longer part of conventional curriculum? Botany? Naturalism? Penmanship? Astronomy? All of these 'disciplines' require a variety of skills and are still in use in the world today so what of them? These ideas for the introduction of 'academic' life skills assumes that you can use them in designing curricula or as after-school activities or at home after school, or perhaps as part of a home-school framework, or to propose as workshops at a festival.

Reading and Writing

Read to kids. To paraphrase the educationalist John Holt, bathe their eyes in text. What I am always moved by when I read Holt's work is the clear sense that most children are able to bring themselves to literacy when they are ready. All we have to do is accompany them on their journey. "Learning to read is easy," he states, "and most children will do it more quickly and better and with more pleasure if they can do it themselves, untaught, untested and helped until when and if they ask for help." (*Learning All the Time*, p.8).

At the right time and pace most children will learn to read. What we can do is make reading a part of our everyday. So many Pagans are bibliophiles that this shouldn't be hard. When you are babysitting a friend's kids, don't turn on the TV, read a book, not necessarily a kid's book, but perhaps a book of beautiful photographs, or a joke book. Demonstrate that books are tools, both pleasurable and informative and that they will give a lifetime of pleasure. As Roald Dahl's Oompa Loompas implore us, "So, please, oh please, we beg, we pray, go throw your TV set away, and in its place you can install, a lovely bookcase on the wall."

The other thing we can do is storytelling. Now, I am not suggesting we all of a sudden learn the Norse myths in dramatic form, but that you perhaps tell stories about your own childhood, about your family, your ancestors. Storytelling combines a multitude of skills, both as a teller and a listener, central to the development of literacy and, of course, for fostering fascination in our kids. What is wonderful about storytelling is that all of us, irrespective of our age or our elemental colouring, love to tell and be told stories. You may find your kid is a better listener than a weaver of tales, but rest assured, storytelling is a strong teacher in the transmission of our ethical and moral foundations. Storytelling is also a tool for passing on family history, our cultural and spirituality without appearing to be 'teaching'. It requires us to create narratives, and thus we give our own children the building blocks to be able to tell their own life stories.

I noticed this recently when we introduced a new babysitter to our household. Ashley is a gorgeous, energetic young woman, a yoga teacher who occasionally dabbles in stand-up comedy. My kids love her in the way in which kids can only love a babysitter and ask you to leave so they can get on with being with Ashley. So much for that period of crying and whimpering we used to have to go through. And what is the wonderful Ashley's secret? Popcorn before bed and stories about her childhood. That's it. Nothing grand, no allowing them to stay up crazy late, or running round the house painting their bottoms blue. Every time she appears at our house they jump up and down and ask her whether she has a new story for them. In the morning, when they recount the stories they sound like, the stories every family has – well, every family in American perhaps! – stories of coyotes, of earthquakes, of going camping with her dad. Often they ask her to tell the same story many times over, giving my kids the opportunity to ask new questions, to experience the sensations of excitement and fear within the story over and over until they have absorbed it.

And yet in the telling of these stories (and the special lullaby that follows) she has enchanted my kids and given them a gift. They now carry special stories about her childhood, and so feel closer to her, and they often use her stories as the root for their own stories about their daily happenings. Storytelling doesn't have to be the great stories of the mythic cycle of Gods and heroes, storytelling can be the everyday tales we tell our kids that build intimacy between us.

Exercise: Storytelling the day

At the table when you eat together, whenever this is, ask your kids to share one story about their day, and listen to it without comment. When they have finished telling, you thank them (even if their story has been rambling, or fictional, or about you!), and go on to tell them one from yours. Ensure every member of your family has had a chance to do this.

Poetry

Poetry is a wonderful gift for kids of all ages, and learning to recite poetry can be a useful skill. It encourages memory and demonstrates the pleasures of language like no other literary form can. Poetry is found everywhere. Yesterday was a beautiful March morning, sunny and clear and we sat eating breakfast quietly to the sound of bird song. Half way through I picked up one of my fave books of poetry to read whilst I finished my tea, and found one I loved, Hatching by Elizabeth Jennings. I read it slowly to the kids. They listened and then I read it again, and whilst we listened to the sound of the birds outside we unpacked this beautiful poem about a baby birds' first foray into the world. Then they finished breakfast and went to play with Lego.

Even if you are not a poetry fan, I bet there is poetry out there that you love. You could start with the works of limericks and the absurdist poets, such as Edward Lear. Such poetry explores the love of sound, shows how generative language is and most importantly makes kids laugh. When we are laughing, learning isn't work. I recall one of the first poems I learnt to recite by Christina Rossetti and when I think about this poem today it makes me shiver, recollecting my child-self's feeling of poignancy as I spoke the words.

Hurt No Living Thing
Hurt no living thing:
Ladybird, nor butterfly,
Nor moth with dusty wing,
Nor cricket chirping cheerily,
Nor grasshopper so light of leap,
Nor dancing gnat, nor beetle fat,
Nor harmless worms that creep.
Christina Rossetti

Have your kids dictate their own improvised poems to you and watch you write them down. Make them books of their own poems and stories. With older children foster a love of creating books – have them make their own collections of stories, rambles, and poems. Poetry forms the basis of much ritual and magical language. To entrain the ear young gives kids a sense of poetic metre and forms that will enable them to participate in ritual with a deeper sense of meaning. To show children that poetry is special but not something to feel excluded from is a key step to building their confidence and understanding the power of language.

Sing and encourage lyrical improvisation. Whether you think you can 'sing' or not, just do it. Singing lifts our mood, it brings us energy, and it can heal. Use your voice, sing whatever you like and whenever you can – sing a song to help them brush their teeth, sing a lullaby, sing pop songs with your teenager whether or not it embarrasses them. Just sing. Be happy to be the crazy singing person cycling along, or pushing the stroller or singing to the radio in the car. Singing connects words to our bodies, teaches us about breath and brings true deep and authentic emotion to the love of words. We sing to our babies and through music and song we teach them speech, connecting words to feelings. Sing-in to things whether you are cooking or cleaning the house sing to bring you to the moment. Singing communicates the basis of language: tone, syntax, rhythm, vocabulary, grammar, resonance and emotion. In certain aboriginal cultures it is believed that in singing we teach children speech – for infants hear all spoken communication as melody. My mum once told me that children don't learn to speak from hearing speech, they learn to sing first and then learn to flatten their sounds. Whether this was to encourage me to sing to my kids, singing often got me through some of the toughest, "What should I do now, it's only 3pm and I have no more craft activities or walks in me?" moments. Think about the early sound infants make – cooing and calling and sound making – it is as close to song as it is to speech, no? Anecdotally I am convinced that the amount of English folk songs that I sung to them as babies promoted their current language use (and unfortunately meant that by the time they could talk, they were asking me about fox hunting) and provided important contexts for words that would otherwise not have been part of their vocabulary. Paganism has such a wonderfully gener- ative musical tradition; there are some beautiful simple chants that can be taught to kids of all ages, and sung or incanted with ease. My boys used to love swinging on the swings in the playground chanting (or rather yelling), "Fly like an eagle soaring so high, circling the universe, on wings of pure light."

Reverie

Lastly, in fostering fascination we must make time for doing nothing. All forms of concrete thinking require real patience and time. Often it requires doing nothing. Unscheduled time has become a rare commodity in many of our lives, and especially in the lives of our children. Allowing kids to self-generate play, or simply sit around staring into space is often considered unproductive. Think about how many times at school you or your friends were told off for staring out of the window! By creating time for this – not down time, which usually involves *doing* something relaxing, but real time of nothing we allow our kids and ourselves space for thinking into ourselves. As adults though we lead the way. This is a perfect excuse for you to model doing very little (this is my kind of book, you are thinking). Sit by a river in quiet, perhaps singing to the water flow, talk to the trees in your garden. This is particularly important for those of us who are not parents, but are in the lives of kids. Seeing such quiet expressed by those in a community or extended family shows a child that this is a common expectation, like brushing your teeth. If we make time for nothing, for unstructured dreaming, our kids will follow.

Language and Talk – The Path to Integrity

Language is one of the primary means of communication between people. It is also one of the most potent and powerful cultural constructs. From the moment a foetus is known they are defined by language. If concrete thinking helps us connect to the world and helps to build relationships with all energetic forms, language is the first cultural structure that enables us to communicate our place within that web of relationships. Our entrance into language is our birth as socialised beings. The languages we learn to understand and to speak will define our experience and understanding of the world. It may define the timbre of our voice and the words we have to express ourselves. It is language that defines us, that marks us for others to define.

This is why language is at the root of cultural expression; different languages express the uniqueness of place and people.

Everything from descriptions of the weather, forms of address, the wonders of pronouns, all express our place in the world and our relationship with the world. It is a means through which the power structures of our society are formed. Consider the basic ways in which we address girls and boys differently. From the early words we teach children to the context and structure of their use, words hold tremendous power. We may tell children to "use their words" when they are expressing a need through whining or punching. When working with young adults, all too aware of the power of words, we are given opportunities to find new ways of communicating together – preferably ways that don't include yelling!

In thinking about our language with kids, awareness of the power of words is paramount. Words, as any good magician knows, shape the world. All things have a true name. When we enter formal magical training or when we undergo an initiation we may take on a new name to express this transition. This is our inner name, one that expresses our true self. Words are keys, they are a means to unlocking knowledge, to understanding the universe, they can heal and reveal but they can also be weapons, tools for violence, subterfuge and pain. Witches, bards, story-tellers all understand some fundamentals about the significance of using words wisely and, for all of us, striving to use words in mindful awareness can be an excellent daily practice.

Here are some principles for your meditation regarding the use of words with young people. Consider how important you think these qualities are to the teaching of word power to kids of all ages and stages. Contemplate on how such qualities can be fostered and encouraged in your relationship with children. Write here how you foster these qualities in your own life, in the lives of the kids you are with. Where do you see room for growth, where are your challenges?

- Honesty
- Integrity
- Clarity
- Inquisitiveness
- Encouragement
- Praise
- Comfort
- Understanding
- Gossip
- Story
- Punishment
- Anger
- Sorrow
- Desire
- Belittlement
- Relationship
- Patience
- Curiosity

Of the above qualities (that I hope you will add to), I want you to consider your ruminations on integrity. Integrity is a nexus word for Pagans. It is a powerful term, expressing a fundamental Pagan ethic. In an ideal world, our use of language both magical and mundane would teach and express connectivity, immanence and integrity. Starhawk writes, "Integrity means consistency; we act in accordance with our thoughts, our images, our speeches: we keep our commitments." (*Dreaming the Dark*, p.35)

This is a powerful teaching for our young folks. If we act and speak with integrity we provide the kids around us with security; they know we are reliable. This is the foundation for trust, honesty and kindness. Most importantly, integrity is foundational if we are to instil in our young their role in future environmental solutions. Further, in being a person of integrity we speak and act clearly, our actions are testament to our beliefs.

So if we say we care about the planet and our kids see us recycling, caring for our friends, choosing to cycle or walk instead of driving, our words clearly express our beliefs. If we make a promise and our kids see us renege on it, then we model for them that words are literally easy, cheap and without power.

The consequences for dishonesty can be a very illuminating process to focus on. If you work with teens you can use this as a foundation for a great set of teachings, both magical and practical (when are they ever separate?) regarding empowerment and self-care. Integrity is inherently a self-directed ethic. It is not about following external rules, and thus it is a way of being that allows for mistakes, ambiguity and uncertainty. Teaching integrity is also the first step in the journey to experiencing the law of threefold return, or karma, or simply in showing "what goes around, comes around".

Our personal integrity has wider consequences, it echoes into the world, creating ripples. I am a person who looks after small animals in distress, you say to a friend, boastful and full of self-import. The universe hears this and sends a small nestling with a broken wing to your garden. What do you do? These are some questions we can pose our older kids, when thinking through the role of integrity in our personal lives and how our own integrity ripples into the world. We can begin to show how our thoughts are connected energetically to our body, and how they are also connected to our actions, our behaviours. They allow us to consider the relationship between thoughts, words and actions, and they also allow us to consider our personal behaviour in a wider context. When we have a teenager who has lied to us about where she stayed last night, we can work through this by using our anger and distress to teach about integrity, honesty and self-care.

Exercise
(For teenagers. Adapt for younger children as appropriate.)

Recall a time when you felt, acted or spoke out of anger to hurt someone, or went back on a promise. Bring the time absolutely to the forefront of you mind. Hear the conversations. Trace that experience back. What anticipated this? What actions or words preceded it? What motivated your words/behaviour? How did it feel? Where in your body did the drive to act come from?

Now, allow the image to fade, and direct your attention to where the memory resides in your body. If you could give it an image or a word, what would it be? Consider whether you want to keep this feeling, whether you felt justified enough to hold onto this energy.

When you are ready, see this transforming into a seed, a pip a bulb. Be aware of how different this feels now. Now this energy has transformed, let us place it in the world; let us make a new intention for integrity for acting from a place of honesty and strength.

Open your eyes, and return to everyday thoughts, and make a commitment right here to do something that will allow this seed to grow. So mote it be!

Words of Power

There are certain phrases and terms that are powerful for Pagans. They have what some magicians call egregore: a synergy of thought. When many people imbue an image or an idea with power over a period of time, it takes on an energy form of its own. Some call it the creation of group mind. Some say this is what is meant by God. Certain phrases, objects and organisations have egregore, the power of collective thought. When we say, "*So mote it be*," at the end of a spell, or to conclude a ceremony, we are stating. "*This shall come to pass*," or, "*It will be as I have stated*". It is both a statement and a request as we ask the world to act in accordance with our desire. We also draw upon the collective energy of that phrase to help the spell on its way.

Likewise Pagans use the word *"Hail"* as a greeting. Although anachronistic to some, this word is so wonderfully rich with memory and ceremony that it both makes us smile and fills us with verve. Such words can also be signifiers to people – a way of checking out if someone is 'on the same path', so we need to use them wisely! *"Blessed Be"* was one of the first definable Pagan statements my kids made, and it wasn't until Summer was five when I realised he thought it meant Bless the Bees. And of course it does, or can mean this! Blessed be, is in many ways our "Amen", our "Cheers!" We use this at the end of a blessing, as a means of consecrating our intent. If you choose to give meal blessings, or do night-time prayers (which we will discuss later) this is the part where everyone can join in, even babes. It is a term as well generally accepted by the entire community so when off to an open festival this is a term our kids will hear regularly.

For many of us the most important elements of word use, are the most simple – the power of pluralising as we call it in our house. Since my kids were little we have spoken about Gods, not God, not Goddess, but Gods, Goddesses. Likewise when we talk about spirits, ancestors, our beloved dead, we talk in stretches of plurality. Polytheism, the multiplicity of Gods, is for many of us the magic of Paganism, and by expressing our reverence for the world's majesty in such terms we reject the binarisms, the oppositions, the duality that seems almost inherent in monotheistic approaches to faith.

For small children who are already experts in concrete thinking, polytheism is a natural concept, for the world is a flow of animate beings. Likewise for those non-deist Pagans, the multiplicity of the natural elements, the magic of earth, air, fire, water, and spirit in wondrous combinations gives us another model of spiritual flow and relationship.

New Enchantments – The Power of Mass Media
Contemporary mass media is more pervasive today than ever

before. Our daily waking, and arguably sleeping selves are bombarded with mass media images with frightening intensity, and children are all too frequently either the target or the victims of it. As a community we are divided on the role that mass media can play in raising our youth. Pagans, as with many subculture groups, are divided on the role and power of mass media, as we have embraced new technologies that allow us to find likeminded folk, and information on our spirituality in safe and secure ways irrespective of where we live.

Yet we are also the victims of incredible misunderstanding, stereotyping, fear mongering and plain old stupidity thanks to the mass media. Wherever we are positioned on the debate regarding the mass media's presentation of our spirituality and those who follow it, we at least have the power to control what, how and when we encounter it (or so we tell ourselves.) As a community of adults we must consider how far-reaching the influence of the mass media, in both form and content, is upon the lives of our kids, and to what extent that influence will play into their capacity to develop mindfulness, concrete thinking and healthy fascination with the world around them.

Screen media is the most significant form of mass entertainment and information media we use. Stop for a moment and consider how much time a day you spend in front of a flat screen – from your phone, iPad, Kindle, to your laptop, your computer at work, your computer at home, and your TV, how much screen time do you have? Is it the last thing you do before going to bed? The first thing you do in the morning? How do you feel in the morning when you have gone to bed watching a movie on your computer, or worked into the night writing emails? Try something. Every night, before going to sleep, stand outside and simply look at the sky for ten minutes. I promise you will wake in the morning less groggy, less tired, and just a little more mentally prepared for the day.

Screen time is a part of current Western lifestyle. You can step away from it, but it is extremely hard. For most of us we struggle with how much time our children should spend in front of screens. And educators also weigh the value of using screens in the classroom. For small children, the American Association of Pediatrics says a combined time of two hours per day is the limit for preschoolers. When I first read this I thought I was mistaken, surely they mean per week? But no – which means there are kids out there, under the age of four, watching more than two hours of screen time every day. I find this really sad and very worrying. TV and screen-based entertainment impresses itself on a child's mind very strongly and it is easy to misjudge a child's capacity to absorb and understand the language of televisual, cinematic and internet entertainment.

The biggest issues with the increased amount of time in front of screens are those that revolve around play. Play is active, requires movement and activity and play is crucial to our emotional development. It is also imaginative and not deter- mined by consumer drives. Watching stories, even the best ones, is neither of these. This is succinctly stated by children's enter- tainer and psychologist Susan Linn in *The Case for Make Believe*, "Across class divides, immersion from infancy in commercialised culture – manifest especially in electronic media and the things it sells – interferes with children's natural impulses for generating their own creations." (p. 27) Cell phones are handed to infants as colourful play rattles. IPads are given to preschoolers to keep them quiet in the post office queue. We put the TV on when we are tired and need to get dinner ready.

The problem with mass media and screen technologies isn't that they are inherently bad or that there isn't good programming available on them, it is that the hardware has permeated every institution in our children's lives. Think about where there are screens today – in doctor's waiting rooms, on the back seat of cars, in classrooms, car parks, airports. In shopping centres and furniture stores. Age four, my youngest son, who went to a lowbrow, inner city, diverse, granola crunchy 'we-raise-butter-flies-and-make-fairy-houses' preschool knew the full gamut of superheroes. Not that he ever watched Spiderman, Superman or Star Wars at home. It spreads like wild fire.

Likewise with girls the princess stage hit like a shock wave, and suddenly every nose picking, dirt-loving tomboy was obsessed with tiaras and high heels. Our children have little time for innocence beyond the reach of the industry of mass media. And for many of us, stemming the tide is a waste of our precious time and resources. Today, as an academic who worked on the power of media images with teens, and as a person who was raised in a family who had an on-off relation with TV, I believe that moderation and vigilance is the best policy with media. I have friends who are anthroposophists and send their children to Steiner school and I applaud them (although I am terrified when these kids come over that my boys will turn into gun wielding ninjas, just to annoy me). I have great sympathy with the 'no media is good media' approach.

Media is there for the distribution of information and products, often the two combined. And to ensure the continuance of an audience to market products at. Television flow, with its seeming uninterrupted transition from programming to advertising (or sponsorship as it is called in Public Service Models, but which ostensibly amounts to the same images for kids) is high-density visual material, and much of it reflects itself in content and tone. I showed my kids *Toy Story*; they found the first one too frightening, so I left it six months and we all sat and watched *Toy Story 2*. As I watched this movie I realised that the entire premise of the movie was about TV; Woody is a character from a TV show, and the evil guy (as my kids called him) is a collector of vintage TV toys. The plot and the character journey is founded on the question as to whether Woody would rather be played with by a child or be put in a museum to be looked at by thousands of children. And the struggle is played out with the backdrop of television characters, Buzz Lightyear, himself a videogame character, rescues Woody and tries to tell him that his play is more important than being famous.

But the irony is that we have already been told that he *is* famous, and that Buzz is too... The levels of complexity in unravelling this single text, deemed appropriate for preschoolers, is simply baffling. Contemporary mass media entertainment wants your children involved in this decoding practise, they want to keep your kids involved and thus every product references other products directly or in those self-reflexive asides so prevalent to contemporary kids' entertainment. And we haven't even started talking about gender roles, sexism, racism and social roles in mass media. Ah, you say, but we don't watch that, we watch the BBC or PBS. We download individual shows from Netflix. It's a step in the right direction, but don't think you can take your eye off the screen for one minute.

Our kids today live in a world saturated with media as never before. And it is all too easy to talk about its use value. Computer skills, for example, are heralded as of central importance for our children to learn, and yet, with the ever-changing technology, it is impossible for us to know whether what children are learning today is actually going to be of any use to them in one, two or five years' time. There has been far too little independent research to prove the effectiveness of computers in classrooms and of teaching computer science to primary school children for us to conclusively say it is a worthy investment. As strong critics of computers in the classroom, Alison Armstrong and Charles Casement argued, "Computer use in the classroom in fact, has been largely a matter of trying to keep up with the pace of technological change, with educational goals running a distant second." (p. 3)

Current research broadly shows it makes scarce difference to children's literacy or numeracy capacity to have them working on computers rather than on paper. Computers are largely designed for an adult mindset, for an adult's thinking and prolonged use would suggest that its interweaving into children's lives has the capacity to stunt their imaginative active play. And the voices that are positive proponents of computer use in early childhood, or even middle childhood cite the 'convenience' and the 'creative opportunities' offered and how significant they will be as kids become adults.

As a culture we have become obsessed with this idea. The introduction of computers into school is justified by arguing that these tools are central to the contemporary workplace. The convenience they propose comes from the capacity to research from one seat, as if finding a book requires more time and effort than is humanly possible! As if all information on a computer is worthy of consideration. I teach college students who increasingly have no sense of the difference between a populist review and a peer-reviewed article. There are fewer checks and balances in place with information gleaned online. As for opportunities, I have always wondered what this has meant, as if by finding information online, there is more capacity to find more "exciting" knowledge. Is this not the case with all research?

The replacement of writing with typing has led to some interesting findings. Firstly, we have to acknowledge that for our kids who suffer from certain visual and/or cerebral disorders, such a shift with its incumbent technology can be entirely positively life altering. For so many of us though, the move from writing to typing has led to some more worrying features in our kids. When we use our hands to hold a pencil and form letters, we are engaged in both a physical and a cerebral action. Armstrong and Casement's argument regarding computer use in schools suggests that the ability to think clearly is linked to the capacity to hear our inner voice, to developing inner speech.

Text, rather than writing, does not enhance this; it does not aid the development of inner speech because it is too fast, less stable, less concrete. Pressing indistinguishable buttons and watching as they appear on the screen, which can be neatly erased with another button, demonstrates an understanding of language that is transient and impermanent. This can be a wonderful liberation for adults, but for children learning to grasp the constructs of language, this is a much more worrying model. I know that for myself and other teachers and educators, we mourn the decrease in basic literacy skills we see in college entrees. Why, we lament, can they not form a sentence? Why can they not follow a logical thought progression? And these are privileged kids, with GPAs of 3.8 and above. What is happening? Is our youth becoming less literate? Then you set them a written exam where they are expected to write long hand, long essay form answers and you begin to understand.

Thinking through an argument requires a clear inner voice and an ability to express that voice using words on the page. Too often the speed of typing can allow words to form into sentences with too little mental intervention! Perhaps that age-old spiritual tool that allows those beyond the grave to speak to us, automatic writing, has come a long way since medium sittings in the salons of post-war London!

I think as Pagans we are often moved by the stories mass media can tell us, and look for our stories reflected in those we find. We also love new technology as Margot Adler's seminal anthropological work *Drawing Down the Moon* showed all those years ago. We are not Luddites, nor are we all techie wizards (although we have a fair few in our community!) but in considering our kids, let's be governed by common sense and by our reverence for fostering fascination and safeguarding our children's imaginative impulse. It is harder to police screen use in older kids and teenagers, particularly as they see our lives so enmeshed with that of various technologies.

I believe that screens should not be a considerable part of children's lives. They should be there – the computer is slowly replacing the television as all media hardware converges and there is increasingly little distinction between them. However, a screen is a screen, and it's a poor replacement for experience, and a limited tool for storytelling, play and education. Let's treat them like power tools – fun, easy, and very useful in certain circumstances, but we don't go round drilling holes all the time.

The New Fairy Land

Screen media technology judiciously used can be enriching additions in the lives of children and teens. They can be family bonding points, raise interesting points for discussion and debate. Nightly family viewing of TV news was often a nexus for the working out of important dilemmas regarding the nature of war, the role of global institutions and the like in my own childhood. For older kids, the exciting and powerful modes of storytelling and education given to us by screen technologies is more able to be balanced with what they read, see, feel and discuss with peers. Where this gets out of balance is where screen media advocates relationships and behaviour that bring our kids out of healthy modes of fascination to become lost in the world of the media.

We can always find examples of where screens have promoted behaviour that may otherwise have lain dormant. In some of the most infamous cases of children's violence towards other children, as in the famous Jamie Bulger Case, or the more recent Edlington Boys Case, prolonged and inappropriate exposure to media violence was cited as a contributing factor to the mental make-up of these boys. Further, I cannot help but think about the awful cases of cyber bullying that we have seen increase in recent years, which have contributed to an escalating number of teen suicides. Likewise the use of cellphones to capture and disseminate intimate or disturbing footage has been a phenomena that is all too commonplace in our teen communities. Questions of privacy, ownership, intimacy, integrity and safety, are all at stake in the issue of mass media.

Mass media is our contemporary virtual fairyland, where dark and mysterious things take place, where people get lost, abandoned, go mad and forget the right order of things. It is also alluring, exciting and visually appealing. It is an important and inescapable part of our cultural landscape. Video games, internet networking and cyberspace allow for multiple constructions of a self. It also allows us to become victims of forces unseen and unknown. As adults in the lives of children, we must now be vigilant to such influences and be aware of the fascination and ever growing capacity such forms have to shape our children's inner lives. And leave us all behind.

An obvious way to ensure that the influence of mass media is tempered is by limiting access, adopting restrictions and by regularly "media-fasting" and by modelling such an approach ourselves. Screens are not portals to other more exciting worlds, but are tools to help navigate the here and now. They are the new appliances and need to be treated as such; used once a day, unplugged when not in use (to stop energy leaks), neither reified nor rejected. Take the same approach as you would to teaching about mushrooming – not all things that look pretty and fascinating are healthy for us. In fact some can give you horrible dreams from which you never recover and some simply make you sick.

From the moment our young folk are engaging with mass media, let's promote media literacy so they are aware of what they are viewing and learn to assess it critically. We began this when my kids were still in nappies, as they stared at the huge billboards advertising Coke or MacDonald's and the like with a variety of clever and very visual motifs. *"It's marketing,"* we would incant, *"marketing wants to sell you something, even when it's hard to work out what it's selling. What do you think that advert is trying to sell?"* Kids are amazingly clever at figuring out the codes of marketing. And they are codes. You can make it a puzzle or a game, but alert children to the reason behind it. In this way our kids can begin to understand that media and marketing does not simply reflect our culture, it creates and sustains it. It wants you to feel unhappy if you don't have another pair of trainers, or have the newest jean cut. Collectively we need to reinforce to our kids that the bombardment of messages they receive regarding success, beauty, and wealth, are all fictions and illusions. They are modern fairy tales. This is useful for older kids, pre-teens and beyond. Play "spot the mug" game, where you look at marketing in hidden places.

Before I had kids I believed that media management was most crucial for girls and young women, and I still hold firm to this point. Our girls are vulnerable in particular ways to the machinery of mass cultural imagery. And I am afraid that no amount of Goddess statuary in your house will alter that. Whilst strong female heroes and heroines are more prevalent in mass media, there is still an overwhelming current of violence and subjugation carried out towards women on the big and the small screen. As the victims of violent crimes, as the victims of abuse and as the victims of culture, girls and women are still too often valued within mainstream media entertainments for their youth, their slimness and their capacity to attract (sexual) attention.

Pagans venerate the female, the flesh and corporeality like no other faith tradition. We do not separate flesh from spirit, but instead see our substance as living proof of the wonders of nature. Thus any stories that seek to limit the expression of desirability needs to be seriously questioned. Some families do this by asserting non-normative models of beauty in their home and their rituals, but mass media will always have a powerful influence.

One approach is to find models within mass media that anchor our values in place. I remember very clearly in the late 1990s when *Buffy the Vampire Slayer* came on the TV scene, and began to be taken seriously by academics as a cultural model of girl power that went beyond the usual gamut of feminine action heroes. I helped organise one of the first UK conferences on the show. Now, there are problems with Buffy's presentation of female empowerment (whole books are dedicated to the shows' complexity) but as a contemporary Artemis, she did pretty well.

Likewise, as we have seen with the *Twilight* saga more recently, many pre-teens eventually lampooned the series, not simply for its intense victimisation and domestication of young women, but through comically recognising its limitations as a story cycle. Comedy can be very useful here, and if you are an educator who can provide spaces for humorous questioning of such media images through lambasting and sarcasm, then we applaud you!

Unfortunately, even in those genres where women are the detectives, the scientists, the cop, the expert, women are also still the victims. Further, female sexuality, despite the increasing plurality shown in mass media, is still limited to certain modes: the mother, the girlfriend, the geek, the ingénue and the whore. When not in narrative media, advertising bombards young women with a vision of the female body where seeing bones is considered sexy and being sexy is what matters. For the sake of our daughters, our nieces, our Goddess children and for the future of our culture we must attempt to interject into this fallacy.

I recently saw the actor and celebrity Ashton Kutcher surrounded by screaming teens, make his acceptance speech at the Teen Awards 2013. In this speech he said, "The sexiest thing in the entire world is being really smart, and being thoughtful and being generous. Everything else is crap – I promise you. It's just crap that people try to sell to you to make you feel like less so don't buy it, be smart, be thoughtful, be generous." Let's not play by the rules and let's take Ashton at his word. We can steer our girls away from becoming overly fascinated or engaged with these fantasies of femininity, and instead give them heroines, models of beauty and power that can inspire them and allow them to live on the insides, rather than showing them that their status depends on how they are perceived by others. When you meet a little girl, don't praise her behaviour or prettiness, ask her what she likes doing in the garden or what she is reading. Ask about her opinion on current affairs and listen to what she has to say.

Likewise for our sons, let's show them that to be brave and powerful means looking after the vulnerable, male and female and everything between. That pulling your weight is important and that means helping out. Being a hero, rather than a superhero, is an important distinction to make. Whilst our kids love to play superhero we can show them real heroes, men and women who go beyond the necessary to do what needs to be done, who are willing to sacrifice their own comfort and their own needs for a greater need. That is where the hero becomes super, when the greater need replaces the individual's hardship.

Air teaches us the big vision, and instead of looking just at our own lives, we are able to, like the air that surrounds our beautiful planet, see everything in a complex pattern of connection and relationship. And from this perspective we can truly soar like an eagle.

Air Activities

Cloud bust	Sing!
Learn about migration patterns of your local birds	Study gravity, atmosphere and weather patterns
Write a riddle and a poem	Make an incense
Smudge your home with sage and feather	Read fairy tales
Make runes	Learn about astrology
In pairs, try mirroring techniques	Listen to birds
Make a recording	Create and fly a kite
Do a project on famous figureheads who represent emancipation and freedom	Practise breath meditation
Start a journal	Raise butterflies
Make up new words	Write a story

Chapter Three

Fire

Creative genius is not the accumulation of knowledge; it is the ability to see patterns in the universe, to detect hidden links between what is and what could be.
Richard Louv, *The Nature Principle*, 2012

Keywords: *Heat, Light, Force, Flame, Fierce, Fry, Sun, Star, Summer, Powerful, Blaze, Create, Destroy, Weapons, Conflict, Laughter, Joy, Games, Fast, Playful, Daring, Will Power, Excess.*

South is Fire, the Noon Fires Burning...

We have a "no gun rule" in our home. So when Summer returns from a play date one day and he has secreted a Lego gun in his pocket (which we only find out about through his brother "telling on him") an almost farcical conversation takes place. With the gravitas and seriousness as befits a moment of truth telling, we try and prise this 5mm weapon of miniature destruction from him, explaining that we don't have guns in the house, even if they are for a Lego alien and less than a centimetre in length. A rule is a rule and unfortunately for Summer and his Lego warrior, must not be broken.

Later that same week, when I pick Boo up from school and sit in the playground to watch him play, all the kids seem to want to do is rush around with pretend weapons. All the adults sigh as we watch them. "It doesn't matter what I do," says Whit, a mum with a son and a young daughter, "everything becomes a gun in the end". It is the cry of almost every parent of a son in this hippy nursery school. None of these parents watch gun wielding TV shows with their kids, none openly owns a gun and yet here are our kids rushing around turning sticks, spades, fingers, anything they can into a weapon. How did we get here?

My family started with a no weapon rule, which quickly deteriorated into a no guns rule, but swords, knives and imaginary lasers seem to be OK. Why? Our thinking is hazy at best – swords take skill, they are no longer weapons used to hurt people (at least not here), and Daddy, as a nurse, sees what guns can do to people. The same cannot be said for lasers. We ask all the teachers we can find about their experience of boys and gun or weapon play and their answers seem unanimous. Nothing can stop it, it is a phase, and it will pass.

As a Pagan, what I find so interesting about this discourse is that weapons are an embodiment of fire. Our relationship with them is similar to our cultural relationship with this element. They embody the forces of safety, power and fear. For many of us they come to represent violence run rampant, and they disclose to us complex questions of who has power, who wants power, and who has no power. Weapons are the currency of such debates for our kids. Weapons are an embodiment of fire. As history teaches us, they both promote and banish fear whilst demonstrating prowess and protection. Fire has the most obvious duality of values; just as it warms, it burns, as it protects, it can kill. Magically speaking, fire is the force of will, it is domination and commanding, it is also illuminating and inspiring. Fire is literally a double-edged sword.

Consuming Fire

In Western society we live with a predominance of fire qualities. We see the living reality of fire in the structures of our government and in our icons of success. Western capitalist economy is the pinnacle of a fire-driven culture – based on consumption, the destruction of natural resources, the gaining of profit; it shows the ways in which fire unchecked can run rampant. The dissonance between the natural world and human culture is framed by the spiritual meaning of the fire element.

Modern consumption removes us from the forces of production and replaces the knowledge of what sustains us with perpetual desire for products that speak our values for us. In a fire-driven culture, our consumption choices are the central way in which we demonstrate our values and our productivity. We are only as good as what we buy.

When consumption patterns aren't defining our values, we are all too often pigeonholed by what we 'do'; by our activities, by how we make money. This is a very modern preoccupation, and one that it is increasingly hard to disavow. A few hundred years ago people were judged by their values; by their passions, their qualities as a person, not upon what activities they could perform. Today success is measured by fame, fortune and getting ahead, and such an archaic notion of value is rarely espoused. Yet when we talk to kids about what it means to be successful, do we want them to think that it is by being consumers? Do we want them to believe that what matters is how much money you make? Is the manner in which we make money of upmost significance to how we are esteemed by our peers? I am hoping that for the majority of us what matters is not *what* we do but that we do it with passion, with love and that it gives us right livelihood. Ideally, we work in good consciousness, we bring our whole selves to our work and that work rewards us, our community and our planet.

Buying and working have unfortunately become interchangeable descriptors of social value and are in many ways indicative of our imbalanced relationship with the element of fire. Think about the constant nagging our kids go through to get us to buy them the newest game/sneakers/doll/smartphone/car. Kids and young adults are the targets of consumer marketing as never before. They are all too aware of this pressure, and unfortunately unaware of how these items come to our stores, how they are made and how their parents have to work to get them! Consider a time when your kids have pressured you to purchase them something. What motivated their desire? Was it a social pressure or a personal need? Would they have asked differently if you had asked, what will be gained by purchasing this? Do you know where it was made? What does it contain? Would they want it differently if they saw the conditions of the people who made it?

Knowledge is power. In our communities we do not shy away from truth, we do not hide in myth to make the truth palatable. Instead, we seek to dive deeper towards the truth. Thus we embrace technology and we embrace science in order to expand our awareness of the magic of the world. When faced with the issues of consumption and desire, we can use this quest for knowledge. Would it help take the passion out of the desire for a kid to look at what happens to those old TVs, cellphones and computers in our drive for bigger, better, faster more? Study the waterways and townships of Ghana that are ravaged with the West's electronic waste, where children grow up with the smell of burning plastic computers in their dreams. Perhaps such knowledge would stem their desire for a new phone every year or a new computer every five years. When it isn't the home hardware but personal items, again knowledge can be power. Set your older kids a task to find out before they ask again, where it was made, who made it and what it is made from. Does it change how they feel about it? Would it help to consider what materials were used to make that new fleece jacket, that new Barbie doll? For older kids this knowledge can be sobering, and certainly make them feel worthier about learning how to curb desire in the face of social and peer pressure. Likewise, it gives them a platform for discussing their choices with other kids – a place of empowerment to fight the endless exchange of desires.

The Solar Cycle

Fire is at the heart of our celebratory traditions in multiple ways – the sun and the hearth fire, the magic of a single candle flame.

Of these, the hearth fire is a place where stories can be told, magic made and festivals celebrated. The hearth fire is a domestic representative of the heart of our solar system, our beautiful star. The sun is the living embodiment of fire's power to heat, bring light and energy to our world. The sun guides our celebratory cycle. Whatever Pagan tradition we are attuned to, the solar cycle marks the passage of the seasons in a very tangible real way. Whether you are deists or not, the sun's influence on our lives is worthy of celebration and honouring. All of the contemporary Pagan sabbats (our major festivals) are connected to fire in some way, whether it is the four great sabbats, the equinoxes and solstices or the fire festivals that welcome the flow of light as it relates to the growing tides in the northern hemisphere. Fire is the heart of our seasonal celebration because it is the element of transformation and as Mother Earth changes from spring to summer from autumn to winter and around again, we recognise that our livelihood is integrally connected to the sun's life giving power here on earth. To me, the first introduction to Paganism for my kids was through the sun's cycle. I remember creating a hearth fire on our kitchen table with tens of candles burning, as we didn't have a fireplace. We watched the sun every day, seeing how the sun and moon are partners in the sky as we journey through a day and a night. The sun and the moon are our companions and the celestial reminder to honour the sources of light and heat.

So much has been written about the rituals and ways of celebrating the sabbats, the sun's dance across the heavens, that I don't want to attempt to add my voice to these (see the Further Reading section at the end of this book some great writing on celebrating the sabbats). Instead I encourage you to think freely and creatively about ways to connect to the turning of the sun's wheel.

When my brothers were very young and I was a teenager, we would go to the local park every solstice and make a sun mandala. From when they were about three and four they learnt how to lay a mandala from found objects on the ground and we made a living sun, here on earth. We would make this sun from sticks and dance around it, as if we were the earth, the moon, and the other planets. As they got older their mandala building became more complex. We made an eight-spoke wheel and used symbols to decorate it, and then we would find flowers with solar affiliations to embellish this work. It was an act of playful meditation and there were some years when it was grand and bold and others when it was detailed and beautiful. Every year it seemed to herald the summer's energy. We would go home and light candles, a drop of sun on earth, and tell stories of how man found fire, both myths and our own imaginings of how early people discovered the ability to make fire.

The Battle for the Sun – A Winter Solstice Tale
By Hannah Johnston

The sun is most revered in Pagan festivals as bringer of warmth and light, ruled by fire. Here is a story you can use to help kids welcome the return of the sun, and the living embodiment of celestial fire in the middle of winter.

It is the deepest part of the winter. For many days the sun has barely risen and has rushed across the sky with such speed that you could blink and miss a whole day. Where you live everyone feels it. People turn the lights on early. They rub their hands together. Everyone is in hats and boots and gloves. And they talk and talk about the cold as if talking about it could keep it away.

And somewhere nearby, perhaps in a field or a forest, maybe at the bottom of your garden or behind an old wall, a gathering has begun. Have you seen it? All the animals are getting together. The robin and the blackbird, the ferret and the fox, even next door's cat seem to be prowling looking for someone to hang out with. The crows congregate in great flocks and fly through the air yelling, "caaaw caaw, sun stands still! Sun stands still!" There is a magic in the air. Everything can feel it.

This is the night of the Winter Solstice.

And on this darkest day, from out of the trees the Holly King comes. Dressed in muddy brown and green, with a scarf as red as blood he comes huffing and puffing. His beard glistens with frost, and his eyes glint with the last of the sun's rays. In one hand he carries a stout club and in the other, a shield. You can hear his heavy footsteps, his boots caked with dirt and he walks as if he is weary of travelling in them.

And from the undergrowth not far away, a glimmer catches your eye. It is the golden hair of the Oak King. He lightly leaps onto the cold earth, his footsteps crushing the old leaves like a deer searching for food. He is lithe and quick, all dressed in the dusty gold and grass green. He carries a long fine spear as strong as an oak and as fine as an icicle.

These two great kings move towards each other. As they see one another across the quiet earth they call a greeting. They have trodden this path before, in another place and during a different season. It is their calling. They will battle in order for the light to return and the life to come again to the land.

"Ha ha old friend! Do you think you'll beat me with that cudgel?!" the Oak King teases as he skips towards the younger champion.

"Hmph," replies the Holly King, tired of the day already. He stops and admires his club, letting the Oak King take in its sturdy strength. But quick as a darting fox, the Oak King's spear is in the air, and glances past the Holly Kings shoulder.

He ROARS: "You, you young upstart – I wasn't ready!" and he turns and runs full pelt towards his foe. Dancing past him the Oak King retrieves his spear and turns to face his fierce opponent. And they charge!

The battle rages. Turning and turning, first one then the other seems to have the upper hand. Wrestling each other with strength and grace until finally, the fatal blow. The spear pierces the Holly King's heart and he falls to the waiting earth below.

"Return Return...." the Oak King sighs softly and kneels beside his brave companion. He places his hand in the old King's.

And quietly, before your very eyes, all the creatures who bore witness to this mighty battle come forward. Large or small, they bring something to honour the brave Holly's death. Small mouse and weevil, house fly and sparrow bring all they can carry to make the Old King a blanket. And soon bryony vine and old man's beard, rosehips and berries, leaves from the ash and the thorn all pile together to make a mound.

The birds chatter and the Oak King smiles as the once dry and crisp blanket turns to soft mulch, and from its centre a pale Holly sprig emerges.

The animals scamper back to their warming homes and the Oak King rises to his feet and faces the sun.

He calls loudly to the dying rays of light: "Sun and Earth, I am your champion. I welcome the growing light." Crows echo his cry.

"Life and light will grow as I do!" And with that he thrusts his spear into the ground and with a shimmer and a spark he is gone.

And so now you know. When you see that Holly bush, the small one growing in the heart of winter, right next to the sapling whose leaves have not yet woken, you know that this is the place where a battle was fought. You know this is the place where the sun was returned to us and where the Oak King was again victorious.

Teaching children how to work with fire is a crucial life skill. My husband often wistfully remembers being asked to lay the fire. His parents trusted him at that age to do this when he had come home from school. This way their Edinburgh flat would be warm enough to enjoy their dinner! Teach your kids how to make a fire, how to handle fire. Not all of us have coal fireplaces any longer, but knowing how to work with fire is a skill – it requires patience, caution and precision. If you go camping, go somewhere where you can try out your fire-making skills – use a lens and paper to start a fire, or rub sticks or use a fire starter such as Gerber Bear Grylls Fire starter or some other traditional means, and see your kids' sense of achievement when they accomplish significant skill.

Toast marshmallows, tell stories and you will quickly find (although I imagine you will have experienced this already) how a fire brings people together, and its blessings of warmth and light relax the mind and open our spirit. Whenever I have experienced a bonfire with my kids, especially during sabbat celebrations or when we have been camping, I watch in wonder as they can spend hours sitting and listening, whereas in any other context sitting still would require real discipline. Fire draws us in to dream. And later, dancing around a fire can be a powerful energy raising technique.

Candles are another way you can teach kids about the power of fire, and they are always a part of our celebrations. As Doreen Valiente wrote in *An ABC of Witchcraft Past and Present;*

> [T]he natural flame of candlelight has been the perpetual accompaniment of magical ceremonies. [...] In the glow of candlelight an ordinary everyday room can take on quite a different appearance from that which it normally possesses. People's faces look different, too. The commonplace is transformed by the alchemy of fire. (pp. 135-136)

Unsurprisingly children are fascinated by candles; they hold a magic all of their own, so distinct from the fire magic found in beautiful home fireplaces or bonfires. If you are a chandler, then please offer your skills to our younger community members! Whether making them with beeswax or tallow (much rarer today), candles make beautiful presents and when made for a purpose such as a birthday or a spell can be warmly received.

Learning how to use matches is the place to start with candle magic, always supervised of course, and then you can show them some wonderful little tricks. Show them how to still the flame, by staring into it, and you will find that they quickly accomplish it (you don't need to tell them in the main it is because their anticipation means they hold their breath, which often causes the flame to lessen its flickering!) Candle magic can be taught to children of all ages. Simple candle gazing, letting pictures form in the mind, and using the flame as a meditation can begin at birth. Turn the lights off and burn candles and see how infants respond to candlelight. Think about the blowing out of candles, the extinguishing of flame is a moment of magic when we blow out birthday candles. Include this in toddlers' magic making.

From the age of about five, younger if your kids are more dexterous, you can teach them how to dress and inscribe candles. In my coven this used to be a maiden's job – often a skill learnt in the coven's 'outer circle' (those not yet initiated, and still in training) and the maidens would learn how to dress a candle with oil, inscribe it, and ready it for use in ritual. Whether inscribed with words or symbols or pictures, placing your desire on a candle in symbolic form helps to bring our mind again to the intention as it burns. This reinforcement can be very useful. Through candle magic we can teach kids the basics of spell-working – the importance of intention, clarity of thought, focusing our need, consideration of consequences and the organisation and workings of magical correspondences. Correspondences are, to rely on the wisdom of the Farrars for a moment:

> ...the word for objects, creatures, substances, plants, deity-forms, quality-concepts and so on which have psychic affinity with each other. A study of correspondences is therefore very helpful in planning spell-working ritual so that everything – accessories, deity-forms invoked, incense, robes if any, colours etc. – can be in tune with the operation and contribute to its power. (*Spells and How they Work*, p.45)

So let's say that they are going to start school and they are nervous. You ask, how do you want to feel walking into that classroom? Happy? Strong? Confident? What colour do you imagine all those feelings? Yellow? Orange? Let's find a deep yellow or an orange candle and we will light it every day for a week before you start school and as it burns, you are going to see yourself walking into that classroom full of smiles, happy and strong and ready for anything. Or, maybe you have a kid who is suffering nightmares. Candle magic can be very powerful for this. What colour takes away things – white contains all colours, black absorbs all colour, or perhaps a brown one, to return your nightmares to the earth, or a gold candle to have the power of the sun lighten your dreams.

Through using candle magic we show kids magical correspondences of the colours and later as they get older and more versed in this simple form of simple spellworking, we can anchor our kids in correspondences of the lunar tides, the colours, the times of day, we can teach them symbols and runic languages.

Ask a teenager to write their fears onto a paper and burn it in the flame. Allow the flame to transform it to dust and ash. There are many ways in which you can use candles as a means of teaching the ethics and practical workings of spells. Young kids get these quickly, older kids see the nuances, and this can lead to many interesting conversations about the nature of ethical living. Most importantly through communicating these foundational building blocks of spells you are showing them that they are active participants in their own lives, connected to all other things and empowered to make changes.

Correspondences – A Quick List for Making Magic With Young Folks

To welcome something new – new moon, Friday, dawn, air, bread, sweets, daisy, rain, a silver penny, yellow, pink, pale blue, maiden, singing, song birds.

To be rid of something– waning moon/dark moon, night time, Saturday, old object, duster, brown, grey, black, running water, sage, ash tree, rowan berries, soil, salt, owl, fox.

To find something – first crescent moon, morning star, Wednesday, air, fire, string, rosemary, bergamot (oranges), bay, chanting, breeze, leaves, blue, brown, mouse, cat, magpie.

To forget something – waning moon, evening, Saturday, mist, water, earth, basil, chamomile, sleep, smoke, grey, silver, violet, raven, cuckoo, goldfish.

To make a wish/project grow – Waxing Moon, midday, Sunday or Thursday, bean plant, acorn, marigold, sunflower, seeds, gold, green, horse, rabbit.

To overcome an obstacle, illness or fear – Waning/Dark Moon, afternoon to evening, Tuesday, pine tree, oak, yew, nettles, caraway, onion, lemon, blue, dark red, white, badger, otter, swan.

The Rules of Spellworking
(From Janet and Stewart Farrar, *Spells and How They Work*, p.19)

1. Never work to harm anyone.
2. Never work to manipulate anyone against his or her own will or natural development.
3. Never assume you know all the factors involved in the situation or person you are working on.
4. Never work for your own gain at someone else's expense.
5. Word your spell precisely and carefully, to leave no loopholes that may result in your inadvertently breaking Rules 1 to 4.

Warm and Cosy Kids
Fire is a beautiful thing. Feeling warm is such a gift, as all of us know who have camped outside under the moon next to a warm fire, or who have got into bed in a freezing house and curled up next to a lover or a child. Happiness is feeling warm, and fire's

most balanced and temperate nature is captured in the heart's love and the warmth we feel when we are in good relationship with others. We all need to be warm. In warmth a seed can grow, in warmth we can relax. Animals' migratory patterns follow the sun's warming path around Mother Earth. Children need to be surrounded by warmth both emotionally and literally, both inside and out, to feel good.

Educationalist and spiritual teacher Rudolf Steiner wrote that for children to grow and to start life well they need three basic things; lots of sleep, to be kept warm at all times and to be well fed. Although I question much of Steiner's philosophy, this seems to be some pretty sound thinking about kids' growth. These elements are essential to children throughout their childhood and children should be kept warm (but not cosseted) both inside and out. When the weather turns colder, dress your kids in layers of warm natural fibres, carry your babies on you and give them soft wool underwear so that their body is not extending that much needed growth energy to simply stay warm. Socks, mittens and hats are lovely gifts for a new baby. If you are so inclined these make perfect Pagan-friendly baby welcoming gifts, as they follow the ancient arts given to us from the fates and they express our desire to allow our little ones to start their life outside warm and safe in the arms of their loved ones. Many of us are crafty knitters or weavers and thrifty too, so such a gift ticks many of our boxes. These are traditional skills bestowed upon us by the Goddesses of old, by the fates themselves, the Moirai, the Norns, the Parcae who some say spin, measure and cut the cloth of our destiny as they weave our lives on the great loom of life. Whilst you are knitting or weaving sing a chant for the child, place your wishes into your stitches and the blanket becomes imbued with all your good intent. Allow your mind to wonder and perhaps you will see something for the child to come or the child new born. Handmade gifts are always special and no matter how simple their design they are the objects that a family cherishes.

Too often I see little ones who are being carried by parents who themselves are wearing socks and shoes and jackets but their babes have tiny naked blue cold feet. Hardy kids don't come from being cold. Hardy kids are made from knowing that the elements are their allies and being out in them – appropriately dressed and fed. Hearty, healthy meals, warm clothing and lots of emotional warmth make for happy, healthy kids.

Fire's Call to Change

As a culture, our relationship with fire needs to change and our kids can help us do this. Fire is not only our desire for ownership, for things, it can be a call to action, and a force for transformation. Recent social upheavals across the globe are testament to fire's capacity to cause change – radical and lasting change. People's will expressed through violence and non violence alike can overthrow old regimes, can question the status quo and can bring to light injustice. The Occupy Movement had, for a short time, a real opportunity to speak out on behalf of those who had no voice – to bring to light issues of disparity between those in the upper echelons of our countries' financial dealings and those whom such dealings directly affected. Likewise, the Arab Spring's continuing evolution is an inspiring reminder of how civil resistance can work to overthrow corrupt and dictatorial regimes.

Such examples show what the influence of fire can be. Both literally and metaphorically these examples demonstrate fire's qualities and how it can be dynamically life enhancing: a new love affair, a blossoming creative outlet, moving house, changing career. Equally fire's influence can be seen in an election period, a ceasefire or a civil rights movement. Whether dramatic and intense or slow burning, the force of fire within our lives is positive if transformative, and can be painful in part, as one thing must die to make room for the new. On the other side of fire's influence are the destructive and the terrible; on a global scale this can global warming, volcanic eruptions, forest fires, epidemics, warfare. On a personal scale this could manifest as violent death, abandonment, betrayal, accident and conflict. Fire is almost impossible to tame, the outcome of its force difficult to control. Yet we can seek to channel it, so its destruction makes way for new growth.

Working with children, how do we approach this choleric element? We can show them how to recognise the power of fire in its various form and functions and how to embrace its transformative nature with courage and conviction. When I see my kids now playing make-believe with weapons, do I try to stop them? Not always, instead I try to frame and understand some of their impulses. Sometime this can be done through recounting stories and tales of bravery, virtue, courage, strength and fear, so that their play helps them understand and come to know the strengths of conflict play. As one mum recently told me, "I can't stop him fighting, so I sent him to Karate, where he is taught how to control his urge to do it." Our pagan ancestors were often warriors, tribal in nature and in habit, and they knew as so many indigenous peoples did, how to balance fire's drive to consume the world with its capacity to cleanse the world.

Daring to Be Different

Being a Pagan requires, at the very least, a daring spirit. To pitch your spirituality and lifestyle beyond those recognised and decreed by mainstream culture takes small daily acts of courage that many of us pay little heed to when we first put our feet on the path. Without knowing it, you were daring in that first moment of identification in saying – "I am a Pagan, I am a witch," or simply, "There must be a better way I can do this". This is an act of courage because every day we dare to espouse values and ethics that fly in the face of social expectations. If we are open about our spirituality we model that we are willing to be different, that we speak our own truths. And to be bold, outspoken or just different means we have courage, because we may face adversity or conflict as a result.

Kids need good models, that much we know. For kids in the "gibbous years", age ten to about fifteen, this is really crucial. Being different within this growing phase can be especially painful and the pressure that kids are under during this time cannot be underestimated. However much we think we can identify with kids this age, we rarely understand the extent to which their experience is different.

We grew up in a different time, when technology was not the mainframe of our lives or where all our social interactions were to some extent mediated for us. The kind of pressures this places on kids today may mean they remove themselves from us earlier and identify more and more with their social groups – in itself a very normal healthy transition, or it may mean they remove themselves from the world – a decidedly more worrisome prospect. Whereas with younger kids we can use myth and story to inspire their understanding of courage and bravery, for kids in later childhood we often need something more tangible and real. This is after all the age of realism, where all those years of playing with fairies and elves are put aside. To help our kids identify their unique difference and to help protect it from the onslaught of social pressure at this age, we can introduce political figures and modern heroines to demonstrate how powerful difference and speaking out is.

Use some controversial, inspiring figures from history and the contemporary time to open up talking points with older kids to get them to start to think about the true meaning of courage, bravery and our right to be different. Here are some ideas to get you started:

The Pankhurst Family (1958+, Britain): Emmeline and her daughters, Sylvia, Christabel and Adela, worked tirelessly for women's suffrage movements in various ways, all demanding the vote for women.

Sacagawea (1788-1812 Shoshone America): A Lemhi Shoshone woman, who overcame immense personal difficulty (being taken and sold to a French Canadian trapper who made her his wife) and went on to accompany the Lewis and Clark Expedition, acting as an interpreter and guide and the only female expedition member in their exploration of the Western United States.

Che Guivera (1928-1967, Argentina): Marxist revolutionary, doctor, diplomat, writer. Che developed guerrilla warfare as a means to try and rid South America of what he saw as capitalist imperialism destroying the unity of South American culture and its economies.

Charles Darwin (1809-1882 Britain): Naturalist who first proposed the theory of natural selection at a time when the trans-mutation of species (one species altering into another) was accepted thinking.

Rosa Parks (1913-2005 USA): Famously, in 1955, Rosa refused to give up her seat to a white man on the bus in Alabama when the white section had been filled. Often called the "Mother of the freedom movement", she became a figurehead in the American Civil Rights Movement.

Aung San Suu Kyi (1945 + Burma): Burmese political leader, and Nobel prize holder, she is the chairperson for the National League for Democracy and was placed under house arrest for 15 years after she challenged the incumbent government and legally won the election. Since her release in 2010 she has tirelessly lobbied against corruption and for democratic process in her country.

Captain Paul Watson (1950+ Canada): Watson is an environ-mentalist and activist who began his career with Greenpeace, but believed non-violent protest didn't go far enough. He went on to form the *Sea Shepherd Conservation Society* for the protection of global marine life. Watson's ships have been known to go to battle with Japanese whaling ships. Wanted for violation of various shipping laws, and having spent time in prison Watson believes that direct action is at times the only way to safeguard protected species.

I recently put a post up on the "book of face", asking friends who inspired them, and I was surprised to see how many people named their family members and friends as those who most inspired them. So many of us feel removed from the machinations of popular culture that it is the inspiration that our own households offer, our neighbourhoods and communities, that have the greatest capacity to move us to action. When I looked at people's answers I found the relationship between inspiration and courage is striking – for many of my friends, those people who gave them inspiration were those who demonstrated a fortitude of will, a courage in the face of adversity – whether through physical exertion, through overcoming addiction, or through great compassion, courage lies at the heart of our personal stories of inspiration.

Exercise

Ask your children to consider who inspires them in their lives? Ask them to tell you stories of those people close to them who they look up to and why? Is their inspiration strong, and how does this strength show itself? Perseverance? Tolerance? Boldness? Do they have the ability to be tricky and wily or beautiful and talented? Are they inspiring because they are unashamed and independently minded (which as every middle year child will already sense, has an element of danger to it)? What qualities do your children believe these inspirational people share with them? What do they want to amplify in their own lives to move them closer to this way of being? How can small changes lead them to inspire others?

As we ask these questions we can begin to understand what

motivates our children whilst allowing us to question what has become the norm in models of success and inspiration. We get to see the lines of force that demonstrate how one act of courage can become the building block of social transformation.

Conflict and Danger

Paganism doesn't shy away from dissent; it embraces dissent as an inevitable yet vibrant part of the multitudinous nature of earth-centred practice. Sybil Leek wrote about this over 30 years ago in *The Complete Art of Witchcraft*: "The most unexplained fact about witchcraft today is that it is a religion with a serious schismatic problem; there are almost as many causes for dissension here as in the Protestant faith" (1971, pg. 15). Although Leek is speaking specifically about the witchcraft community many moons ago, the debates over differences in ritual traditions remain in contemporary life as a Pagan.

It is perhaps a necessary part of growth. Yet, despite this push-pull within our communities, we continue to evolve and generate thinkers, poets, ritualists and activists. What insight does this dynamic offer us regarding the purpose and power of conflict?

Difference is an inevitable part of life – we are not always going to agree with each other all the time. Some dissent must be always accounted for, and some people like nothing more that disagreeing for its own sake. Allowing for healthy dissent stops our thinking from stagnating – it can ensure that Pagan spirituality evolves and can rise to the challenges of the common times. For example, in the broad Pagan community there has been ongoing discussion of the ethics of meat eating, which with the forms of intensive farming today have become a serious question for those of us intending to tread lightly on the earth.

What these discussions can show us, in their form is that might is *not* right. Starhawk most famously discussed this in her description of Power Over, the form of patriarchal authority that pervades our contemporary models of power structures. Here

Power Over articulates that those who are bigger, stronger, louder or richer or prettier (more of anything that patriarchy values), has a natural right to dominate those who do not. These forms of cultural, emotional and spiritual domination and oppression have no place in Paganism.

Democracy teaches us that everyone has the right to speak. At the heart of modern democracy is the understanding that every person has a right to be heard, a right to equality of voice at a given stage of decision-making. As Aristotle stated, "Democracy is when the indigent and not the men of property, are the rulers." How this is interpreted is of course debatable (and a great project to undertake with your middle-schoolers). At the root of the normative idea of democracy is that having more, or being more, should not give you more right to make decisions over others.

This leads to questions regarding force, and its appropriate use. Violence is rarely a viable option. For small children dealing in absolutes it is infinitely easier when it comes to discussing the role of violence and conflict to state that violence is never right. However, as you will know if you work with or raise kids over the age of six, they will offer you a plethora of examples where violence is used to demonstrate valour, protection and honour. Are we to dismiss the myths of old, the tales of the great Sagas? The wonders of King Arthur and the Knights of the Round Table? Should we avoid discussion of great battles, or proud warrior clans and tribal Chiefs?

Likewise, you and your tribe may have been the victims of violence, of generations of oppression. Do you live in a neighbourhood where crime is the norm and children's ongoing exposure to it leaves you feeling despondent? Perhaps you are a proud military family, who sees the role of force as necessary in an ever-changing and volatile world.

Such variation in our community means that we are unlikely to reach unanimous consensus on the question of whether violence is a viable option. Is violence in the name of self-defence justified? Is violence against oppression justified? I am going to quote from an old friend here, Robin, a writer and a member of Occupy Boston. When I asked her this question she replied:

> I think it's very complicated. It's not that it's justified, it's that people become so sick with whatever that they can't stop themselves. Gandhi was once asked to be critical of a man who broke into a British government office and killed some officials there. His answer was that he couldn't be hateful towards the man, or even be dismissive of his actions; the man had become so infected by the evil that he lived under that he became like them, and he was more saddened by it than anything else.

When Summer became fascinated with the story of Robin Hood we had lengthy discussions about the use of force and this is what he realised. Heroic characters and traditions from which they come are rooted in an understanding of violence as the unnecessary exertion of force against the powerless. This is opposed to justifiable defensive force, often against a powerful oppressor. Our history overflows with stories of battles, war, heroes and heroines, combat conflict, and many of these help us to understand how power works, and how violence and force can be justified, in self-defence and on a grander scale, for the emancipation from oppression. By telling our kids the story of Robin Hood and King Arthur we can contextualise the question of force by emphasising the importance of valour, of mercy and compassion. The energy of fire must be tempered by water.

I think of Captain Paul Watson currently aboard the Sea Shepherd. This man was one of the original founders of Greenpeace, but found that their stance of complete nonviolence meant that he was asked to stand by and watch as many of our planet's beautiful and endangered marine wildlife were illegally hunted and killed. Consequently he used international laws, including the United Nations World Charter for Nature, as a means of condoning the illegal whaling and seal killing. Using direct action, *Sea Shepherd* deliberately rams whaling boats. Such controversial tactics raise several hackles. What makes *Sea Shepherd* different to other pirates operating outside the law on the high seas, you may ask? What gives such vigilantism the right to damage the property of other nations' fleets? Cpt. Watson's attempt is first and foremost to hold those criminal protagonists accountable. Further, Cpt. Watson and his crew advocate for creatures that have no voice of their own, and they justify direct action on behalf of those vulnerable creatures. Whether we agree with his methods or not, his compassionate impulse is brought to action through fire.

I personally find that issues around conflict are the hardest aspects of educating and raising kids. For those of us working in dynamic groups, we have worked long and hard at conflict resolution and the work of Judy Harrow, Starhawk, Emma Restall Orr amongst others have inspired us to see empowering models of conflict resolution in adult situations, magical communities and real world protests. Yet when dealing with unruly toddlers, petulant middle schoolers and violent and abusive teens it is easy to lose our way and forget the basic principles that Pagans aspire to. Helping our kids navigate the daily battles of feeling powerless – whilst we try and find our way through the sticky territory of power struggles – is a tall order. Added to this, we live in a time when our approach to parenting is often defined in part by our attitude towards conflict (think about the differences in approach between attachment parenting and Tiger Mothering) and well, it gets messy!

A child's will is an essential part of them. It needs clear channels. If you have a kid as I do who has an excess of will, it is intensely useful and needs all our patience. We can instil limits and channel its use in appropriate ways. Importantly we try to be consistent. Conflict with kids so often arises from fatigue, low blood sugar, and inconsistency. By giving a child a clear set of expectations that can evolve and grow with them, we give them nourishing soil to act as a foundation. Then, of course, we can model the conflict resolution we aspire to see in the kids we work and live around. In your family, coven, and neighbourhood be as transparent as you can with your kids about points of conflict, and show them not just the point of dissention but also the process of its resolution.

As we all know, boundaries befit the child. Set limits, stick to them and if they are broken allow the consequences to truly reflect the behaviour. In magical thinking this is cause and effect in action. For Summer who brought home the inappropriate Lego gun, his consequence was not being able to borrow toys from friends' houses until further notice, until trust was once more restored.

A child who is constantly repeating the same challenging behaviour, like a motif in a dream, is communicating something to you about her needs. A kid who is constantly making friends with kids who are abrasive and bullying may be telling you she feels disempowered in other areas of her life. Or a boy who runs down the street after your repeated admonishments may be asking for your trust and needs more independence. Our job as guardians of the kids we live with is to try to listen with an open heart. One of the biggest challenges we may face when our children demonstrate violent or dangerous behaviour towards others or themselves is to not rise to their anger, but to listen to what their angry behaviour is telling us about their feelings. Anger is a symptom not a source feeling.

The Question of Harm

When fire is out of balance in our lives and in our culture, it leads us down a path beset with challenge, fear and even violence. No matter whether they are 4 or 14, as caretakers we are faced with the terrifying reality of our own limitations when our children become the victim or the perpetrator of harm. How can we hold both love and compassion for our child and steer them out of harm's way? How can we prevent youth violence? When our charges have been the victim of violence of any variety and to any degree, it is easy to react with fear and anger. Children's vulnerability to violence makes all of us accountable.

Violence towards children is a barometer for social wealth and happiness. In times and places plagued by economic and social recession, by limited opportunities and resources, violence towards and by children is a tangible reality. The majority of violence that children face is in their own homes. As one American report states, "One in ten children in the U.S. are exposed to domestic violence, and the majority of them are under six years old." (http://www.urbanchildinstitute.org/articles/research-to-policy/overviews/domestic-violence-hurts-children-even-when-they-are-not-direct, accessed 27/08/13).

Violence can take many forms. Witnessing domestic violence, parental bullying, sexual abuse, neglect and outright physical harm towards children by their caretakers, parents, teachers and neighbours is a reality of the world we live in. Most adults want to be loving and kind towards the children in their lives, but some are simply unable to cope with the burden placed upon them. Some adults are angry and children are an easy target and some have unresolved mental health disorders that make it difficult to know how to appropriately be with children.

It is likely that someone you know, a child or an adult, is walking a line across this tricky terrain. It could be a parent with post-partum depression who can't stop yelling at her kids. A neighbour who does not heed your silent signals to steer clear of your kids, or perhaps an unhappy child at school who is displaying signs of trauma and harm. Violence can be found everywhere, and it is our job to be cognisant to the fact that it could be as rife within our community as within others.

How can we help? Magically we can ask the powers of the

world to bring resolution and calm to families and children in need, but it is our number one job to ensure the protection of children at risk. National organisation such as the NSPCC and Pagan based organisations such as Pagans Against Child Abuse (PACA) in the US are set up to educate, inform and create a safe place for dialogue and intervention regarding child abuse. The Pagan Federation in the UK is working hard to put the same supports in place for British Pagan families. Unfortunately our community is large and fractured, and there are many people who proclaim themselves Druid, Wiccan or Pagan without the safety net of a community's endorsement. This is both one of the strengths and the difficulties with our faith tradition. Back in 2010, internet pioneer Jason Pitzel-Waters wrote several articles on the relationship between the Pagan community and abuse cases, and posed some important points for us all. He said:

> A vast percentage of modern Pagans aren't part of any estab-
> lished group, or are members of groups and traditions so
> small they hardly count as "established" on any national or
> even regional scale. This creates a culture where we tend to
> ascribe a certain amount of legitimacy to any individual
> practitioner as a common courtesy, which creates fertile
> grounds for those who want to abuse that trust. I'm not saying
> we should stop trusting, or that everyone should join a
> national organization if they want to be taken seriously, only
> that our decentralized nature makes us uniquely vulnerable to
> con-men and monsters. (http://www. patheos.com/blogs
> /wildhunt/2010/04/child-abusing-druid-sentenced-to-12-
> years-in-prison.html, accessed 04/2010).

Our spirituality's place in culture requires us to be particularly vigilant towards the possibilities for power abuse and due to the unconventional nature of many who follow this path we must practise heightened awareness at all times.

What can we do to help families and kids who have been involved in violence either directly or indirectly, or who might be at risk? Firstly we must ensure that the relevant authorities are informed. In addition to the recommendations laid out by the CDC and other national organisations such as the NSPCC, STRYVE (www.safeyouth.gov) and the Stop Bullying Now Campaign (www.stopbullyingnow.hrsa.gov), I have found through my own work with kids and in talking to educators and therapists who work with children, that Pagans have much to bring to the healing process. Firstly, nature is a powerful ally. If your kids have been the victim of violence at home or school, find opportunities that take them into green spaces. Survival skills, camping, Scouts, volunteering on a farm or alongside animals and plants can be great ways to relieve disturbed kids. Such activities put kids back into their bodies, get them connected to their feelings and give them a place to process what has happened without having to talk about it.

When kids have gone through upset of any kind, they need respite. Simplify – allow them to rest, encourage sleep, good food and rejuvenation where you can. Slow the pace of life right down. Let them spend time with animals, who have a more natural relationship to their rhythms than we do. This can be incredibly healing and can help them release emotions safely. Be out in the sun, and under the moon. Allow the restorative power of the celestial bodies to do their work. Then you can begin to emphasise rhythm again, returning them to a place of earth. Give structure, lay expectations clearly and build predictability.

Even for a wayward teenager this can be important; to know that there will be dinner on the table at six o'clock whether she chooses to join you. Then, when they are ready, you can encourage them to get involved – to get active – find obviously positive outlets for the expression of will. Limit the number of people around your kids when possible. Over population in a child's life can be a source of stress. Instead encourage those healthy, close relationships. Encourage your kids to find a cause or an organisation that sees them and appreciates their gifts.

This simple outline has been explained to me in so many ways by so many talented and gifted educators that it strikes me that the structure of healing works like a ritual – to find balance and peace again, children often need quiet, peace, understanding, food, rest, then rhythm, purpose and activity. All of these pointers aim to contain fire, to reinstate the rhythm and peace of earth and water – to bring comfort, healing and calm. For children who have been the victim of domestic or peer violence, substantial forms of healing are necessary.

When our child is not the victim but the perpetrator, the solutions can be surprisingly similar. Faced with the challenges of a difficult and perhaps challenging child our instinct even as a guardian, may be to withdraw and withhold. We may feel embarrassed, let down or simply angry. Why my kid? We ask ourselves, just as we do when our child is a victim of challenging behaviour. As caregivers in whatever capacity, we are asked to recognise a cry for attention over a real psychological disturbance that needs immediate help.

If a child we know has done something that seems to go against everything we believe we have shown them, how do we approach them with compassion and understanding? The media tells us that anti-social behaviour and criminality in kids comes from parents – and whilst this may hold true in cases, there are multifaceted reasons why children get off track. If we reach out to those families and look holistically at the problem of youth criminality we can find places of compassion within us. We need to strive towards creative ways of changing the sickness in our culture that gives such fertile soil for damaging expressions of self.

Young adults trying out identities can be drawn to those who seem to offer excitement and energy in the face of apathy and boredom. Juvenile systems the world over are not full of bad kids, they are full of kids who made bad choices and who took some wrong turns. Some kids who feel powerless in their own lives search for ways to feel powerful by taking it from others. What we can offer is another path to power.

Luckily many of us were once difficult children! I know that I was given numerous chances from adult musicians and Pagans who offered me something far more enticing than drugs, alcohol or the high from starvation – they showed me the path to magic.

Some of the best ways in which kids who have been out on that edge have found ways back are through healing techniques that ground and centre them. Consider programs like the thera-peutic program in Harris CO in the USA, rehabilitating violent teens within the criminal justice system using HEEL, a treatment program with dogs. And, as one journalist writes about Harris' novel approach to bringing troubled teens back to the community, "there's the gardening program, which teaches patience, nurturing, and most importantly the ability to land a job." (http://abclocal.go.com/ktrk/story?section=news/local&id= 8545325, accessed 26/08/13). Therapeutic horticulture (or what we might call magical gardening!) is finding its way into prisons, rehabilitation centres and hospitals across the world as we realise the power that growing things has on serotonin levels in the brain, leading to heightened positivity, self-confidence and calm.

A 2011 study at a juvenile rehabilitation center in south-western Ohio with a gardening program showed that horti-culture therapy helped the kids see themselves in a more positive light and helped them better manage their emotional and behavioral problems. And most of the kids said they would continue gardening after the program, according to the findings in the *Journal of Therapeutic Horticulture*. (http://www. npr.org/blogs/thesalt/2012/02/17/147050691/can-gardening-help-troubled-minds-heal, accessed 20/08/13).

These responses, a far cry from the 1990s' and early noughts' boot camp approaches to rehabilitating teens, recognise that healing comes when we are in deeper connection to Mother Earth.

When fire energy runs rampant it often turns inwards. Knowing a kid with an addiction or self-abuse disorder can be terrifying for all those around them who want to love and support them. For young adults struggling with the myriad problems that come with entering our culture there are various ways in which some of those hard circumstances can be avoided. Drugs, alcohol, self-harm are all ways in which our kids internalise the challenges of adulthood as they stand on the threshold of independence. Addiction is often a symptom of not having a purpose. We all need to feel that what we are doing matters.

The writer Paul Garrigan has talked about the link between addiction and the loss of purpose from a distinctly spiritual perspective (paulgarrigan.com). He suggests that personal purpose is the motivation for will. We cannot put energy or willpower behind an endeavour without a purpose, without us knowing what it is and why it is we are doing it. Purpose then gives us meaning, and allows us to bring our whole selves to an endeavour. Will and purpose, motivation and action are all qualities of fire needed for us to lead healthy happy lives.

Paganism has so much to offer vulnerable kids, especially those who are searching for a brighter, exciting life. Too often our young folk are entranced by the bright lights of mainstream culture only to find that this is not the true sacred flame of fire but the glimmer of a ghost light, a will-'o-the wisp, that seems to offer brightness but can lead to greater unhappiness. We can replace the desire for wealth, fame and desirability, all expressions of consumer success, with the promise of magic – with the power than comes from within. When you are a radiant person, illuminated by knowing who you are, you walk and act in the knowledge of your connection with the universe. This is what Paganism can offer.

Kids need to be allowed to express their will, but obviously need to do it in appropriate and safe ways. Allowing kids to express the full range of their feelings is essential to their mental health. By denying their rage, frustration and anger, we lock it away and it will reappear elsewhere. We live in an image driven, violence-infused mass media culture – our older kids and teens know this better than we, and the stress it creates in them cannot be underestimated. Our young people are told daily that what they have is not enough and we should not be surprised when so many of the crimes we see our kids committing are those against themselves, others and property. The myth of happiness revolves around what they can get, and it is turning in on itself. This needs to change.

Think about this elementally – what do you do when a fire is running rampant? Give it no fuel, wait till it has run its course, or put it out with water. Love, compassion, rhythmic activity and nature are your best allies during these troubled periods. Give kids something to care about, something that has real value to replace the gnawing hunger promoted by advertising and media industries. Community-based organisations that aim to support, up-skill and integrate urban youth such as the Urban Youth Gardening program at Beech Creek Gardens USA, or the Horticultural Society of New York's pioneering program with at risk teens or Britain's Woodcraft Folk (woodcraftfolk.org.uk) or Youth at Risk (youthatrisk.org.uk) offer great models of how to help kids find purpose, activity and connect them to their communities in meaningful ways.

Fire brings complete metamorphosis, sometimes in the most destructive and tragic ways. Accidents, violence, acts of war, these are some of fire's faces and those hardest to look upon and work with. We witness fire's fate befall those around us every day, the whole of the news media is built on the premise of such stories as newsworthy. Such news shocks us, rocks us and changes our place in the world. Until they happen to us directly though, it is hard to comprehend the true meaning of fire's profound ability to change or erase us. And when it happens to kids, how do we hold them in such a terrifying place? Buddhists believe that pain and suffering is a consequence of this existence, that it is in part a consequence of desire, and that only by living a life of nonattachment can we look beyond the individual life patterns to live freely. Christians believe that our pain and suffering comes from our origin as sinners, and that God decides what it is we need to experience in order to teach us.

Pagans generally do not hold with a belief of non-attachment, nor do we care much for the concepts of sin or divine retribution. Instead, as we live in more complex entangled webs with the world around us, we are often arguably closer to sources of pain and suffering. When awful things happen, we strive to understand that we are a tiny part of a whole and all the colours of our life, heartache pain, suffering fear, anger, destruction are an integral part of the life cycle. It doesn't mean we have to like it or that it's easy, but we see it as part of the journey of every living organism.

Perhaps a butterfly experiences deep apprehension as it awaits its transformation from pupa to butterfly. Perhaps the black bear feels heartache knowing that there won't be enough food to let all its cubs live through the late spring. Pain is a part of being animate (who knows, perhaps inanimate beings experience it too, when a mountain is blast mined, does it cry out in pain?) and we can neither hide nor run from it. We can only acknowledge it and find a way through. This is where our magic, our belief in the transformative power of energy work can help.

It reminds me of a time I was late night facebooking a friend. I had known this young man for many years and knew him to be learned, earnest, funny and committed. And yet in our conversation on this night, he was in such heartache and pain that he let it all spill – he had HIV which he was managing successfully but left him tired and depleted, a partner he loved deeply but who was abusive and precarious, and importantly he felt he had little support and little magic in his life. How, he wrote, can I continue? This is just too hard.

As my heart opened, I remembered that once my own mentor Eric had said to me, "This is a hard path and it isn't for the many". Now I think he was saying that unlike so many spiritualities we have no perfect answer for changing or handling pain and heartache, no secret code to unlock it. This is what makes our path hard. It comes to us, and we must bear it, we must carry it whilst remaining open to the beauty and life around us. This dichotomy is hard to live, easy to say. It doesn't offer a cure-all, it is not a fix-it faith. It is an honest reflection of the power of time and trust. That is what makes us strong, and that is the strength of magic. That is what I told my friend, keep reaching out, and remember you are the power, you have the magic. You are the Goddess.

Growing Creativity

There are two giggling kids on my porch. Sophia has come over for a home-school day and I am trying to corral her and my boy Summer into doing some visualisation before we do some painting. We are standing on our front porch in the beautiful sunlight, with our eyes closed. I can hear them jiffling as I try and set the tone with quiet calm words. Yet still they giggle. The birds are singing and everywhere the air feels busy. The warm weather has arrived.

"Send your roots into the ground beneath your feet," I say. Summer farts and both of them let out a gaffaw.

"Feel the warmth of the sun across your body now. Like a tree you have roots and your branches are reaching to the warmth of the sun. Pull the heat and the light in through your new leaves, pull it to your heart. Let the sun's warmth glow and grow there, in your heart. Feel it: red, orange, yellow, spreading its warmth throughout your body, and seeping down, down into the earth beneath you, into your roots." They are quiet and still now, brows slightly furrowed.

"This is the sun within you, and we are going to go and express the beautiful warm radiance of its glow when we open our eyes."

When we open our eyes the kids are glowing, literally beaming and we skip inside and all three of us use watercolours to make a beautiful sunrise painting over an imagined landscape. We use water on water paints, so that it appears that land and sky, sun and cloud and earth are all blending together. On this bright morning, two kids have connected to the creative impulse and the magic of the sun.

At the heart of Pagan philosophy is the spirit of creativity. At the centre of our vision of the world is the reverence of the earth's capacity for generative evolution. Also, as a new spirituality still finding our feet, we are constantly in the process of reinvention and creation of rituals and traditions. We take Mother Earth as our guide, as our holy book. She is the ultimate standard of creative recycling. Mother Earth is the definitive recycler; pretty much whatever is thrown at her, she can handle. Acts of creation that are so mundane are the manner and mode of the miraculous for us. A seed, a tiny speck is placed in the ground, given light and water and it becomes food. That food becomes waste, which is then broken down to become enriching soil, to grow food again as well as provide habitat for some of the world's most useful and fascinating creatures. When people tell me they don't believe in magic, I say they aren't looking closely enough. Magic is something you can do, but it is also all around us.

Summertime seems to have come early this year, sneaking in the middle of the rainy May-time and so we already have bees and butterflies lazily pootling around our garden. Boo, my youngest, is completely awe-struck by how a caterpillar becomes a butterfly. He cannot get his head round it and in watching his wonder, I too am captivated by this act of magical alteration.

How does the caterpillar know when it's time, why does this tiny, seemingly inconsequential insect go through one of the animal kingdom's most radical transformations? What purpose does this serve? Why are they so beautiful? It seems to be Mother Earth's way of reminding us that magic is in the very fabric of our world. In Boo's astonishment I can see the wonder of creation and its ongoing achievements. Nature is the mistress of creative enterprise.

When we think about creativity today we often think of those who have more artistry or drama than the rest of us. "Oh, he's such a creative person," we say about someone who has designed his or her home with flair and originality. Somehow the evolution of the term creativity as a quality has led to a very narrow conception. Creativity through the process of education in schools is linked to particular subjects, and only those that are so often eradicated from the over stretched school systems.

Ken Robinson, ambassador of arts education, an activist and commentator has spoken and written extensively about the eradication of creativity from our school system and the worrying trend of ousting creativity from our educational emphasis in favour of test taking and academics. Children, he says, are essentially creative, they are inherently so, and unfortunately we as adults grow *out* of creativity as we become further enculturated. In *Out of Our Minds: Learning to be Creative* Robinson contends that this stems in part from the hierarchy of subjects in the traditional school system. Creativity is ideologically linked to arts subjects like music, drama and art that are increasingly absent from curricula. Today, Robinson argues, our model of education delivery is outmoded and will not prepare our kids for the challenges they will face. What we need instead of a rote, test-based system is an educational model that privileges creativity at the basis of learning, not dependent on the arbitrary nature of school subjects. Creativity requires risk, vision and divergent thinking. To paraphrase his well-known

Ted Talk, "As a human function it [creativity] is essential to our happiness as individuals, but also to our survival as a species."

As Pagans, the creative impulse, the force of inspiration is revered, and named sacred for those of us who are Druids.

The modern Druid symbol of Awen

It is Awen, the fire in the head, the force of poetic inspiration. Similarly, for many Wiccans creativity is the cornerstone of will, capturing and transforming thought into action or manifestation. Some understand creativity as the authentic nature of the divine. The Gods and Goddesses are found in every act of creative expression. This is why ritual is so sacred to Pagans. Through it we come into closer relationship with the spark of the divine within us, the force of creative manifestation. We understand that our creativity is magic, the force of fire at work in the world. It is the spark of an idea turned to action. In magical traditions from all over the world, fire is a ruling element of manifestation. Hence so many ritual transitions are formed around a fire, a flame or smoke. Manifestation is the visible result of magical or spiritual work.

When I first told my kids that I was a witch and that their aunt, their Nona, their great Grandpaw were also witches, diviners and magic makers and that further back in our family we can find a variety of oddball eccentrics, the first thing my eldest son wanted me to do was demonstrate my "witchy-ness", by making something happen. The list of possible demonstrations he offered included making things appear or disappear, making something invisible, or making something move. At such a young age and raised pretty free of commercial culture, their way of understanding this idea of familial magic was to ask what I could *do*, the capacity to create, to manifest is at the heart of our collective consciousness about magic. We can harness this awareness when teaching our kids about the relationship between creativity and magic.

This is like baking bread. Magic is making bread; a loaf of bread is the result of mixing ingredients, the labour of kneading, giving it time to rise, and heat to bake it. Baking bread is making magic because it requires the right conditions, ingredients, formulae, and, importantly, heat to see growth and completion. To stretch this metaphor then, creativity and manifestation (and I use these terms interchangeably, one mundane and the other magical) are fostered by certain conditions. Creativity is shaped by environment – just as fire is shaped by earth, by its fuel, its location and the surrounding elements. It takes knowledge (air) ingredients (earth) a little love (water) and a lot of work and action (fire). And sometimes, if you let yourself be inspired, you could make something both nourishing and beautiful. Creative endeavour is the heart of Pagan practice. Consider how you can bring greater creativity to your family, school and community.

Exercise: Honouring Your Creative Achievements

List your creative achievements. Ensure that you consider the small things as well as the large. This could be making a new recipe, building a fort for your toddler, to designing a website, choreographing a Maypole dance or birthing a child. List every creative act you have done this year and then those major creative achievements that have defined your life. Meditate on those acts of creation and how they have enriched your life and the lives of others. Put this list on your altar with a red or gold candle. Burn the candle for seven nights.

The Power of Play

Creativity is a valuable resource. And its fundamental outlet is play. For many Pagans their journey to a Pagan spirituality was in part motivated by the desire to capture more play in their lives. For some, magical thinking and perhaps ritual and magical action are all a form of play, or maybe we never stopped perceiving the world as a gigantic expression of playtime!

Play is central to our understanding of fire's creative nature. Play is a simple word and one we revere and frequently hear when our kids are under the age of five. Play-based schooling has been a significant part of the preschool agenda since the 1970s when it was recognised that, in environments where kids are encouraged to play, they learn life skills with enjoyment and efficiency. Play-based education, particularly in nursery or preschools, takes play as the learning model. And it works. Through play children learn both social and intellectual skills often simultaneously.

Renowned psychoanalyst and children's doctor Donald Winnicott described play as essential to children's well-being. Play, he said, enables the development of the dream potential, allowing us to express our hopes, wishes, fears and anxieties and allows us to work on our problems hundreds of times without real world consequences. Through play we develop our social and emotional backbone. For children, play develops divergent thinking, whether solitary or collaborative. Seminal professor and play specialist Brian Sutton-Smith has spent his life writing and teaching on the importance of play. Play, he says, is crucial to being human. It is not simply the work of children, we all need it in order to remain optimistic and healthy. He says, "[T]he opposite of play... isn't work. It's depression. To play is to act out and be wilful, as if one is assured of one's prospects." (p.198). If play were a currency then our young would be determining our society's GOP – and at the moment, it would look pretty dire.

Play is like breathing. It comes naturally to us. We are born with an innate knowledge of how to do it and if adults give kids enough room to do it children will play all the time. Play happens within boundaries, often set when children are very small by adults ("you must stay in the garden" or "no we are just getting the blocks out now") or by ability and so much like ritual the rules of play state that in order for play to be deep there must be a safe place for it to happen. If these are in place then open-ended, make-believe fantasy play can be the most powerful educative technique available to us.

Unfortunately our culture has become fixated on the mechanisms of play, most specifically on the commercial opportunities of play. Toys. I know I am guilty of this, that somewhere I struggle with the inner dialogue that says if my kids have more toys, or the right toys they will play "more". When I step back from this voice and look at what my boys and the kids around us are drawn to playing with I realise that their favourite toys are pretty commercial free: balls, sticks, more balls, more sticks... string, shovels, scissors, building blocks (Lego included), themselves and the space they are in. Play is simply better with less – and limited props, limited space, create challenges to be overcome creatively, giving kids opportunities to expand games in previously unseen ways. Play needs limits and it needs form. In these ways it mirrors our rituals.

Yet something seems to happen when kids turn five. Our mainstream education systems no longer invest in play as a form of knowledge sharing and learning. Instead play is the province of unusual, independent schools that follow a specific play-based method; Summerhill in the UK, Sudbury Valley or the Albany Free School in the US, for example.

Suddenly play is eccentric in schools and proper knowledge gaining happens around tables, sat, listening to a teacher and filling out worksheets. Today most of us have to place our kids in a system where their learning is filtered through what Robinson refers to as the "hierarchy of subjects". Important subjects maths, science, technology, English are taught through workbooks. Subjects that could create opportunities for play through their historical relationship to creativity, art, drama, music, dance are considered 'soft' and all too frequently underfunded and under resourced.

Even when they are found in traditional school environments (and I am referring to public rather than private school systems) they are often delivered in formats that don't allow creativity to ripen. For example, in 45-minute classroom blocks where kids are asked to sit still, write, stay indoors, and control their bodies. Do you find it easy to be creative in such limited time? Then as they are perhaps starting to get the creative juices flowing they have to transition to another class, perhaps algebra, perhaps French.

Despite needing boundaries and context, creativity is not a tap to be turned on and off, and such a way of teaching does not allow creativity to flourish. Such an approach teases creativity with the promise of expression only to quell it when it has just begun to flow. Imagine a system of education that is premised on capturing and encouraging this creative impulse. Imagine instead if school were unhampered by the strictures of academic subjects, with unlimited time to see a project through, where every child's unique approach to the project was valid was considered. What would school look like if this were the foundation? What would kids learn?

If Awen, the spark of inspiration, the divine impulse, was the means by which a child's aptitude was 'measured', our children might acquire the skills necessary to solve the problems they will be asked to face. They would be allowed to see the divine in a line of code. Artists, dancers and engineers would work together to find the perfect design for a wind farm. Think of the alliances our kids would make if they were encouraged to explore the intersections of subjects because creativity was the driving force between them? Interdisciplinary work would be the norm, not the exciting exception. Such an educational model may seem pie in the sky, but fundamentally it all starts with play, and play can be encouraged anywhere. Play is crucial to creativity and of course to magic – many people believe that being good at magic is a consequence of play.

Let's encourage kids to play. Get down on the floor and play with Lego, learn card games, let them play in the rain in the garden. Start small – ask your kids' school, or if you are a teacher, ask if you can have a period in a day for kids to free play – or project based play *irrespective of their age*. My best memories of school are the 1 hour 10 minutes outside lunchtime break we had where all manner of complex games were developed, right into our middle school years. We had the time to do it and we used it wisely. Allow experimentation that is open ended, increase break times, and encourage creativity in all subjects – including maths and sciences. At home the best way to encourage creativity is to create a conducive environment. Give your kids lots of time to be active – activity, walking, climbing trees, swinging on swings. Running about may look like the expulsion of youthful vigour to us, but in fact activity is crucial to allow the brain to think creatively.

Richard Louv's books on nature deficit disorder describe the necessary relationship between activity, nature and creativity. This is a sacred triumvirate and one, he reminds us, that has given us some of the most brilliant minds on earth – Einstein, Emerson, Van Gogh, Dante, Da Vinci. When people are allowed to playfully explore, Awen flows.

If imaginative or free form fantasy play is difficult in your household, or you aren't sure where to start then consider playing structured games. Now, my friends will laugh at me for saying this as I am not a board game person. I play backgammon with my husband (because I have been on a winning streak for the past five years) and every other game under duress. I find they release the worst in me, making me competitive and ugly. However, I play cards with Summer and games of Pictionary and charades can reduce me to tears of hysterical laughter.

Strong bonding and moments of ingenuity and independence arise when families play together. They are also excellent spiritual training grounds as they enhance concentration, memory, intuition (which card is she holding? what will his next move be?) and co-operation. Parlour games, as they used to be called, are often games of fancy and good for kids and adults alike. Why did we stop playing games together? Give it a try and I promise that games playing with the kids you know will lead to all kinds of revelations about yourself and the people you love. They need few props, can happen anywhere and can be entirely improvised. For Pagan educators, these games help teach all kinds of control skills – control behaviour, help to control emotions, resist impulses, exert self-control and become self-disciplined. Many would say these are skills necessary to becoming fully formed social subjects. Here are some games that my family love, and that give us family playtime when we need it!

Hide and Seek

Practise your ability to be quiet and be invisible.

One person is the finder and counts to 10/20/100 whilst everyone else goes and hides. Once you have been found you can help the finder as long as you don't have prior knowledge of where everyone else is hiding!

Charades

This can be adapted to all kinds of groups and is super for developing awareness and listening skills with pre-teens.

Divide the players into two teams, although you can play this with just two people. Choose a secret word or phrase – songs, actors, films books etc. Then the person who knows it must act it out without speaking, using only actions. The guessers have a certain amount of time they must be able to guess the phrase in. There are a variety of different rules for Charades and it is worth checking these out further if you aren't sure.

Chinese Whispers
Hilarious, even for groups of adults.

Sit in a circle. One person starts. Choose a word or phrase and whisper it in the next person's ear and they in turn pass on what they heard to the next person. If you are only doing this in a small group allow the whisper to go round several times before you say it aloud. One person starts deciding on a word or phrase and whispers it to the next and so on and so on.

Travellers' Alphabet
Go round the alphabet with each person stating a destination that begins with the next letter in the alphabet. For example; I am going to Algeria, I am going to the Bahamas, I am going to Crete etc. You can play this with towns, cities, countries, or even change it completely and make it not a Travellers Alphabet, but perhaps a Gastro Alphabet, or a Nature Alphabet e.g. I am an Apple Tree, I am a Butterfly, I am a Cougar…

Consequences
Each person takes a turn choosing a word or phrase for one of 11 questions, in this order. You can alter this in many interesting ways, choose animals instead of people, replace what they wore with what they did… the list is endless.

1. Adjective for man/woman
2. Man's/woman's name
3. Adjective for woman/man
4. Woman's/man's name

5. Where they met
6. He wore
7. She wore
8. He said to her
9. She said to him
10. The consequence was... (a description of what happened after)
11. What the world said

Murder in the Dark / Wink Murder/ Lonely Ghost

For slightly older children, this is a fun game despite its macabre name. One person is the 'murderer', often decided by handing out cards and assigning one to the murderer (we used to use the Jack of Hearts), then they wink at all other people in the group. If you are winked at, you must count to five before falling over, as if dead.

This goes on until one person thinks they know who the murderer is and says, "I accuse..." then someone must second them without knowing and both must simultaneously point at who they think is the murderer. If they both point to the person who admits to being the murderer then the game is over, and they are the victor. If they disagree or are incorrect the game continues. Many variants of this game are available.

Blind Man's Buff

Played outside or inside in a spacious setting, this is great fun for getting the 'blind man' to expand their awareness and listening. Make sure this is done somewhere without wires and treacherous low tables, such as a living room, or even better a lawn or garden area. One person is the blindfolded 'blind man' whilst all other players must stay close and attempt to remain out of reach whilst teasing the blind man as to how to get them.

I Packed my Bag...

We play this on car journeys. It's a great memory game and often ends in laughter. It helps to make the time go and can be played with kids as young as five. Taking turns, each player describes something they are going to take on a journey, but must remember everything that the previous players have placed in their bag. As the list gets longer it gets harder to remember every person's items and they can become more outlandish!

Lastly, we must consider the importance of rough and tumble. Most kids enjoy vigorous play but rough and tumble play – wrestling, fighting or rolling around with little purpose other than to annoy someone (usually an adult) – is truly crucial for today's kids. There is now a body of research that shows that this activity correlates to maturity in the frontal lobes of the brain. However, in a society where vigorous activity is the prime province of competitive sport, this form of unauthorised play has been shunned. Some researchers have made some interesting connections between the growing intolerance of roughhousing with the increased number of kids diagnosed with ADD and ADHD (see Panksepp 1999, Fergus P. Hughes 2009 and the seminal work of Brian Sutton-Smith).

Roughhousing, for both boys and girls, should be on the national curriculum. It puts kids in their bodies in a way that teaches them body awareness, compassion and self-regulation. If you are not a natural roughhouser, start with tickle fights or pillow fights. Rough and tumble is exciting because it tests our limits, and it allows us to be fierce in a safe way with people who love us.

For girls this kind of play is so valuable as it can show them how to be fierce within their bodies. For boys, particularly at points of testosterone surging, it can be a safe way to find their new limits and channel their urge to hit things! If you need more persuasion on the importance of rough and tumble look at Pam

Jarvis's article "Rough and Tumble" play: Lessons in life, *Evolutional Psychology*, 4, 330-346, and Steve Biddulph's great book *Raising Boys: Why Boys are Different and How to Help Them.*

It is much harder to encourage play in older kids or young adults; when you think about kids running around, playing airplane, or dressing up as a pirate, you probably imagine a kid under the age of seven. How can we continue to foster such play in older kids, especially in the face of the commercial markets that aggressively interpolate them? Organisations like Children of the Earth (USA) and the Scouts/Guides and Woodcraft Folk (UK) have adapted to the current needs of our older kids, and in part respond to the growing movement of educationalists who recognise the relationship between creative play, nature, and kids' mental and physical health. Kids, older kids especially, equally need to have creative time in nature to play, skill share, and learn about natural survivalism. Wilderness exploration, camping, and nature retreats for urban dwellers are obvious ways we can encourage this in our kids.

Enabling our kids to see the strength in creativity opens ways you can foster creative activity to fit their nature. It could be you have a very water child, who will need to do a lot of drama as her form of play, and fashion design, and may want to spend an awful lot of time in front of the mirror putting on make-up. For a water/fire kid, design and theatre, the more adult edge of make-believe will be important. Let them design rituals, make complex and beautiful altars or make their own runes. For an air/fire kid, see if jewellery making or chemistry is of interest. Encourage them to rollerblade or skateboard, reclaiming the streets!

If you know real earth kids, set them a problem – they love tackling problems. Give them a car that doesn't work and watch them fix it, dig a garden, set them survival challenges in wild spaces. If they have the right amount of fire in the mix, they could become a fantastic wilderness activity leader.

For older kids, creativity often flourishes when it responds to need, and when kids feel that their play (or work) is valued and serving a purpose. By offering and encouraging real skills that enhance their creative impulse and allow them to connect with others in a creative relational way we can demonstrate how play is essential to life. If you want a justification for continued active play in our kids' lives, remember the attributes it enhances:

- Original and divergent thinking
- Problem solving capacities
- Compassionate, empathetic learning
- Environmental awareness

Often inspiration and creativity spring forth through an imbalance that needs to be rectified. Poverty can often breed acts of creativity that defy their harsh surroundings. And it appears that our kids may have to face a lack of natural resources that we in our lifetimes will not – issues over water, power sources, air purity are real issues that our kids and our grandkids will have to tackle, and we need to encourage the necessary skills to solve these Herculean problems.

We know that the solutions to these issues will have to come from creative and innovative sources; the devising of new technologies, the redefining of existing resources, the replacement of certain cultural values. Pagan youth can be at the forefront of these decisions, offering unique perspectives and skills if we extend a spiritual pedagogy into their everyday lives. If our values as parents, caregivers and educators speak to our reverence for the elements, and the divine nature of manifestation and creativity we can truly empower them to be shapers of the world's future.

To recap then, we can aid creativity by encouraging fire traits. Here is a list of some of those traits we can encourage kids to follow:

- RISK TAKING: Let them stretch their capability. Let them

try to do more than you think them capable of. Let them experience trial and failure, and help them to get up and try again. Experimentation. I am not advocating you tell your 15-year-old to try drugs and see if they can drive whilst under the influence. Reckless behaviour is not risk taking. Risk taking requires calculation; it takes knowledge, and courage. It is the visionquest, and it means that there are times when you defy the odds. Let your five-year-old walk down the road and back by themselves, to listen to the birds. Let your nine-year-old ride their bike to school with friends. Set parameters, but allow them to push themselves.

- FOSTERING PASSIONS: Often kids' passions seem meaningless or odd to us. My eldest went through a phase of collecting odd bits of found metal. It drove me crazy – his room was covered in seemingly treacherous bits of rusting metal, and yet, he was crazy about it, and it allowed him to imagine all sorts of machines he might make. Let kids see your passions, let them see what gets you excited and what you are passionate about, whether it's gardening, numbers or yard sales!

- DREAMING: No innovation and no creative expression can grow without dreamtime. Kids need time to think and dream within. They also need sleep to let their ideas and dream percolate. Remove the TV from their bedroom; maintain a quiet time as part of your daily or weekend rhythm. Structure less and dream more. Ask your older kids to keep a dream record or diary, whether written or drawn or recorded. Encourage them to view their reveries and dreams seriously.

- ACTIVITY: Daily time outside and ideally in nature: cycling to school, feeding the chickens, weeding the garden, playing at the park after dark or cross country running. Physical activity outside will help develop their sensual awareness and physical health and give them time to stimulate their creative juices.

- REBELLION: Allow your kids to feel good about being different and doing different things. Give them strong models of people who stuck to their own way of doing things. Let them see your rebellious side. Let loose (even if it embarrasses them a little!) We could call this "self-expression". Encourage all activities that give your kids self-expression, the form doesn't matter – algebra or ballet, gardening or singing. Reflect back to your kids what you see as their expressive strengths.

Lighting candles, sitting by a fire and honouring the sun are simple intrinsic ways in which we right the balance between our lives and the power of fire. May our children find this balance already within their blood and breath, so it comes as second nature to know the true meaning of passion, success and love in fire's warm embrace.

Fire Activities

Build a bonfire	Make a solar wheel
Run a race	Go on a date
Protest something you feel passionate about	Conduct a science experiment
Create a birthday ritual	Play!
Dress a candle	Design and knit booties for a new baby
Hug someone in need	Settle an argument
Play rough and tumble	Have a party

Chapter Four

Water

Keywords: *Life, Grace, Beauty, Love, Compassion, Help, Rain, Fog, Mist, Precipitation, Drop, Flow, Stream, Ocean, River, Tributary, Honour, Sacrifice, Giving, Generosity, Open, Releasing, Fluid...*

West is Water, the Tide Begun...

Water is the origin of all life. We all begin in the dark waters of the womb, just as all earthly life began in the primordial waters of the world. Water is sacred, it is finite and without it life cannot flourish. If you want to amaze a kid, give them a glass of water and remind them that it's the same water that the dinosaurs drank. Within Pagan traditions, water is the element associated with cleansing, healing and blessings. Water connects us to the moon and the oceans; it holds our memories and as such marks the passage of time with every moon and every tide.

One of the most important elements of water's teaching is its ability to connect us to each other. It circulates around Mother Earth with a grace and beauty that we can aspire to. It fluidly connects across time and place, as we might seek to live in harmonious relationships with all our global relations.

I am standing in a hall with over 100 young people, aged between eight and 16 years old. It is close to Samhain, and as it's 11am there is a dim and misty light from the windows that line the hall. I have been invited to a Unitarian Universalist church to lead a Samhain ritual for the youth group, and the excitement and anticipation is palpable. Some of them are looking at me in wonder, some with a little apprehension. Maybe I am the first witch they have seen. Maybe the idea of a Hallowe'en 'ritual' makes them nervous. A couple of times the little ones come up and ask if I am a 'real' witch and when I bend down to smile at them they giggle and clutch at each other.

"We are going to celebrate the coming of winter," I say, "are you ready for it?"

We have designed the ritual simply and we shake out before we start to get rid of some of the nerves and the buzz that seems to be in the air. Then we take hands. Almost immediately the circle energy is phenomenal – so much presence just fizzing around. It crosses my mind that this number of uninitiated untrained adults would never have this kind of energy. We start a hum that quickly turns to a chant calling the elements, then the divine source. These are UU kids, so they call out all the names of Gods and Goddesses and spirits and angels they know. Their voices rise slowly and by some unseen cue they begin to step forward.

Each of us holds a leaf, fallen from the beautiful old maples outside. These are the remains of the old year, of the summer gone, in their yellow, red and orange glory. They say their own words quietly as they place this leaf in a pile by the archway – some crumble theirs to dust happy to see the year gone, some gently and lovingly placing it into the basket.

A chant continues, "It's the blood of the ancients that flows through our veins, and the forms pass, but the circle of life remains."

They step through the archway to be blessed with water and incense before circling into the winter and the new year. And we remember. When all have passed through, we tell the spirits of our dead who stand at the threshold that they are not forgotten, that we carry them in our hearts and our blessings. We speak their names aloud. Some of the children softly cry, remembering pets that have passed or loved ones gone. They acknowledge their ancestors. Then we spiral together into the new year, and shout out all the qualities we want to grow in this darkness, where the year will germinate, the darkness that holds all possibilities for new life. We hold hands and in a snaking undulating line we look each other in the eyes as we call out: "Hope! Friends! Finishing projects!" In the spiral we see that everything we do comes back to us, that in moving forward we take the past with us. We move in cycles. We see our friends, then they are gone, then we see them again. The spiral reminds us of how life works, ebbing and flowing. The energy peaks and troughs, another chant begins as the spiral unwinds. *"The dawning of a new day is coming; golden light is flowing all over the earth..."*

Afterwards, as I am taking the basket of leaves outside to the wind, a little girl comes up and quietly says how she hopes she can be a witch when she is grown up and teach people to sing songs and do dances. My work is done.

Water teaches us to move with the flow – it teaches us how to adapt, how to release and how to change. Like the ritual I describe above, which is nothing like the high ritual form I was taught as a Wiccan or a priestess within the Fellowship of Isis, for these wonderful young folk it worked. It had the authenticity we aim for, the energy we can only hope for and it tapped the needs of those present. Water teaches us how to respond to need like no other element can. It calls us to be sensitive to others and to recognise how we are all in relationship with each other. Water shows us how every being is connected through seen and unseen ways.

For many Pagans today the element of water is a nexus point for concern and care. Ruled by the moon, water is intricately tied to our striving for greater sensitivity, compassion and healing. It rules over our intuition, the sixth sense that can help us live in greater awareness of those around us. It guides our compassion so that once we are aware of what is going on around us we can look beyond the self to the greater patterns at work. At its best, being in touch with the esoteric qualities of water can enable us to more deeply understand and care for those in need. And by being in touch with water at both an elemental and a metaphorical level fosters healing which can transform that deep knowledge into action.

Water Children

Children who are ruled by water are our dreamers. They are often naturally sensitive to the moods of people and places. Perhaps at times oblique, water children can seem remote, distant, and somehow less tangibly of this world than other children. They may seem to be ever on the boundaries of the fairy kingdom. Being a water child in today's society is hard. There is little credence given to their unique perspective. It would benefit us all to learn from these children. They are the clingy children, the one who is still tantrumming when all the other children have settled. They are literally soft too, often fair featured and their skin may feel cool and soft to touch.

As babies they are their best, able to stay in the warm embrace of parent, falling asleep easily, moving and changing as their needs are met. But as young children they will seem to cry a lot, and they can find the rhythms and needs of their body hard to remember. Instead of embracing this, as these kids get older we often label them as difficult, dreamers, lazy, moody and manipulative. They can find school a real challenge, when the social talents they have to connect people to each other can make them targets for bullies or malicious gossip. They are highly distractible and often infuriatingly vague about what they have done today or what they should be doing. However, they can tell you in detail about who said what to whom and who hurt whose feelings and what they were thinking about having for dinner.

For water children information is a flow, and they find it hard to learn in the prescribed and linear fashion we have developed in mainstream education. They are perfect candidates for Steiner education or homeschooling, which may temperamentally suit them much better as long as their social needs are met. In other cultures water children would have the opportunity to develop their talents in devotional, healing or social roles. In our competitive fire-dominated culture, water children have to either sink or swim. On the challenging side, when their energetic flow gets stuck or in some way muddied, water children may become highly deceitful and manipulative. They are masters of emotional terrain.

If their water energy is not channelled as teenagers (especially girls), water kids often 'drop out'. Water, when it is out of balance, can also lead kids into addiction and self-loathing tendencies that go beyond those usual in the difficult teen years. To try to support them we need to help them build a clan – they need their people like no others. They may be the odd Emo kids, or the thespians. Whatever their alternative choice is (and it is likely to be an alternative group they choose), water children and young adults need to find their 'spark' and have that recognised by the group in order to stay healthy and connected.

If you have a water kid, or your child is going through a surge of water energy, you can help. Firstly, let them sleep. A lot. And encourage them to drink a lot of water to help them ground. Encouraging hydration, rest and affection are almost the perfect cure alls. Secondly, they need beauty like no other. The arts and music are medicine to them – watch what happens when you play them Mozart, or Beethoven, or Mike Oldfield. Like you did, every teenager goes through the phase of listening to songs of misery and fear, heartbreak and fate – I found Joni Mitchel, Jon Martyn and British folk music.

At this age, all our young folks are connecting to the surge of water in their psychic selves. Let them release it. Requiems are often a favourite I have found. Use Bach flower remedies if you can. These are amazingly effective – and Judy Howard's book *Growing up with Bach Flower Remedies* should be a must on every adult's bookshelf if you are working with or raising kids.

All children are drawn to water, and whether we have a child who is energetically akin to water or not, all of our children would benefit from being in better relationship with this element. Watching a baby in the bath or a toddler in a sprinkler, or, as I did yesterday, watch two nine-year-old boys scooter in the rain for the joy of it, water soothes and invigorates the body and the mind. Its capacity to calm us comes from our earliest experience within the mother's body, held in the warm darkness of water, where we breathed water rather than air.

Our Bodies and Water

Our bodies are made up of water. A newborn baby is 75 per cent water and our water content decreases as we grow. However, even as adults, about 60 per cent of our body is water and 70 per cent of our brain is water. To stay healthy in mind and body and spirit, water is crucial. Then consider that about 70 per cent of the planet is covered in ocean, which in turn contains 98 per cent of the world's water and we see how water is in constant relationship with us. The cycle of water, the flow of water within us and around us is one of nature's most magical models of global transformation.

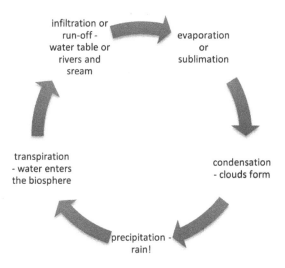

This extraordinary cycle, where matter is transformed into

vapour, where liquid becomes gas and ice feeds plants, is one of Mother Nature's greatest alchemical magics. It teaches us a great lesson in the earth's ability to conserve energy and create a self-sustaining system of health. To understand this beyond the head though we have to be out in it!

Don't let the rain stop you walking, don't let it ruin plans. Instead adapt them to include revelling in the wonders of this process and use the rain to teach us about being adaptable. Bless the water you drink, recognise that every mouthful is a precious resource that has come to you through multiple processes both natural and manmade. Once we see the water as precious we are less likely to leave the tap running or leave endless sprinklers on in our gardens during the summer. At a time such as this where drought plagues so much of Britain, and where water rates are high and our waterways are suffering from pollution and overwork, let's bring our attention to the ways in which we are reliant upon this most basic of human needs.

10 Lessons in Water

1. Stand in the mist
2. Jump in puddles
3. Measure rain fall in a measuring jug
4. Create a grey water system in your home
5. Practise cloud busting (see below)
6. Learn to swim
7. Watch raindrops on a window pain
8. Cry when you need to and let your kids see you
9. Catch snowflakes
10. Go to the ocean whenever you can

Exercise: Cloud Busting for all ages

Lie on your back on a cloudy day, full of billowy cumulous clouds. Choose one and stare at it, imagining it dispersing into fine vapour. Maintain your attention, perhaps incanting inward, and slowly you will see it begin to dissolve.

Pregnancy and Birth – Becoming the Ocean

In some tribal cultures, the full moon is called the pregnant moon, as her ever-changing face is round and full, like the belly of a woman carrying a child. From ancient times, the relationship between a woman's pregnant body, the moon and the ocean has been recognised and honoured.

When a woman is pregnant, she in some ways returns to a being of water. Like our primordial ancestors, we share both energetically and physically a relationship with the birth of the world – the amoeba that first crawled on land came from water and the child that grows in a woman is literally cradled in water.

Today it can be hard to hold onto the sacred nature of pregnancy. When women's bodies are the territory for political and religious rhetoric that suggests the mother is a vessel ruled by the state or by God, we have to work hard to go deeper in our understanding of this blessed time. Further, when pregnancy is defined by consumption and lifestyle choices, it seems less sacred, and more a full-time job! Some of us may also face this time with deeper trepidation as we make choices regarding whether a pregnancy and motherhood is viable. Without judgment, water helps us to both accept and release our old selves and look forward to our evolving new selves.

First Three Moons (First Trimester 0-14 Weeks)

Sickness, nausea and tiredness plague this first flush of pregnancy. The first pulse of water makes us queasy. We have to find our new pregnancy legs! This is the time to sink into the awareness of your changed self. Overjoyed or anxious, this can be a time of intense nervousness surrounding pregnancy. This is the time of choices, and the time when miscarriages and abortions most commonly occur. Give way to the flow of emotion at this time. This first phase is understood as a period of releasing and dreaming your new self. Stay well hydrated and meditate on the waxing moon during this phase. Get fit, gently exercise and drink peppermint tea, take your folic acid and multi vitamins. If you are a vegan/vegetarian get your iron intake up – lots of leafy greens, legumes and beans. Turn inwards a little, pay attention to your body changing and most of all, relax!

Middle Three Moons (Second Trimester 15-29 Weeks)

Your body is visibly changing and your clothes won't fit, and you may start to feel heavy. The baby within will start to move, and the abstract idea of pregnancy in the first phase becomes a reality as those little flutters and later kicks make you aware of who you carry within you. This is often called the blossoming time, when your sensuality is right on the surface of your skin. Now you may have told everyone, and you may find yourself inundated with questions and opinions – what kind of birth are you having? When are you going to take maternity? How long for? Do you want a boy or a girl? Where will you have your baby? Don't let the questions bamboozle you. You have time to work this all out. If you don't like being the centre of attention ensure you have enough alone time or time with a partner or friend to process these questions.

Your sex drive may go through the roof and despite your changing swollen self, you may feel full of energy and a lust for life. Now is time to dowse or divine for the sex of the child, an ancient way of finding out the gender. Use a pendulum over your belly and see which way the crystal swings. Circles for a girl, back and forth for a boy. You will start to slow down now, and may receive some vivid and telling dreams. Keep a dream journal, but importantly, whatever the weather get outside, be in nature. Swim and walk, do things that make you feel joyous and connect to your body through rhythm. You may find that if you drum into trance that your baby moves with you. Revel in this last phase when the new water within you is in balance with your old self. You are in harmony, you and the child within in blessed symbiosis.

Final Three Moons (Third Trimester 30-42+ Weeks)

Now is the time when you feel the waters rise within you. You may be very emotional; tears and laughter are intermingled and sometimes simultaneous. Let this be, see it and release it. This is you becoming anew. Meditate now on the true heart of love – this is one of the deepest teachings of water – how to love without knowledge or condition.

Your relationship with the child within will hopefully now be defined – you will have a sense of who this person is, what their rhythms are. Create a ritual for welcoming the new phase of motherhood, allow your belly to be tattooed with henna and have a party to celebrate this most profound physical and spiritual transformation.

Dream and visualise a birth free from complication and anxiety. If you have difficulties in your pregnancy now is the time to look deeply at these and see what they can teach you about the nature of parenthood and the spirit of this child. For example, with my eldest son I had a placenta previa. Luckily, it resolved by the time I went into labour, but the process taught me a lot about releasing expectations and that my son would have his own, sometimes rather last-minute, way of doing things.

The Baby Moon (Birth and the First Three Moons Postpartum)

Whilst I advocate for the most natural birth possible, as it is ideal for both mum and baby, we are incredibly lucky to live in a time when we have the ability to call upon medical intervention should it be necessary. Many wonderful women and children I know would not be here today if it weren't for the presence of emergency midwifery and obstetric care. But birth is neither an emergency nor an illness, it is a natural and normal process and if we are prepared and healthy the odds are we can have a perfectly natural birth.

In the process of bringing forth life, we become like the great mother of us all –it can be a most profound experience, unparalleled in our lifetime. For many women the insights and wonders of birth stay with them throughout their lives. In approaching your birthing, knowledge is power, so research the process of birth, what happens in a woman's body. But a wise woman would do well to balance book knowledge with women's stories. Ask your close friends about their experiences. You may quickly find that your body and this new life are not under the command of your mind's desires. Birth is wondrous but not always predictable. Sometimes things happen, and you cannot blame yourself if you don't have the birth of your dreams.

Birth is sacred work and water can be your friend. Whether you choose to use a bath or a birthing pool, or you shower or have your brow mopped and are fed ice cubes, when we are birthing we are made aware of the healing and soothing power of water. We also need to take in water – stay hydrated and let yourself be like water, unfettered, free, following only the pulse or tidal rhythm of your body. Water is a birthing woman's ally. Across the world water deities, Goddesses a plenty are called and prayed to, to assist the birthing woman: Yemaya, Isis, Hathor, Oshun, Hera, Brigid. Before you give birth, research those Goddesses that inspire you. Then when you come to being in labour, chanting the name and qualities of your guardian mother can be incredibly helpful to allow you to move with the flow of your body as it pulses to release the child within.

Incantation for a Birthing Woman

The moon she dances,
Like the waves, like the waves on the shore

Making circles, making circles, like the waves, like the waves on the shore...
(By Prana Chants)

New techniques for birthing, such as hypno-birthing (which I used for the birth of my youngest boy) use deep relaxation to help us birth without fear and pain. For those amongst us carrying the scars of sexual abuse, body dysmorphia or fear around childbirth, I would strongly recommend this approach. It is Pagan friendly and very healing.

In labour, we touch on our true nature and this can be incredibly insightful. In a way we hand ourselves over to the higher force of nature. For many of us this is more of a challenge than we might expect! We write birth plans, we know what we want, we may even hope for certain 'outcomes'. We can learn from the element of water here. If you listen to other women's birthing stories you will hear that there is a guiding principle between their varying accounts. Whether we are able to let ourselves trust to the power of our body and give ourselves to nature's great pulse is a deep teaching of birth. This is true for the birthing woman but also those who surround and support her. It takes strength, quiet, a relinquishing of ego and the ability to meaningfully listen to the needs of another beyond words. This is a moment of initiation for all concerned, and if we are lucky we can come through it transformed.

Whatever your birth experience is, whether you use pain relief, or end up having an emergency caesarean section, you will be transfigured – the maiden becomes a mother, the midwife/doula/birth helper becomes the healer, the man becomes a father. Much like the other magical initiations or social rituals we may undertake, bringing a child into the world is a commitment to life and to the future of our planet.

This change in identity and cultural status can be most welcomed but the post partum period can be unsettling. It is easy to forget the importance of rest and recuperation in those moons directly following the birth. You may not have time to meditate, you may not be inclined to ritual or relaxation, you may only want sleep and to 'get back to normal'. I would urge you, and those around a new mother, to stress the importance of taking time, of moving with the flow of the 'baby moon' and not rushing.

Conduct a baby welcoming ritual (see the one given in Chapter One). This will help with your milk flow – too many women get home from hospital and start cleaning and cooking, up and about and then are surprised when their baby finds breastfeeding challenging. Stop, relax, take the time to just be. During this phase, you are moving from the water element to being back in earth – like many phases of elemental transition, what is needed is deep rest from the world's pressures.

Recently I had the fortune to be in France with a friend's family. A new mum was there, with her two-month-old. This beautiful and relaxed young French woman looked like the model of maternal ease and when I asked her how her transition had been she said that in the week after the birth of her daughter, she just slept. She didn't get out of bed, she didn't do chores or housework, she didn't change a diaper. Her mother and her boyfriend did all the work. She slept and held her baby. She said, "I wanted to be really rested so that when I did get up I wasn't angry with the baby for making me tired." This clear logic made so much sense I applauded her ability to assess her limits, her needs and then parent in a way that set them off to a good start as a family.

If you can, go outside every day, just sit outside if the weather is good or if it's bad, bundle up and get a breath of air. Resist the urge to enter the world quickly but don't coop yourself up– like the old 'lie in' period where a new mother was cared for, fed, and ensured that her and the baby were safe and thriving. Although this may sound excessive today, I have seen women in supermarkets shopping three days after their baby was born. I took my eldest son out when he was only ten days old (I was hosting a conference at Harvard at the time) and my husband and I got home and cried with the strain it had taken on us.

Early parenthood is not a macho endeavour, it is not a competition of who can get their body back the fastest, who can get their life back and start work the soonest. This may be what the mainstream wants to sell us, but let's try and resist. Let's encourage mothers to stay home, to rest; let's applaud those that do whether it's their first baby or fifth. They are blessed in their changed status. They are deeply connected to the pulse of life in its raw wilderness, and as such they hold a hallowed place within our community.

If there is a family in your community that is welcoming a new child, rally round; organise a meal rota so they don't have to cook those first weeks home. This is a huge gift, and one that we as Pagans know the value of!

I remember when a friend brought me a meal after my second son was born. A large lasagne dish arrived on my doorstep and never had a meal tasted so good. Iron rich, hearty and grounding, a lasagne can use left-over veggies, or you can pack it with foods specific to the needs of the new mum/family: spinach or kidney beans for an iron rich vegetarian option, or of course some lovely organic beef for a meat option. See Peg's Green Salad below as a great side idea.

If a mum has baby blues give her a fish-based side, or a lovely cabbage and caraway warm salad, or a walnut and goat cheese salad. For desert take something with chocolate. Dark chocolate, especially where the cocoa solids are 70 per cent or more, can help improve mood by increasing the serotonin levels in the brain. So a little chocolate is a good thing!

Chicken soup is delicious and a cure all especially with a nice loaf of crusty bread. Make the stock by boiling a litre of water with the cooked chicken carcass, and after it has simmered for an hour add in an onion, two carrots, three sticks of celery, a pipkin of salt and some fresh basil. Bring to the boil gently, then leave to simmer. Remove any surface fat and serve. There are more rejuvenating recipes by Peg Aloi below.

If cooking isn't your thing, find other ways to help – babysit the older children perhaps, or offer to clean their kitchen or weed their allotment. These are much better gifts than another packet of babygros, and they support the resting period of the mother and the new grown family. In this way we allow mum/s/dad/s to fully focus on their new arrival.

Simple New Mum Meals – Recipes by Peg Aloi

Peg's Hearty Soup

A filling, delicious soup packed with vitamins and thrifty too, made from just four basic ingredients! And it can be frozen, and it's terrific warmed up.

You need:
Onions, chopped
Potatoes, cubed
Bacon, cut into chunks
Carrots, sliced
Salt and pepper to taste

Sauté the bacon until mostly crisp. Leave some of the fat in the pot, as this is where you will sauté the vegetables. Add the onions, sauté until translucent, then the potatoes and carrots. Stir to coat the vegetables. Add enough water to accommodate your soup needs, and cook on low heat until the carrots and potatoes are soft. Before serving, use a whisk or potato masher to gently smash the vegetables and thicken the soup. Salt and pepper to taste. You may also make this soup without bacon; use oil or butter to sauté the vegetables.

Easy Cheesy Vegetable Pie (or Quiche)

This is very easy for brunch, lunch, dinner or supper. Milk for a nursing mother is nourishing, and you can add spinach for an iron rich option. May be eaten cold, at room temperature or heated.

You need:
1 frozen piecrust (the more wholesome the better)
Cheese of your choice (Cheddar, Swiss, Red Leicester)
4-5 eggs
1 cup milk
Greek yogurt (optional)
Pinch of nutmeg
Sautéed vegetables (onion is traditional; combine with baby spinach,greens, broccoli, cauliflower, mushrooms, chopped tomatoes, and fresh herbs); season to taste.

Grate the cheese and cover the bottom of the pie shell. Layer the sautéed vegetables or spinach over it. Make a custard from the eggs and milk; this can be thickened with a bit of Greek yogurt if desired. Pour over the top. Sprinkle nutmeg or white pepper over the top. Bake at 375 Fahrenheit/180 Celsius for 35 minutes or until set in the middle. Let it sit for at least 20 minutes before cutting.

Fresh Garden Greens Salad

Your kids will love helping make this salad by picking the greens you've grown in pots or your garden. It's easy to make variations, and if you add more protein it's hearty enough for lunch. This is a very healthy salad with healthy fats from avocado, and liver-boosting lemon juice.

You need:
Greens and lettuces, washed and dried gently

Additional vegetables if available: cherry tomatoes, sliced cucumbers, red onion, peppers, and green beans
Cubed cheese (I like a soft cheese, goat's cheese or mozzarella)
(For meat option you can add cubed ham, cold chicken, salami or turkey)
1 sliced avocado
Dressing: fresh lemon juice, olive oil, seasoning (fresh garlic, salt and pepper is nice, add a touch of maple syrup or use orange juice if the dressing is too tart.)

Combine the vegetables and toss lightly with half the dressing. Add the cheese and/or meat, and dress and toss lightly again. Then add the avocado slices on top to serve.

If it's a hot summer why not make fresh lemonade? Combine an equal volume of fresh lemons, water and a little less sugar and add some fresh mint to taste. Scones are incredibly grounding and comforting I find, whatever the season. For colder days, ginger cookies can be excellent option for new mums. Ginger helps aid circulation and lessens any post partum nausea. Flapjack made from whole oats helps fight off depression, soothe digestion and is an all-round super food.

For some new mums, the period after birth can be especially difficult and they don't bounce back. When baby blues becomes something more profound then it is crucial that someone advocates for the mother suffering. Post-natal depression or PPD is a hormonal and emotional disruption that needs understanding and support. It is very isolating and without treatment can lead to years of family disruption. It interferes with the bonding process between mum and baby.

If you feel that you may be suffering, if you have dark thoughts towards yourself or your baby, reach out to someone and go to see a doctor immediately. Help is available and you will be surprised when you begin to open up how many other women have suffered. If you are in the UK and you want to find resources and support go to, www.pni.org.uk and if you are in the US look at www.postpartumprogress.com. It is also worth remembering that a new baby doesn't only disrupt the well-being of mum, but also all the surrounding family. Everyone needs a little extra love and care, and that's where a loving and understanding community becomes essential.

Post Partum Checklist

If you have the following symptoms persistently for more than two weeks after birth, talk to someone and get some help:

- Depressed mood – sadness, tearfulness, hopelessness, anxiety.
- Loss of pleasure in most of your daily activities.
- Appetite and weight change.
- Problems sleeping even when your baby is sleeping.
- Noticeable change in how you walk and talk.
- Extreme tiredness and loss of energy.
- Feelings of worthlessness or guilt with no reasonable cause.
- Difficulty concentrating and making decisions.
- Thoughts about death or suicide. Some women with have fleeting, frightening thoughts of harming their babies. These tend to be fearful thoughts, rather than urges to harm.

All being well, at about 12 weeks, the new family will begin to feel more solid. You may feel as if you have landed and if baby is thriving you can start to take up some old and perhaps new activities. Some women go back to work at this point, and those mums really need all the support a community can offer them as they make this transition. If work is not on the horizon yet, then you can take some time building rhythm with baby if you haven't already started this.

One of the things you can do, irrespective of whether you are going back to work or staying home, is build a household shrine to bring your focus to embracing your new family. Build it with representatives of water and earth as you move into this new phase, perhaps with figures of mother Goddesses and candles and pictures of the extended family. This can be a place you can visit at stressful times, or to acknowledge those precious benchmark moments, first smile, first roll, first tummy push up.

The Moon

Esbat festivals are the Pagan rituals most associated with witch-craft traditions past and present. Within almost all contemporary witchcraft traditions, the full moon celebrations (known as esbats) are the time when a coven or solitary practitioner honours the moon, the feminine divine or Goddess and performs acts of divination and magic.

As the beautiful sacred poem by seminal Witch, author and poet Doreen Valiente states… "Once in the month and better it be when the moon is full, there you shall assemble, you who are fain to learn all sorcery yet have not won its deepest secrets…." This *Charge of the Goddess* calls in the Goddess energy, it is an invitation to move into deep empathy with the sacred power of the moon. Whilst I do not advocate children's active participation in Wiccan/witchcraft ritual (it is after all a mystery religion), there are elements that we can share with our kids, irrespective of their age. Attuning our kids to the energy of the full moon or any moon phase can start at any age. When my kids were babes in arms I would take them outside on full moon nights and chant to then under the light. *"Mother moon shine down on me, I am you and you are me, and we are part of everything, we are part of everything."* As they got older we would make wishes to the moon, and now we write her poems and light a special candle to honour her beautiful glow.

As they grow, children's relationship with the moon phases can become more complex. Teach children the name of each full moon, drawn from whichever tradition you feel a kinship with. And teach them the names of the different moon phases, and then you can slowly introduce little pieces of folk magic and magical thinking concepts that go with each. The moon is gibbous – what are you growing? What do you need help with to finish a project? The moon is just new, a tiny crescent waxing – new ideas, turn over a penny in your pocket for bringing wealth. Waning moon – think about how you can solve that problem with a friend, what do you need to forget and let go of, what can you change in your behaviour? Once begun, this kind of thinking is incredibly valuable and seamlessly attunes our kids' thinking to the moon's phases. If you are a teacher, put up a moon phase chart in the class room, and every day ask someone to move the pointer along to where the moon is now.

When kids move into the pre-pubescent years, they can begin to use full moon nights to explore magical skills. Why not start a young adult moon meditation group? It is a wonderful way of quietly attending to the moon's changes and the body's changes. By conducting a simple moon meditation, such as the one included later in this chapter, you can begin to explore the relationship between the moon's changing nature and our own. Dowsing, water blessings, and dream journals are also ways of inspiring older kids and teens to connect to the water element and the moon's influence upon our psychic selves in a magical way.

Blessing Water for Consecration
(This is based on the salt water consecration in Wiccan ritual)

Place your index and middle finger into the water receptacle.

Say: *"Blessed is this water, without impurity, May all it touches be blessed in the name of the Old Ones."*

Teach this to our young folk and they can use the sacred water to bless objects, people and spaces. It is excellent if you are blessing a home, or a first pack of tarot cards or a dream journal.

Full Moon Meditation

By introducing a moon meditation, we lay the foundations for Drawing Down the Moon skills if your kids should choose to take a more active ritual role in witchcraft traditions or Paganism in their teens or adulthood. Here we connect them to the moon's light, energy and power, and build connection between their body and the celestial bodies. I have used language that would make this applicable to primary school kids.

Please adapt this as you see fit. If you are working with older kids or young adults, you can add deeper symbolism and an encounter with a priestess of the moon, a moon animal (hare, wolf, cat, owl) or perhaps the Moon Goddess herself. For more adept children, leave longer spaces (indicated by ...) in order to give them time to build the imaginary and psychic frameworks more complexly. Read the following slowly and calmly in a warm and quiet environment.

Close your eyes, allow your breathing to settle. In and out... Now feel your whole body relax, sink into the chair/ground beneath you. It's as if your body is turning to butter, spreading and melting slowly. First your feet, then your legs, your torso, down your arms and your chest, your hands, and each finger, now up through your neck and into your face and your head, a warm soft feeling.

Now you are relaxed, imagine you are standing at the edge of the sea/ocean... It is dusk, when the sun is setting, and the sand is warm from the day and pretty much everyone else has gone home. You are there with people you love, and you are looking up as the sun is settling spreading beautiful warm colours across the sky. You can breathe in the warmth of the day, down into your belly...

Now you look up into the sky above where the sun is going down, you turn and see high in the sky the moon – she is out and she is already

BIG, *a big beautiful round moon. This is the full moon, and she seems to be catching the last glimpses of the sun as he sets. And as it gets darker and darker the light changes around you… and the moon's light shines across the sand. How is the moon's light different to the sun's?*

You are still lovely and warm and relaxed on the beach. You decide to moon-bathe, so you lie down on the warm sand and face the moon, letting her light pour all over you. And as you do this, something wonderful starts to happen… It's like the moon has a special moonbeam just for you. You begin to tingle, and feel as if you were floating up, up on a moonbeam… The moon's face is shining down on you, making you feel loved and special in her light. All your worries disappear, all your aches and pains go. You are floating in the light of a moonbeam. At last, as she climbs higher the feeling leaves you, as her beam of light moves on to another person. But for that moment you were in the light of the full moon, she gave you her blessing…

Back on the sand, you know it's time to come back now. Bring your attention back to your breathing, and allow the beach to fade from your mind… Wiggle your toes, stretch your arms and legs… Come back to this room, and when you are ready open your eyes and join us again.

Hazel Twig Dowsing

On a day close to a full moon around Beltane or Midsummer as you can, find a hazel tree, who has its root in water (or if you live in the fens, then pretty much anywhere!) Find a branch shaped like the letter Y. Ask the tree for the branch to help you learn to walk in the old ways of wisdom, and make an offering to the tree – this could be something delicious – honey, apple cider, or something traditional like a silver penny pushed beneath the soil at its roots, or perhaps a ball of seed to hang upon its branches for the birds. Carefully cut the twig.

Now, holding lightly onto the V of the twig, allow the longest length of the rod to guide you. You can use a hazel rod for finding energy or ley lines, but they are especially good for finding water. However, you must train the rod. You can do this by focusing your intent (much easier for youngsters than us oldies) on water – fill your mind with it – also go to a place where you know there is water. As you move, if you hold the rod lightly, you should feel a vibration in the end of the rod as if it starts to wiggle up and down, your hands may also begin to feel 'fuzzy'.

The more you do this, the more sensitive you will become and the more effective the rod, so if the first time is a letdown don't give up!

Making a Full Moon Incense

Incense making can be a quiet and thoughtful enterprise, allowing for reflection and involving all the senses as you make decisions about which herbs, resins and spices to include and exclude. There are some wonderful books on incense making, the most well known being Scott Cunningham's *The Complete Book of Incenses Oils and Brews*.

I suggest choosing ingredients that are in your home cupboard, and when possible native. Although frankincense and myrrh are beautiful ingredients used in sacred incense, current economic and tapping practices of the *Boswellia papyrifera* in Ethiopia and Somalia in Eastern Africa, where most frankincense (and myrrh) comes from, is leading to the Boswellia tree's decline. If you choose to use it at all, treat it as a truly valuable jewel of the African earth and know where your sacred resins are sourced.

You need:
(Sandalwood/frankincense 2 parts– optional)
Orris Root – 1 part
Mugwort – 2 parts
Jasmine oil/flowers (1 drop/1 part)
Cucumber seeds – part
Rose – 2 parts
Lemon peel/rind – ½ part

Other plants/trees/flowers ruled by the moon include: cleavers, clary sage, saxifrage, willow tree, wintergreen, pumpkin, poppy, loosestrife, chickweed, lily, and iris. These are lovely to decorate a moon shrine or altar or to make an incense or moon bag to carry for moon power. Rose and jasmine oil, and a weak cup of mugwort tea, are also good, in small part for menstruation pain or discomfort.

Water Gazing

On a full moon or a dark moon fill a large bowl with water. Bless the water. Sit it on a table with a candle flame behind it. Dim the lights, ask your child to look into the bowl and ask what they see there, perhaps they see the candle flickering, perhaps in their mind's eye they see a person or an image. Perhaps they see nothing but their own reflection. Note down their observations and practise this the next week. Sometimes with younger kids this exercise can bring up feelings about something that has happened or something they are thinking about. Go with their responses to the water gazing. Make a note and try again next month.

Healing - The Gift of Water

Healing lies in the province of water. When we have a family, health and healing reach new levels of importance. Having the ability to take care of your family's health without always resorting to antibiotics and a long wait in the doctor's surgery is very empowering. We don't all need to be doctors or nurses or even have a first aid qualification (although this is a really good idea) to explore our healing skills with our growing family, or community.

Whether we are parents or teachers or an adult friend of children, safeguarding their health is key to their general well-being. This starts by ensuring they have a balanced diet, enough sleep and rest (ever diminishing in the lives of many kids) and cleanliness. Many Pagans are interested and skilled in healing arts such as massage, energy and crystal healing, herbalism and homeopathy and now is the time when you can delicately apply this knowledge. Also, some kids naturally take to certain healing arts.

Earth kids are great at first aid knowledge, earth/water kids are keen at massage, whilst earth/fire kids make strong crystal healers. Fire kids can be very interested in all forms of energy healing, and although healing doesn't come naturally to them they are often eager receivers of alternative types of medicine. For air kids, basic herbalism and homeopathy, systematised healing systems, work well. Air/fire kids are good at retaining and applying knowledge and like the historical aspects of these healing paths. Water kids find hands-on healing very natural, and are also very sensitive to alternative healing types, homeopathy and Bach flower remedies are good to use on them and to teach them about too.

Making teas and tisanes are great for all kids to learn. Making tea is a ritual in and of itself and much revered as a spiritual tradition in many of the world's oldest cultures. We all know how a good cup of tea is a useful remedy in almost every situation. Our friends Sam and Vlad have been growing their own herbs, veg and coffee plants for many years now and, as I laughingly say to them, come the zombie apocalypse we will all go to their house because when all else is lost a cup of coffee or herbal tea will be the last bastion of human civilisation.

For very small children, chamomile tea with honey can be a great remedy for insomnia or anxiety. For aches and chills or a sore throat, sage leaves with honey, or a squeezed lemon with a teaspoon of honey can be just what the body needs. Here is a small list of other herbal teas you can make with kids, and can use with kids safely. For best tea-making practice, place the fresh or dried herbs into a pot. For one person you might look to use a teaspoon of dried herbs, or a handful of fresh to a mug of hot water. Ensure you bring the water fully to the boil, and then pour directly onto the herbs. Leave it to steep for five minutes then strain and add honey/lemon to taste. Of course, I cannot say they will make your child or you 'well' again, but they are old remedies that are worth a try.

Peppermint tea is excellent for headaches, and getting rid of excess wind and bloating. It is also good for reducing fevers by cooling the body down. It helps bring up mucus if your wee one has a cough or cold. Drink this if you are breastfeeding and the baby has a lot of gas/wind.

Chamomile flower tea is good as a digestif and also good for kids' earache, both as a drink and to make a warm compress from the tea and hold it to the child's head. Let this cool then apply it to sunburn to help soothe the skin. Make lemon balm tea for teens to lessen tension or pre-exam nerves, and it also lifts depression in kids (and adults!) – take it as a tea or put a bunch in the bath.

Dill or catnip tea is very good for hiccups. Comfrey and chamomile teas are excellent as facial rinses to heal acne or facial redness/soreness. Chamomile tea is also good to help kids relax and sleep. Lavender flowers can be great for kids who suffer restless nights, and you can make a dream pillow, or a lovely bunch to tie up in their bedrooms somewhere. Lavender oil, as I discuss below, is a must-have and a couple of drops of this can ease an ear infection.

Family First Aid

Being married to an Emergency Room nurse we have first aid kits that are the envy of our friends. However, what I rely on again and again are not only the array of bandages and plasters and pain killers we have, but a small cupboard of useful remedies.

Witch Hazel (Topical Treatment)

Good for cuts, abrasions, swellings, and post partum for pesky haemorrhoids. It's also gentler on the skin than other over the counter antibacterial solutions. Some people also use arnica cream/pillules for similar problems with bumps and bruises. Witch hazel also benefits from being great for nosebleeds. Hold a cold compress with some witch hazel to the nose. Remember that now the recommendation is *not* to tilt the head back.

Lavender Oil (Topical)

The best remedy for burns, lavender oil is antiseptic so it's good for insect stings and bites, but there's not much that lavender oil isn't good for. Be careful on baby skin, mix it with a carrier oil, but it can be excellent for rashes, to ease bronchial spasms and to aid sleeping. We use it in an oil burner at night to ensure good dreams. There was fear regarding the use of lavender and tea tree oil and its potential for hormonal disruption on boys when a study came out that discussed the enlarged breasts of three boys. This research has since been disproven but always be cautious using these potent remedies on children.

Tea Tree Oil (Topical)

Excellent on fungal infections including warts, in fact our doctor recommended this saying it was equal in efficacy to the painful dry ice treatment. Apply tea tree twice daily to the wart. Tea tree is also good on cold sores and on all kinds of problem skin such as acne. It is shown to be effective topically against bacteria, viruses, fungal infections and its limits are as yet unknown. Tea tree oil is great to burn in an oil burner for a child who has a cough, cold or chest infection.

Eucalyptus Oil (Topical)

Use a few drops in a burner when you have kids with a lot of upper respiratory congestion. Also lovely to burn after a child has been ill as it fumigates and cleanses a space.

Honey
Another cure all, add this to teas for its antibacterial properties, but it is also excellent to use directly on wounds to clean and aid healing.

Oil of Cloves
For toothache there's nothing better. Put a couple of drops of on a cotton ball and apply directly to the area.

Salt
A natural preservative and also a natural cleaning agent. Good sea salt should always be in the cupboard of every Pagan household and it can be used to make saline solution to clean the throat or mouth of mouth ulcers or gum infection and toothache, or even a sore throat, and a paste of salt water can be applied directly to a bee sting to take the sting/itch away.

Ginger
Chew a little bit of crystallised ginger for travel sickness or drink ginger ale after a bout of vomiting. Ginger has wonderful anti nausea and sickness properties.

Calendula (Topical)
These beautiful marigold flowers are excellent for any skin conditions, including minor abrasions and scrapes, bruises, and aching muscles, also for cold or wind burn. We use calendula cream a lot. An infusion of marigold flowers can be used as a compress on the eyes for pink eye/conjunctivitis.

Aloe Vera (Topical)
Excellent on burns, after-sun skin care and dry skin or psoriasis.

Rescue Remedy

We use a lot of Bach flower remedies in our home and I would thoroughly recommend you researching this if you have a child who is sensitive and open to them. However, rescue remedy should be in your bag at all times. For shock and pain there is nothing better.

Remedies for Childhood Illnesses

Headlice: Author and aromatherapist Maggie Tisserand's recipe has been used in my family home for decades. It's pretty much a mixture of 25 drops of each of the following: Rosemary, Lavender, Eucalyptus and Geranium Oils. Add these to a half a cup of vegetable oil, spread evenly over the hair and leave covered in a shower cap for two hours. Comb with a fine-toothed comb. Repeat in three days.

Threadworm (also called pinworm): This common and rather irritating childhood illness requires the whole family be treated. Firstly, to keep them at bay, encourage good self-care cleaning and eat a lot of carrots, oranges and pomegranates. Use half a cup of witch hazel in the bath at night for a week. Wash all bed linen and clothing and ensure good hand washing skills are in operation at all times.

Eczema: Introduce dandelion, nettles and chickweed to the diet and make a tisane and soothe the skin with this once a day.

Warts: Tea tree oil or garlic applied twice daily directly to the wart.

Colic: Make sure you know that it's colic your baby is complaining of, so go and see the doctor or health visitor first. Nursing mums can drink fennel or chamomile tea or rub chamomile tisane directly onto baby's tummy.

Acne: If it's oily skin acne then drink chamomile tea and carrot juice, if it's dry skin related then apply rose oil and witch hazel and drink dandelion tea.

PMS/menstrual pain: Warm compress applied to the lower

abdomen with chamomile or fennel seed tea.

Cystitis: Hydrate! Cranberry juice (not the juice drink, but fresh cranberry), and take chamomile and salt sitz baths. You can also use bicarbonate of soda and water topically (which also happens to be great on stings, whether from nettles or insects!) If you get a fever go to the doctor immediately.

Thrush: Eat live yoghurt, and plenty of garlic. You can even apply yoghurt directly to the site. Avoid sugary foods.

Anxiety: Lemon balm tea. Cut out screen technology for a few days, early nights and eat lots of fresh fruit and veggies.

Insomnia: Dependent upon its cause, of course, but lemon balm tea and chamomile are good places to start.

Compassionate Relating

As many of us know, the best form of healing is often the warm embrace of a loved one. Touch and kindness are ways we heal rifts, dry tears and demonstrate our care for each other. All of us want a culture where compassionate kids are the norm. One of the greatest challenges of our time is ensuring that the effects of poverty, poor education and low living standards do not interfere with our kids' ability to relate compassionately and affectionately to the world around them. Being able to relate well to another person is a learnt skill and some of us are better at it than others. Our relationships are the means through which we ultimately leave our mark on the world.

In considering Pagan ethical principles, being in good relationship is paramount. For example, if we (rather reductively) believe that the foundation of Christian ethics include *faith and forgiveness* and that in Judaism it includes *loving kindness and divine service,* and in Islam *good character* and Buddhism *compassionate non harm,* then the Pagan foundation might be *immanence and relationship.* Wiccan and Pagan author Yvonne Aburrow wrote recently on the blog site Patheos:

I think the foundation of Pagan ethics is the idea that everything is sacred, because the Divine is / deities are immanent in
everything. The stories and mythologies that we share illus-
trate the idea of deities and spirits being involved in the
world, and of people taking care of each other and of animals
and plants. These are the illustrations of that basic insight.
(http://www.patheos.com/blogs/sermonsfromthemound/2013
/04/foundation-of-pagan-ethics. Accessed 01/09/2013)

Immanence is the knowledge that everything that exists in nature
is sacred, and we are part of that great river of relationship with
all living things. This river is the divine. Demonstrating true
kindness is the means by which we honour all our relations. It is
this foundation we seek to bring our children into relationship
with. And a way we can approach this is by nurturing empathy
with all the world's beings.

Psychologists tell us that empathy is not a 'born' response.
Babies, infants and toddlers are not empathic beings. Perhaps if
we have water kids they may show early signs of empathy. At
about age five though children begin to demonstrate empathy and
are able to extrapolate from their own experience to that of others.
Sometimes young children are able to mimic empathic responses
– kiss a hurt, make sorry noises – but when does this move from
mirroring to experiencing empathy? Can you recall an early
example of your child-self experiencing empathy? Perhaps it was
with a friend or stranger, perhaps you witnessed something that
upset you? It could be connected to an experience with an animal
or insect. Can you get deep into the memory? Flesh out your recollection and see how you feel. Hot? Tense? Tearful? Strange?
Empathy is the doorway to the deep water, to the deepest
emotional self. Once we open that doorway the hope is that the
illumination into others that it brings will lead to a broader and
broader understanding of the world. Thus from empathy comes
the foundation of connected relationships. It takes a lot of

empathy, a deep and considered empathic self, to feel the needs of Mother Earth and compel us to action on her behalf.

Nurturing Empathic Children

Many young children connect to the vulnerability of animals far easier than they might connect to a young friend or sibling or adult. Allowing kids to build relationships with animals, rather than simply viewing them behind cages, encouragingly gives rise to children's caretaking and empathy. We value and praise empathic moments, moments of unprovoked kindness or sadness towards another living thing.

I saw a moment like this the other day. In my home we have had a summer learning about bees, and we have a plethora of bees in our back garden, of all species and all types. Their perpetual industry is amazing to witness, and the facts about how they communicate, pollinate and make honey are fascinating to my boys. They are also insects with whom we can on some level communicate – if you emit an air of calm they will happily work around you. Yet, in rolling around the grass playing, a bee stung Summer, and he shrieked loudly when he pulled the stinger from his arm. I thought that this was a consequence of the pain but as he frantically searched through the grass I realised his shriek was the realisation that the bee would now die. Tears followed as he explained to me that he had never meant to kill the bee. I wondered at his capacity for such empathy towards this wee thing. This is part of the ethic of reciprocity – the understanding that we have a reciprocal relationship with everything on Mother Earth.

Other ways of increasing the opportunities for empathy come from involvement with the arts – with forms of beauty that may stir within our young folk feelings and emotions. This is one reason why exposure to dance, fine art, live music and nature is so beneficial. We do not know what will move our kids, but we pursue the opportunity by standing for hours in a museum queue in the school holidays or paying to go to see the Nutcracker ballet at Yule, despite it costing virtually a month's wages; we value the arts because they enrich and develop our children's emotional lives and their deeper spiritual instincts.

In some of the most distressing cases involving children's violence, we repeatedly hear disturbingly familiar scenarios. Although these are by no means indicators, we find that children and young adults for whom empathy is not forthcoming often grow in environments plagued by poverty, lack of access to education, poor opportunities for advancement and frequently a diet of consumer culture unchecked by guardians, school or community leaders.

State schools across Britain and public schools in America all too frequently relegate liberal arts subjects to the second tier of subjects, little understanding that this could be a contributing factor to the sense of alienation and despondency our young people have. Because when we are educated in and about the arts, we also have a stake in their creation. Making art in all its forms, whether through dance, music, painting, theatre or sculpture, allows us to express our emotional selves, it is if you like active empathic work. It is no wonder that children who have demonstrated aggressive or harmful behaviour towards others are given intensive art and music therapy and often talk therapy is tempered with creative expression in order to give these children a language with which they can express their deep feelings.

For kids who need deeper journeying into empathy we must first show them kindness, affection, attention and respect. If we understand that each of us is a reflection of the divine, made by Mother Earth and that our relationship with each person goes beyond personality, we must look to see our fellow human beings as truly capable of change and evolution, and strive towards their happiness.

If young people can take care of themselves, then they are

ready for responsibility. This can breed trust, which can in turn lead to their ability to care for others, which is a pathway to empathy. When kids are given responsibility, to care for an animal, a garden, something that requires their best selves, they see that they are valued and needed and have a way to contribute. Give your kid a patch of the garden, let them collect snails, or walk your dog and when you witness a moment of kindness, warmly and verbally value it. Also, asking kids how they feel about such encounters (especially if you are not a parent) and then listening quietly to whatever their answer is can build bonds of trust. Ask how an exchange made them feel, ask why they seem sad, ask how their days was – simple questions asked seriously, not simply as a pleasantry gives kids the opportunity to begin to unpack and understand their emotional responses.

Questions to Promote Empathic Awareness
How do you feel about ____?
How would you have liked to see_____ happen?
How do you think ____ and ____ felt about it?
How do you feel about their feelings?
If you had to do_____ again, would you do anything differently?
How would that change how you feel now?
How would that change how they might feel now?

In Canada and now in the UK, the charitable organisation *Roots of Empathy,* founded by Mary Gordon, has developed an evidence-based teaching programme for elementary children that has been rolled out in schools to help develop empathy in school children. This pioneering programme uses engagement with an infant and parent over many weeks to promote emotional knowledge and development. In its mission statement it says:

At the heart of the program are a neighbourhood infant and parent who visit the classroom every three weeks over the school year. A trained Roots of Empathy Instructor coaches students to observe the baby's development and to label the baby's feelings. In this experiential learning, the baby is the "Teacher" and a lever, which the instructor uses to help children identify and reflect on their own feelings and the feelings of others. This "emotional literacy" taught in the program lays the foundation for more safe and caring classrooms, where children are the "Changers". They are more competent in understanding their own feelings and the feelings of others (empathy) and are therefore less likely to physically, psychologically and emotionally hurt each other through bullying and other cruelties... Empathy is a key ingredient to responsible citizenship and responsive parenting.

(http://www.rootsofempathy.org/en/what-we-do/about-our-program.html, accessed 11/7/13).

Bonding is an empathic skill that we continue to learn throughout our lives, but when we instil this in our young folks we nurture kindness in our future citizens.

I want to give you a little cautionary tale of what the consequences of raising empathically attuned kids can be – and, like the last, this one also involves insects! One evening I had made dinner. It was summer time and flies plagued our dining room. We were having our usual dinnertime banter and I was joking about the flies as they buzzed by.

One landed on the table by the food and in a fit of pique I hit it with a book next to my plate, not expecting to actually squash one of these pesky fast flies. As I lifted the book I realised a fly was squashed and both my boys started to wail. They were inconsolable. Between sobs they admonished me for killing a fly that "wasn't even half my size".

Boo, tears streaking down his face told me I should feel ashamed, and in that despite the fly being a germ-carrying insect not high on my list of loveable household insects I acknowledged that it was a creature and that I had thoughtlessly killed it at dinnertime. Summer chastised my inequity: "You should at least have let it see the book, to give it a chance!" Their fervour for the dead fly showed me two things – that in valuing empathy my children made no differentiation between killing a fly and any other creature. That I had done this glibly hurt them – my protestations that it was an accident had no purchase.

I was both incredibly proud of their capacity for empathy but also sad this had resulted in my own shame. Solemnly I apologised. We took the squashed fly outside and laid it under the rose tree and said prayers whilst I apologised to its spirit.

And still today, the 'fly incident' is not forgotten and is raised to make a point about my poor judgment and still causes them to look at me with both pity and sadness. It has also raised some other interesting questions – Summer asked recently why road kill is not a punishable offence under the law. "Why don't the police come and arrest them?" he asked one day after seeing a dead badger in the road. In the minds of our young these tough ethical questions is empathy that recognises no differentiation between living things.

Having a highly empathic child can be a blessing and a curse. How can you tell if your child is naturally highly empathic? Here are the recognised indicators of highly empathic people (HEPs):

- Highly imaginative
- Intense curiosity about others
- Inspiring to others
- Challenge prejudice and assumed assumptions
- Eager for new experiences
- Listen hard to others – pay attention

- Excellent in groups – social butterflies!
- Disregard social conventions

You can also expect highly empathic children to be attuned to the spirit world. They may see or sense presences from a young age, they may be sensitive to people and places and highly attuned to their own needs. You may arrange a play date only to have them play up the minute they arrive. Or you may plan a lovely family trip but they cannot go because they haven't found their special charm or cuddly toy. They are easily moved, but also extremely clever and can play a situation to their emotional advantage. They are emotionally astute but do not always understand their own motivations for doing something. Beware that in their empathy they don't play you!

Highly empathic kids need attention and affection. Listen to them but don't give them too much room to linger or dwell. Don't over schedule them. They need a really healthy diet as they may be frequently sick and in another time may have been described as sickly. As teenagers or younger they may opt to be vegetarian or vegan so vitamin rich foods are essential. They may have an overwhelming urge to travel and see the world as they get older.

Ultimately, although the path for highly empathic water children is hard in Western society, know that they are essential to the balance and well-being of our world, that they bring social change, creativity and the ability to make alliances like no others, and although they may not attain worldly success as a fire/air child might, they will become the adults that we need if the world is to be healed from our increasingly destructive consumption of resources and people.

Kids in Circle

Magic makes the world go round. And magic only happens when people relate to each other. Enabling our kids to relate is one of those parenting/guardianship benchmarks. Teaching all our kids to articulate their emotional life should be a highest priority for those of us considering the sanctity of Mother Earth and all our relations. If making magic is the art of focusing willpower to cohese with intention, then both parts of that equation require knowledge of the deep emotional self in order to hone an honourable intention and harmoniously shape willpower accordingly. Helping our kids to be in good relationship with the beings around them helps us all, and may teach us about living in honesty and love.

We began 'family circle' time when my youngest, Boo, got to about five. When big issues came up in our family we would 'round table' them (King Arthur ruled the mythic imagination of our household at the time). Someone would hold a crystal or stone (something beach-worn is our preference, as it sits smooth in the hand) and speak, and all others would be silent. Each person in the family would have their say and then we would commit to resolving the issue before putting the stone back on the altar.

This takes the Native American Talking Stick ritual and strips it right down, and I can vouch for it working minor miracles. Problems about bedtime, discipline, TV, worries about school and friends, changes in timetable, work life, poor sibling relationships can be aired safely. The key rule is no judgment and no responding or speaking whilst another is speaking. And trust me, once the rules are in place, kids will hold you to them.

This is an excellent technique to use in large community groups of multiple ages, and can be done by allowing each person to take a turn or by the speaker replacing the stone to the centre to see who wishes to speak next. No accusations, no bullying, and no leaving the circle until it's finished – those are our family rules. This kind of circle activity can be great for problem solving in a classroom or in a community group and I have seen it in small spaces with a family of four or in large meetings of 100. Whatever the number the process is the same –

enter in love, be here in love and leave in love.

Connecting kids to speaking from the heart is a wonderful gift to give them. Love, and all that comes from love, is an expression of water's purest form. Allowing kids emotional expression cultivates their capacity to listen-in to their responses. This in turn will help them pay attention to their instincts and their impressions and develop those listening skills that will later help them 'To Know' themselves and the truth in others.

This leads us to consider the questions of children and magic. Throughout this book I have been cautious in discussing how kids are included in adult magical traditions. Paganism does not require active participation in active magical work, although many Pagans will choose a path that develops this. Being a Pagan is in essence being a person who follows the rhythms and patterns of Mother Earth and reveres the sacred nature of life. But kids are natural magic makers, and they are sensitive to the dynamic powers of natural magic all around us. You will find them enacting pieces of sympathetic magic without any assistance from us adults. I will discuss this further in the next chapter.

So what about when kids want more, and where do we stand on this issue of teaching kids active magic? Some kids want more, they want to bless salt, they want to cast a circle, they want to help sick friends with spell working and they want to make magic. Let's not interfere with the magic they do as small children – they have their own way, and let's keep that for them and not impose adult structures. But there are seeds we can sow that can prove beneficial later.

Until a child reaches seven, showing developing awareness, meditation and all ways of encouraging fascination are enough. But teaching kids to be in circle, and to make or cast an energy circle is one piece of 'formal' Pagan magic that I think is invaluable for children. It can be used anywhere, and can begin as a simple visualisation at the beginning and become more elaborate as they become more adept. This is basic energy work, simple, safe and effective. I have taught Summer this and he uses it almost daily now. This is how we began:

Close your eyes, feel your feet rooted to the ground, and feel Mother Earth holding you, supporting your feet. All her love and warmth is spreading up from your toes up, up through your body and her loving warmth, that earth warmth, is making your body soft and relaxed. Up through your chest and down your arms, your face and your neck all warm and relaxed with the loving energy of mother earth. Now, that energy is collecting in a ball just below your belly button. It is a beautiful ball of orange, and from this begins to spread a beautiful shimmering web, it is making a bubble all around you. Feel it, like being out on a warm sunny day. This is a circle of energy around you, and when it is complete, you can say, "Circle around me, always protect me. So Mote It Be".

This is a simple grounding and centering circle casting. We do not deconstruct the energy sphere once made, I have found that kids will do this when the purpose has dissipated, but I always say how energy work sometimes takes our own energy so we always drink and eat a little something afterwards, to ensure they don't feel light headed. This has not happened, however, and we have used this in various circumstances. And once you have gone through it about three times, they can begin to take the reins, especially if they have uncluttered minds and they are between six and nine years old. Older than that may in fact be more challenging as they may have more questions for you! What we now do is use different colours of energy, if Summer is practising his invisibility he will turn the core energy blue/green. If he is working on feeling confident it will be orange/yellow, or if he is helping us bubble the car before a long journey he often uses pink.

Ultimately all acts of creativity can be understood as magic.

Magic is everywhere, and follows the path of love. In wanting our kids to encounter magic in their lives beyond the formalities of form and ritual, we can encourage them in a magical worldview, and we can open their hearts to feeling and joy. This means allowing them to express their heart. Love is the ultimate means through which water expands and nurtures the magical garden.

Water Activities

Shout to the ocean

Tell someone how you feel

Dress up!

Get active to save marine life
– protect the whales!

Be a good friend

Make ice lollies

Meditate on the meaning of love

Volunteer for a local charity

Go pond dipping

Take an acting class

Learn some hands on healing

Do some ink on water
painting or use watercolours

Help out in your neighbourhood

Care for a baby

Play Pooh Sticks

Write a blessing

Chapter Five

Spirit

Mum I don't want to let go of the balloon because then the Gods will get it and they will keep it for themselves
Boo, aged three

Key words: *Spirit, God, Gods, Goddess, Universe, Nature, Life-force, Qi, Chi, Maya, Energy, Mother Earth, Mana, Ancestors, Beloved Dead, Supreme Intelligence, Ascended Masters, Cosmos, Buddha, Brahmin, Nirvana*

In the Centre of All Things

Spirit – the enlivening force of the universe that runs through all things, animate, inanimate and beyond. It is the force that moves the tides, the numinous energy in nature. In Paganism we name this Goddess or give different forms of this energy different names that reflect the nature of this power: the Gods, elementals, divas, Old Ones. Spirit is found in the wild places and those cultivated, it is the extraordinary force that tells a caterpillar when to make a chrysalis. It is the animating energy that brings our planet in this universe, a consciousness. Spirit is Gaia. Pagans and earth faith folk understand and attempt to live in a way that draws us nearer to understanding our place in this great cosmic pattern. We endeavour to live and work in a way that demonstrates an awareness and reverence for this life force.

This life-force is the flow of magic through our universe. All of the ideas I have suggested throughout this book are ways I hope we can bring ourselves in harmony with the life-forces and place positive magic more firmly into the fabric of our family, our home, our schools and our community. Our celebratory cycles model the patterns of flow within the universe, the eternal

229

circles and spirals, the branches and waves that pulse with life and death in endless tides.

The circle is at the core of our discussion of spirit, as within many Pagan traditions (particularly Wiccan), we say that spirit lives at the centre of the circle of life. Within ceremonies and ritual, the direction of spirit is at the axis, the heart of all things. The circle is the symbol of spirit, as the circle around the pentagram shows how all the elements are combined in a never-ending round. The circle has no beginning, no end, no above and no below. In three dimensions the circle becomes a sphere, beautifully proportioned to be a shape with no edges, with no hierarchy. It is both a place of safety and it is a sign of unity. We use circles to meet, to work magic, to dream:

> The circle flows eternally, one circle continues into another the circle puts everyone on the basis of equality. The circle provides you with your own place of safety. The circle holds energy for you as you generate it, concentrating it by confining it like a cooking pot.
> (Shan, *Circlework*, p. 32)

What Do We Believe?

In bringing children to the table of our spirituality, we often have to tackle those big questions regarding the nature of spirit without the certainty of other religious traditions. Children can always find the cracks in your answers and they ask the most sublime questions on the machinations of the Gods' work. I have certainly found that I struggle to simplify the answers I had always given adults when teenagers asked me, "So, you're a Pagan, what do you actually believe?"

This question is highly personal. No two Pagans would answer the same way! It seemed to require a definitive answer, a certainty, whilst I have always felt that what I believe matches my experience, and so was constantly in a state of growth and change. However, as a species we like definitions, and I have found that with kids, some sense of definition helps anchor our discussion of the moral, ethical and environmental aspects of Paganism.

To small kids I say something like, "I am a Pagan, and Pagans believe that the earth is sacred, we call her Goddess and Mother Earth and we celebrate her and all her changes through the seasons." For older kids I expand this, "I am a Pagan and I hold the earth sacred. I know that the world is full of spirit or energy, which I call Goddess, but also by different names. I celebrate outside, often in nature. Pagans don't have a church or a temple as we make sacred circles in which to honour and revere the turning tides of the earth's seasons." I will say more if they ask anything, and it tends to be that this answer is enough. Funnily enough I say pretty much the same when kids ask me what witches believe!

When Pagans talk about spirit they are often referring to the animating forces of the universe, the tides of energy that sweep sometimes unseen through our world. This differs to the notion of soul (itself a rather overused term used in monotheistic faith traditions more frequently than earth-centred ones), in that for some Pagans, the soul is the unique blueprint of memory and matrix passed down through ancestors across generations. The soul can be the specific manifestation of energy, tied to a place, a family or a person. The soul then can be a preponderance of spirit energy, that which remains.

This can make sense of some of those extraordinary moments of life and birth; we may see that the body lives on, there may still be life spirit present, but the soul could have passed. For anyone witnessing a person on the brink of death maintained by a machine, this may ring true. Likewise, some children are born with strong soul and spirit in them, and for some, the soul enters some time after birth. For some native peoples, the soul is said to enter with the first breath, for others, after the first 100 days the soul has finally descended into the body.

I often think about the question of the soul when I am thinking about orchids. I love orchids and have harboured a dream that in my dotage I will grow an orchid garden (and collect old hats, and smoke unfiltered camel cigarettes, but that's for another discussion!) In my current and decidedly amateur propagation of orchids I have noticed that certain orchids have very distinctive personalities or temperaments. Perhaps these plants and I share notable qualities that allow me to see beyond their 'orchidness' to something else. Is it that these orchids, replete with life-force, with spirit, also have some form of soul, in greater strength than others? Is there an orchid soul, shared by the genus, which holds the memories specific to that genus encoded in the strings of DNA? Some would say yes, the plant is germinated with a fore-knowledge of its blossoming.

Most significantly of course, and importantly for me and my love of orchids, it is not the intricacies of labelling the differences between definitions of soul and spirit, but how these concepts bring us into communication with the plant realm. Imagine how we might move through the world differently if we considered the soul of every plant and tree, the soul of a beehive or an anthill, the soul of the ocean, complete with multitudinous life forms.

How would you change your choices if this were the case? Vegetarians, vegans and fruitarians alike have considered these questions (and some meat eaters too of course!) and answered them in their consumption choices. All life-force contains spirit – every pebble, every molecule is an integral part of planetary consciousness, is part of Mother Earth's living self. Human inter-vention can shape, use or define the value of each being in a variety of ways but such definitions are of human relevance alone.

Perhaps we need to turn the table and try to see how the earth defines her relationships, the points of connection between species and genus. If the drives for value were divorced from the drives for profit, and instead seen as the quota of planetary nourishment, how would we relate to the species that live around us? How would we consider the value of flowers for example? Flowers nourish insects through their pollen and nectar, they nourish us through their beauty and their perfume and they provide habitat whilst their decaying blooms make mud for more plants. If we considered flowers in this way would we make flower growing a point of education for our kids, would we let them mindlessly pull the heads off the flowers in our locale?

If we say that the God Pan watches over the plants and animals and that fairies inhabit many flowers, a living representation of the soul of that plant, how would we go about relating to that plant? In considering this, we imagine a whole new way of relating to flowers. We might grow children better attuned to the earth's cyclical turn and to flowers' numinous nature, so that even the smallest flower is worthy of our honest attention.

Blessing on the Soul of a Fellow Earth Dweller

To be said to a tree/plant/flower/stone whose presence moves you.

Greetings friend
Greetings of green and gold and all that is good
I see you
I reach to you across the space between us
I offer my blessing to you—
That you will know contentment in your state
That you will know the passage of time and your place within it
You are a face of the Gods/Goddess
Blessed Be

The Issue of God

Kids are sponges. It's true. All the stuff you *don't* want them to know about, they seem to collect like dew from the morning air. Superheroes, profanities, names of specific artillery, space weapons, Disney characters, by the time they are five it seems they have learnt a veritable pantheon of characters that had nothing to do with you. You blame play dates, preschool, friends, the universe, but it all ends up in their thirsty mind.

It's the same way it seems with God. We pick up the notion of God seemingly by osmosis. Dr Ana-Maria Rizzuto (in Robert Cles *The Spiritual Life of Children* p. 45) discusses this omnipresent "God representation" that grows within children during the formative years. She suggests that a child's relationship with this "God" is defined by the exposure and context of religious belief surrounding the child. Yet her research suggests that it seems to be present from the point at which a child begins to communicate with the world. This supports an anecdotal truism that a good friend and UU minister Robin Bartlett once told me, "When it comes to spiritual ideas and religious teaching, if you don't get in there first, someone else will".

For those of you with toddlers in your life, you may already have experienced the notion that God is one of many magical beings that inhabit their expanding consciousness. The challenge, therefore, with introducing the concept of deity may be not to introduce the notion of God but to pluralise it. Further, we can focus on connecting this 'spirit impulse' to the self, so that our kids' early perceptions of the divine connects to the tangible world around them rather than to a disembodied God figure that inhabits a purely celestial region. Better that Gods live in the garden than in heaven.

Pagans often describe their relationship with the divine as a relationship based on immanence, that the Old Ones are in all things at all time. Modern Paganism is generally not a faith of transcendence; many of our practices allow us to move deeper *into* rather than beyond the mundane word. We understand that the Gods, the Goddess, the spirits are numinous, within all things. And nothing within nature is of greater or lesser spiritual value than any other thing. Everything has a place. As a spirituality of immanence, we have no persons better equipped to talk to the Gods than ourselves.

When this is combined with polytheism, the understanding that there are many, many faces to spirit, there are many Gods and Goddesses flowing through the matrix of the universe, we see the value of pluralism and diversity embodied in our relationship with every living thing. To introduce these concepts to kids in a non-dogmatic way, where the focus is still on exploration, allowing kids to come to their own sense of the divine (especially considering so many of us oldies are evolving our perceptions of divinity), is in part defined by our own terms. Here is a framework to help navigate the exploration of divine concepts at different phases and different ages of your kids:

Zero to three years: Keep it simple and family focused. Introduce terms – Gods, Goddesses, and particularly the notion of pluralism (Goddesses) and numinosity (the Gods are with us and all around us at all times). Talk to them about the Gods through prayer and ritual, such as shrine building. All life is precious. Here we can lay the foundations for the beginnings of immanent thought. Allow them to experience the wonders of the elements in nature: late night walks with lanterns, bonfires, a waterfall, the forest. Emersion in the natural world gives them strong foundations for connecting with the deep spirit of nature.

Three to seven years: During this age phase you can begin to concretely link deity to nature's seasons. As the cycles turn begin to discuss specific Gods and Goddesses: Oak King and Holly King, Mother Earth, Father Sky. Story is key here, and experience. Allow your children to develop their own way of talking to the Gods, encourage their self-generated relationship, petitioning, wishes, blessings. The Godesses are within nature. Try to restrain the outside world's definition of monotheism as much as you can and although you don't have to introduce pantheism yet (which can be confusing) allow the sense that there are many faces to the divine to permeate your family life!

Seven to ten years: Open the rich world of pantheons and rather than making these about 'history' as they are so often taught in school, connect these to the here and now, the everyday. Most particularly discover the association between Gods, Goddesses and place. The legends and myths of your place can be incredibly useful here – in the UK, for example, you may want to work a project on King Arthur as the King under the Hill, or Robin Hood, Lady Godiva and Boudicca. Discover what images of the divine are specific to your country, your place of origin, and your culture. Begin the acknowledgement that different deities have different qualities and rulerships.

Ten to twelve years: During this phase children are beginning to understand the relationship between polytheism and the concepts of unification. Having worked so hard on the various systems of pantheon, you can begin to explore the idea that these are all facets of a single energy, that the spirit that runs through the universe is an animating force. This is a good time to conduct projects on world religions – focus on points of difference and similarity between religions. Explore places of worship from across spiritual traditions and other forms of ritual or celebration from other religious traditions – go to a synagogue, a mosque, visit churches of all persuasions, and groves, and talk to the people who worship and teach and priest in these places. As Karen Armstrong, religious historian and advocate for compassion said in her Ted talk, *Let's Revive the Golden Rule*, "Religious teaching must always lead to action". (http://www. ted.com/talks/karen_armstrong_let_s_revive_the_golden_rule. html).

Thirteen-plus: At this point you can begin to pose moral dilemmas and begin to work more closely with moral and ethical concepts. Pose ethical themes such as reciprocity, charity, suicide, population control and freedom of speech. Young people at this age will have a defined concept of deity and you can encourage them in their own relationship with deity should they choose to have one.

One of the biggest questions you may have to tackle once children start to consider the place of the Old Ones is what they look like, how to think and imagine them. Do we need to anthropomorphise the divine? This is a serious question for those of us guiding children's understanding of the divine. We are naturally inclined as a species to understand other species in our own image, by our own terms. We do this to our pets, so perhaps it is no surprise that we do this with our Gods too. I think that when it comes to considering the many faces of the divine, we share much with Buddhists, Hindus and other shamanic cultures. The problem so many of us have in answering this succinctly is that the images of the divine that we construct tend to reflect dominant cultural expectations or experiences of holiness.

Pagans need to be especially clear that we are not replicating the many problematic limiting images of masculinity and femininity onto the divine. Too many images of skinny, nymph-like maiden Goddesses abound. Too many sky God characterisations look frighteningly like the Hebrew Yahweh. So many of us grew up with an embedded notion of God as a kindly/wrathful and generally emotionally inconsistent parental figure, wearing a white beard, a little like Father Christmas only on a throne in the sky. We work hard to purge ourselves of this image of God, but run the risk of replacing it with a mother Goddess, bountiful/disinterested in human affairs, who sits benignly on an earthy throne. Although this may be a start, in the end this image of the divine threatens to limit the potentials for divinity.

If we truly perceive the divine as numinous, as all around us, then we need to look around us for images of the divine. Shamanic traditions and more recently the many strands of feminist spirituality have captured this well. In shamanic traditions the Gods come to us in many forms, animal, vegetable, and human, and it is our sensitivity to their presence that marks our ability to honour and celebrate them. In this way the depictions of the divine are truly plural and responsive to the environment, the landscape and that which dwells within it. However, and this may be Pagan heresy I am about to commit, I suggest that we do not need to anthropomorphise deity.

We choose to see the Gods in our image because we recognise the worldly and political implications this has, and so often it allows us to connect more deeply with the spirit of the universe. But the spirit of the wild place is not sexed or gendered. When I say to my kids that Pan looks after the little creatures, they have a self-created image of a tender and caring God, a God who to many looks wild and imposing in their mind but who runs through the forest ensuring life is maintained, and watching over little lost animals. What a powerful concept of God this is, and what a departure from the standard biblical image. I use the terms Gods and Goddesses daily – "Good Gods!' I say when something unusual or extraordinary happens, to claim the plural, cracking open any concept of monotheism. Our language defines shapes and creates the way we see the world. It may be, as psychoanalyst Jacques Lacan stated, the process through which we become individuals and separate from our mother. Through changing our language we allow new forms of divinity to be possible in the minds and hearts of our children, and we allow them to come to a possibly more enlightened view of the spirit of nature.

A few years ago we lived down the road from a beautiful modern Catholic church. This church abuts a friary and a nunnery and so is a bustling and exciting place. From the time my kids were small we walked past this busy religious neighbourhood at least once a day. And my kids learnt to walk up stairs by walking up the church's front steps. My eldest son loves this place. He senses that it is a holy place. He often asked questions as we looked at the front of the building with its relief of Mary in prize position at the top of the church's doorway.

One day he exclaimed, "Mummy – it's the Goddess!" (Exclaimed when a brown robed monk was walking by of course…)

And I answered, "Yes, Mary is a Goddess, but this is a Christian church so they don't call her Goddess, they call her the mother of God."

"Why?"

"Because Christians believe in one God. They are not too into Goddesses."

"Why?"

At this I felt I had backed myself into a theological cul-de-sac with a four-year-old. In stating this I had complicated the matter for him and had defined and perhaps squashed his instinctive understanding. What I should have done is asserted he was right and left it at that. And of course my lesson was, sometimes, less explanation is a good thing. If we allow our children to determine the concept of the divine, instead of imposing them we may find some interesting answers. And I would encourage you to try de-anthropomorphising your concept of deity, instead look at the head of a beautiful rose, a running river, the force of the ocean. We can praise *her*, using a female pronoun because we know that like the miracle performed within a woman's body, from her all life springs forth. We share much in common with pantheists and humanists, whose spirituality is guided by the blueprint of Mother Earth. Akin to Pagans, Pantheists see nature as miraculous and do not reject the revelations of science but embrace them. Whilst however we see that there is divinity everywhere, pantheists and humanists see no need for deity, and instead state that the wonders of nature are enough (http://www.pantheism.net/ sourced 18/11/13).

We call to the Gods in many shapes and guises – a rabbit, a hound, a bear or a mountain because we refuse the singularity of monotheism, because the strength and wisdom to be a man is found in many guises. See a running hare and say, "Ah, there goes Ostara." Small acts such as these can have profound implications.

For those of us raising or teaching children within specific magical or cultural Pagan traditions, part of your journey may be to introduce your kids to the rich myths and stories, images and representations your tradition reveres. What happens if you allow your kids to come up with their own images, and allow you to open these to questions? Instead of reading them these stories, try storytelling, try telling them without pictures first, to see what images come to their mind. When you are working on a new pantheon, look at images of the people who live there the landscape itself, the culture, and then allow your kids to be inspired to show you what the Goddess of this place would look like. Allow your voice to weave the tales first before you let other interpretations in. And if you have been working with books, put these away. Help your charge to learn to tell these stories themselves, let them become part of them, as then we allow new visions to emerge from the synthesis between the tale itself and the person telling.

In all of our explorations with deity, as our children grow we can encourage many kinds of knowledge about the world of the spirit – head knowledge about the divine and the honouring structures through which different people in different places come to experience the divine and heart knowledge. It is important not to psychologise this process of knowing for kids but to keep them in touch with the essence of awe. Awe is essential for them to grow and develop their personal relationship with the divine. In order to foster awe, adults can make a commitment to give our kids experiences that facilitate awe. These can be as simple as witnessing a thing of great beauty made by nature or by human hand and to experience it directly. Being around animals, in places of natural grandeur and in small ways, being swept into a song or a piece of music all open the doorway to awe. Play to children's senses and you begin to open them to the inspiring power of awe.

Exercise: School /Community Art Project (Age 5 +)

Set the project to the group as a whole. State questions such as, "Today we are going to explore what the Gods look like," or "What does Goddess look like?" or "Imagine God," and ask everyone to make a piece of art that shows what they think about when they think about the Gods, or God or the Goddess. Provide a range of materials, including traditional art and craft materials, but also bring in some non-conventional art materials from outside – twigs, mud, grass, flowers. Give them free rein to really express their responses, but try to keep talk to a minimum to allow them to go deep inside.

This is a very personal project so not one to do in groups. Allow up to an hour, or more for older kids. When everyone has made something, allow them to explain their process, and then you can build a shrine to all the Gods and Goddesses with the art they have created. You may be surprised with the results.

Paths to Power

Many Pagan and magical traditions have a framework for exploring our relationship with the world's abundant energy, which we call the Paths to Power. The purpose of these is to train the body and the mind in the ways one can raise energy to be focused for magical work. Power as we understand isn't a sort of macho personal electricity, but instead a way of working with natural forces. The majority of these have their basis in the creative and expressive arts – music and silence, movement and stillness.

These are the eight paths to power as found in the seminal work of modern Wicca's founding father Gerald Gardener and they share many elements with spiritual and shamanic traditions from across the globe. I am always surprised that divination is not a separate path to power, and that there was not a path that honoured the ability to care for others as a path to spiritual power and energy. Healing for example I would place under caretaking and is a means of energy working. If I were to re-write the paths to power for contemporary Pagans it would go something like this:

- Meditation/concentration
- Trance
- Divination
- Ritual/spells
- Chant and incantation
- Dance
- Gardening and growing
- Caretaking

At the root of this framework is the essential idea that by focusing and directing the energy of our minds and bodies we can energise our desire for transformation and positively change the world. Further, through these various paths we align ourselves more closely with the Gods by placing our life-force in harmony with the world's turning cycles and energies. In doing this we move closer to a life of calm contentment, of knowing ourselves.

We can start approaching the paths to power with children through introducing the basic concepts of grounding and meditation as outlined in previous chapters. These are exercises that meet the child's needs at their stage of development and allow them to connect to a deeper sense of personal strength. It may seem impossible to get small children to sit still for a moment, let alone consider meditation with them. If you are lucky enough to have a child who is capable of sitting quietly and breathing rhythmically, then we all want to know your secret! Many girls, I have heard, take to simple breath meditation much easier than boys, who seem to be in perpetual motion. Whatever the particular gifts of the child or children you work with are the key to introducing meditation is, don't expect miracles, and praise, praise, praise!

Consider that your child probably goes into a form of meditative focus every time you read them their favourite story, or every time they curl into a cosy chair to read an old favourite book. You know they know the story inside out, they may be able to read it themselves, and yet they love the sound of you doing it. Likewise, if you have ever watched a child in front of the TV you know they are capable of trance. Whether you like this kind of trance or not is another question entirely! You can introduce kids to meditation at any age and begin by simply introducing quiet focused time. Have a daily period with no computer no radio or TV and where you can be 100 per cent focused with them. From here then, you can introduce breath work. Singing helps this hugely, as it requires your kids to be conscious of how they breathe.

As part of your daily quiet focused time, build in some fun deep breathing. You can also use this as an excellent way of helping kids navigate intense periods of frustration – I taught my kids an exercise when they were five or so by saying each time they felt that horrid frustration rising in their belly they were to use their deep belly breaths to blow it away and let the spirits of the air carry it away. In this way we show them that when they focus on and change their breathing, they can change how they feel. Such exercises are so simple and yet profoundly empowering to little people who are often at the mercy of their emotions.

Then for older or more adept kids, a daily family meditation, if only for two minutes at breakfast is a good way to integrate meditation into the web of your day. Take a moment before eating to hold hands and in silence breathe. For the first few times expect laughter, giggles, jokes etc. But then you find you have held it for 30 seconds, then the next day 34 seconds and so on. Kids respond to these moments of connection. If your kids find it hard to do this, accompany the meditation with a hum to sharpen focus and eliminate surrounding noise and allow you to sync your breath.

Another way to encourage the beginnings of trance is to allow children unmediated time to creatively experiment. When we allow kids the opportunity to creatively experiment we allow them to open the door to dream time, to light trance from which innovation, problem solving and the voice of our deep selves, our Goddess self, can speak. When I first considered this section I was camping with a family we are close friends with. The daughter, the same age as my eldest son, has always had an astounding capacity for visual representation. We sat in our campsite in the Berkshires, nestled amongst the early autumn trees.

A storm had passed through the night and the morning was bright and fresh, the pines and the birches glistening with the last of the rain. Morning, when you are camping, is the best time, to my mind. Everyone wakes with the excitement of having been outside, the kids are rested and excited about the day and rambling around the woods in their pyjamas.

On that occasion, the three boys that our two families have were a sea of motion, clambering over branches, falling over roots, crying, laughing, chatting together. And Sophia was sat at the table quietly and intensely drawing. As I watched her I witnessed her descend through levels of trance, drawing her way through all her experiences garnered during our time camping. In the end she managed to block out all sound and her focus was entirely narrowed on the pen and the paper. I called her name many times, her brother and friends were within inches of her, yelling and running about. In watching her I saw a valuable lesson regarding trance. She was moving herself from the everyday reality to the trance reality, because she was in a place that fosters this kind of concentration and because, despite the noise, she was doing something she loves. She had come loose of the everyday world and moved deeper into concentration.

When we know what our children love to do, what allows them to truly express themselves, we can create opportunities for them to explore this deeply. For Sophia it is visual representation – art and pattern. She is a child of air. For your kids it may be kinaesthetic, that your child needs to run or dance. For some it is in storytelling, in listening to a tale being woven. For fire and earth kids finding meditative expression can be more of a challenge, but I have found that these kids respond wonderfully to making things – complex Lego creations, a sun wheel from sticks, a spider's web from string, placing paper all over the floor and giving them paint on plates, using their body as a tool. Any activity that fosters their own deep silence is worth nurturing.

This is another time for us to consider the elemental matrix of our kids to help us determine the way to foster their meditative and trance nature. Sophia is a child with a lot of air; she loves patterns and music, and learning about laws and rules. She laughs a lot, and loves reading. She will, I predict, find great solace in science and music as an older child. If your child is air/fire they will need a focused and probably repetitive activity to allow them to find their trance self – martial arts, gymnastics, circle dance, yoga, archery or through performance arts and you will have to work hard to stop them falling into the trance of video gaming. For water kids it may be writing endlessly in journals, in acting, playing an instrument or being in a space of great beauty. For earth children, they will find this natural trance in places of natural beauty also, but it will strike them differently. They may also find it through physical and mental endurance and challenge – hiking, cycling over distances, sport.

When approaching grounding, the basis for rooting ourselves to our body, kids have much to teach us as adults! Most kids aged zero to four years old are naturally grounded, and by encouraging self-care and supporting the body's routines we help them maintain this. Many kids aged four to seven are in a constant state of movement and so we can help balance them by bringing their attention to stillness, and use imaginative games to foster their groundedness. Being or thinking-in to various other beings or objects is a great way to start this. Remember 'being a tree' or playing sleeping lions?

We can extend this to teach them the basic grounding by maintaining their focus on individual body parts, in a simplified form. I have successfully used a pre-bed visualisation with my boys since they were very small, a very simple sinking countdown leading to a landscape of dreams which helps transition them to bed and helps my highly strung older son settle. If you keep it simple you can introduce breath meditation (tell them it's what Yoda does...) They will really come to enjoy it. Adding this to lots of time for imaginative play and for quiet time is key here. And importantly, ensure they are getting enough sleep. Sleep is underrated but so important to ensure healthy, grounded and calm kids.

For children aged seven to about twelve we can really begin to introduce more complex forms of grounding, as they have both enough physical control and will find the opportunity to imaginatively construct universes interesting and enjoyable. Many parents and teachers begin guided visualisation and pathworking with children at this point. I strongly recommend using Pete Jenning's book *Pathworking* as he has some super pathworkings and meditations here that can be adapted for children. *Calm Kids* by Lorraine Murray is also an excellent resource.

For kids age twelve-plus we almost have to go back to exercises that help maintain a focus on the body. For young adults, from this point on (and for many much earlier) they are undergoing significant biological change alongside feeling the increased impact of culture of the perception of self. This means that it can be incredibly valuable to teach our pre-teens and tweens strong anchoring and grounding techniques. Bring them back to their body, allow them to feel this positively, and encourage girls and boys to expand their sense of space and self-awareness.

For kids over the age of about eight, we can introduce some of the meditative or trance skills that move beyond the realm of the sensual to that of the cerebral. Contemplation is a great gift and one often overlooked by today's rushing attitude. When we take a ten-year-old to a museum there is the urge to rush around it and see everything. However, when we do this, we do ourselves disservice. We have no time to really look, to really consider what it is we are in the presence of. In times gone by, people on vacation would visit a city and may spend many days in one museum or gallery, considering the work of an artist over a period of time. Today kids are pummelled through as many activities as possible as this is what supposedly equates to having a good time or learning something new; rushing through museums with the sole purpose of filling out worksheets in order to get grades.

Does this encourage young folks to really see, to be able to contemplate something? To allow art to speak to us requires quiet, time, and a non-rushing attitude. It may take multiple visits to gather a feeling or a sense of our opinion about it. Go to a gallery and say, "OK let's find one piece that really speaks to us and let's just sit with it, for the time we are here." Such an attitude is not only reserved for beautiful buildings, museums and galleries, but can also be applied to our kids' relationship with the outdoors.

Older kids really benefit from taking time, from you slowing the pace, turning off the phone and just sitting in a place, observing, contemplating, and being. If you do it, although it may seem strange and at first disconcerting, you will quickly find that they will mirror you. You may also find that these become lasting memories for them. See less, appreciate more.

The Many Mancies

Divination, or the power of the many 'mancies', is the means by which we can use specific tools in order to truly see into the present and future or see the past with a different perspective. From the Latin it literally means "to foresee" and also to be inspired by God. Linked to augury and prophesy, divination requires means that are occult or supernatural in order to uncover hidden knowledge. There are therefore as many divination forms as there are cultures and traditions. All forms of divination grow from cultural and spiritual traditions. Today divination is often psychologized and successfully used to help gain insight and perspective into a specific life issue.

Many of you may be wondering why I have included divination in a book about kids, as divination is one of the most powerful and arguably adult skills in a Pagan's bag of tricks, and not one to be lightly considered. We may not want to teach our kids the full use of tarot cards before they are adults, but divination allows our kids a way of understanding and considering consequences, of growing empathy and compassion and can encourage different perspectives. It can also, if handled well, enhance children's intuitive ability.

An excellent method of developing divination and intuition skills is dowsing. This is a fascinating, simple and often mind-blowing skill that still has very tangible practical applications. I remember watching a team who worked for the electricity company in Boston show up with a van, and out popped a guy who began to walk up and down the street with two bent metal rods. Excitedly I ran out to the front door and exclaimed that he was dowsing.

"Excuse me Ma'am?" he replied, entirely befuddled by my exclamation.

When I asked him what he was doing he told me the rods

showed him where the pipes were laid, and that this is how 'they' knew where the water pipes were in the road. Brilliant! I thought. My kids can actually see that one of mum's hippy things has a macho purpose!

Kids can be exceptionally good at the rod form of dowsing, and it allows them to work on clearing their mind, and can also help them to create maps of their neighbourhood. Get them to walk the street you live on looking for water or gas or energy lines and come home and make a map of these.

Older kids, particularly over the age of about eight or so can also be taught to use a pendulum, which can help find lost objects, answer questions and can be used both seriously and easily.

As with so many trance and simple divination tools that can answer questions, when using these with young kids, it is important not to allow them to be overused. The debate always arises as to whether these 'work' and I am never sure how to answer such questions.

In my 20 years of using various forms of divination I would say my findings have been accurate – often it is my interpretation that has been off, not the message I have been given. Such devices simply tap into our subconscious knowledge and our tiny movements influence the swing of the pendulum. At times, they have been uncannily accurate. If you really want to know whether they work, use them in the way they were meant – to find lost objects, or to trace water lines. In this way our questions should be clear and the answers truly one dimensional. For all other forms of question we have to use more complex methods of divination.

Exercise: Pendulum Dowsing
Find a crystal or holey stone, an old necklace or just about anything that can be attached to a piece of cord or a chain and swing freely. Find the set swing used for yes and no – either hold

the "YES" in your mind and see which way it swings or ask it a question you already know the answer to – for example, "Is my name_____?" for yes, and "Am I a gerbil?" for no!

As a kid of about ten I was utterly fascinated with all forms of fortune telling. I found a huge old second-hand book published in the 1920s about different forms of fortune telling and I ate it up. From phrenology to chirology, to astrology and numerology, the notion that there were patterns everywhere in the world and that if I were attentive to them, they would give me knowledge about my circumstances was utterly enchanting. Despite hating maths at school, I became fascinated with numerology and astrology and began to teach myself the foundations of these forms of divination, looking at numbers everywhere and attempting complex equations to see if I would have a good day or not.

Divination can often imbue older kids with a sense of control over the universe, especially when it seems particularly fraught or changeable. I would generally not advise introducing any structured form of divination to children under the age of about 12, although I have seen some exceptionally gifted children use crystals, numbers and patterned cards at younger ages. Astrology, tarot, and rune reading require a maturity in that more often than not, the reader needs experience of the world to understand what the tool is communicating. However, I do believe that we can teach children basic skills that facilitate some excellent dreamers and diviners later on in teen and adult life. Divination requires moral fortitude, intuition, sometimes simple lateral thinking and sometimes great leaps of faith. It also builds on the foundations for magical work we have already discussed – groundedness, focus, and good listening.

Much of the time divination is in fact an exchange between people; good diviners also need to be good with patterns, good with people and responsive to their environment. Here are some great, simple exercises that can place kids on the path of being sensitive listeners and intuitive individuals, all useful traits irrespective of whether they become diviners or not. I would advise linking your divination practice to certain phases of the moon.

Zener Cards (All Moon Phases)

These are great fun to try and kids can be surprisingly good at it once they have clicked in to the kind of attention it requires. Designed in the 1930s as a means to conduct ESP experiments you start by placing the cards face down and pick a card. Ask your child to guess what shape you are holding or thinking of. With practise you will improve. Zener cards make fun, playful games out of projection and reception. If you don't fancy using Zener cards try numbers or colours.

Aura Reading (Full Moon)

Again this can be excellent fun and a really practical skill, teaching kids sensitivity to energy in people. Show your kids how to hold their hands about three inches away from a person or pet and feel the warmth coming from their body. Then ask them to see if they can detect any changes in temperature or imagine any colours as they move their hand around the person/animal. It can also be fun to sit in a semi-dark room, and you sit against a light coloured wall and ask your child to look towards you with unfocussed eyes. Can they see anything above your head? Do they notice anything?

Candle, Water and Crystal Gazing (Waning/Dark Moon)

This can be hard for some kids, but is particularly good for water kids, and can help to tap into their dream world. For earth kids this can be a challenging form of exercise but one that could be really useful to allow them to quiet their mind and dream awake! In a dark room light a candle, a single flame, or fill a dark bowl with water to the brim. Then, stare into the flame or the water, and see what comes into your mind and if you see anything form on the surface of the water. Tell them it may look like a mist but look closer and see if it makes any shapes.

Dice (All Moon Phases)

These are so much fun. And so underused to my mind. Dice can help teach numbers, maths and choice making. Create or adapt your own key. For example, ask a question and if you throw 1= yes 2= no 3= not yet 4= ask again 5= it has already come to pass 6= it was never meant to be.

Augury (All Phases – Dependent Upon Seasons)

Look for patterns around you – learn the superstitions and folklore of your country, your geography, and your neigh-bourhood. My kids spot magpies wherever we go – 1 for sorrow, 2 for joy, 3 for a girl, 4 for a boy, 5 for silver, 6 for gold, 7 for a secret never to be told. The folklore of your local area can be your guide when it comes to this kind of augury and it can be a doorway to learning about local folk traditions and local and national history.

Dream Work (Best Around Full/Dark Moon)

Build a tradition of telling your dreams every morning, and then when kids are old enough, encourage them to keep a diary or a dream journal and record their dreams. Encourage them to have regular periods of reflection, to go back and look at those dreams and see whether they make sense of anything that was happening at the time or since.

There are, unfortunately, many divination systems so archaic in form and meaning that they are close to useless to us today. Many of these forms are painfully flawed due to the period in which they were used and developed or as a consequence of their initial use. They can be bigoted or prejudicial in many ways – either racist (phrenology for example) or sexist (traditional palmistry). When introducing kids to any of these methods, be conscious of their history, which could be a history of oppression where such spiritual tools were used to maintain power systems and prejudice no longer appropriate.

Different Strokes for Different Folks

Divination often shows us that people do things in very different ways and that all of our experiences are a result of our unique pattern as beings on Mother Earth right now. Difference leads us to consider diversity and diversity is a significant key to living in a viable, sustainable world. Unfortunately though, there is much misunderstanding about the strengths in diversity. Diversity has become a shorthand for evoking racial difference, cultural ignorance and religious intolerance. We often hear diversity referred to when in fact we are unable to say something due to our lack of understanding or knowledge. I heard it used recently in this way when a neighbour was discussing the merits of a local swimming pool. " Oh yes," he said when I asked his opinion about a certain pool, "that one is nice but it has lots of *diversity*."

Now the Pagan community knows difference and diversity very well – there are as many kinds of Paganisms as there are apple trees – Heathenry, Druidry, Wicca (and there are many traditions of Wicca), Witches, practitioners of Asatru, Shamans, Priestesses and Priests of all forms and then all those who consider themselves Pagans without adherence to any particular religious or magical tradition. Getting us to agree on anything can be hard! However, through difference strength can be found. We share basic common values, but we don't have to be, think or practice the same way in order to take shade under the great umbrella of Paganism.

Learning how to give our kids an understanding of the importance of diversity whilst also imbuing them with pride and certainty in their own identity is not a dynamic one can easily 'teach' but is fostered by attitude and environment. The kind of kids your kids hang out with, the everyday influences that sustain them will all be contributing factors to their conception of diversity. Paganism has often held its doors open to people of various colours and creeds, yet it cannot be denied that most contemporary Pagans are mostly white and lower/middle class. We may have to work to find sources of inspiration for the creation of diversity for our kids.

This can be as simple as breaking the gender loop – this has of course become something of a hot topic of late as stories regarding parents choosing to raise their children 'gender neutral' plague the tabloid newspapers and blogosphere as an example of the world turned mad. Whilst I may share the sentiment (on both sides), what is interesting within these debates is how it raises the insecurities of many parents' and children's organisations regarding the role of identity in kids.

I remember the exact week when it seemed that by morphic resonance every four-year-old girl in my sons' preschool became a pink-adorned fairy princess. We can attempt to shelter our kids from such influences and give them different stories to compete, but ultimately this is easier to discuss than to embody. To my mind what is important is not whether our girls dress as pink fairies or our boys want to be savage gun-toting soldiers, or vice versa, but that they recognise that there is a choice, and that the diversity of these choices is respected by the institutions and activities that they engage with. Easier said than done, but we are called to try.

So, if you are or you are close to a non-heterosexual, non-normative, non-nuclear family, letting your urban kids roam, if you let your boys wear flowers and your girls get dirty and shout, if you are an interracial family choosing to adopt, or a Pagan-Christian family, you are embodying diversity from the ground up. For the rest of us, we are going to have to work to model diversity as part of our spirituality and necessary if our culture is not to become stagnant and dull. And if our faith is really ready to stand the test of time then we have to think very hard about the role that social and cultural diversity plays in the forms and functions of our spirituality.

Here we turn to the world to seek sources of inspiration – what does it mean to be female in the animal kingdom? What model of family do we find if we consider Bonobo monkeys, or an ant colony? How does a forest, or a marshland model diversity in its entire imperfect, shifting richness? Pagans and earth path folk have numerous models for embodying diversity as a framework for social organisation and personal identity, for we have the rich variety of the natural world to show us that in every place survival is premised on adaptation and diversity. If we can embody this basis, social justice becomes an imperative.

Exercise (Age 7+): Diversity around us

Consider your local landscape. Do you live within marshland, seashore, forest, woodland or mountains? Take a day trip to explore some of this, and make a note as you walk of all the life you come into contact with whilst you are out. How many types of tree can you name? Can you name them by their bark, their leaf shape, their flowers? How many insects do you find, and can you identify them? How many mammals and species of bird inhabit this area? How do they manage to live together in this landscape?

Come home/back to school and make a visual representation of all the types of life that inhabit your region/local area. Talk about how they live together, how does this area manage to balance all those needs? What role do we have in this landscape?

Chant, Dance and Incantation

Chanting is a simple and powerful path to power and one I have also discussed in the section on singing earlier. Chanting is focused vocalisation; it can be singing, but it can be incantation. It is the weaving of energy using the voice and whereas so many people have concerns over their ability to sing, everyone can learn to chant. So many spiritual traditions have chant as a form of prayer, as a means of contacting the divine that it may seem obvious to you that chanting is a powerful form of magic making and one that we often see our children do unprovoked.

Chanting and incanting are the combination of vocalisation and rhythm, and they stir the deep bloodlines within us. Chants speak of cultural heritage and age, place and self. We hear the power in the echoes of nursery rhymes. Teach your children chants and you give them powerful magical skills – teach them the songs and rhymes of your culture and place but also teach them the chants of magic.

Chants can also be a great thing for kids to learn and compose – a simple two or four-line refrain, with a rhythmic melody, can allow kids of all ages to be spontaneous or more choreographed composers. Teenagers and young adults can be excellent chant makers, creating chants to be both sung and incanted for all kinds of occasions. If there is a special event, such as a rite of passage, or a seasonal event, ask your teen if they would create an ensemble of chants, or a chant and accompanying dance. These can be played by a band or sung by one voice. What is key is repetition. The chant repeats over and over, allowing the energy of words and melody to grow and diminish as befits the occasion. They can often be intoned repeatedly on one note.

Chants To Know

See the wonderful books and CD, *Prana Chants* by the Prana

collective http://www.thatroundhouse.info/music.htm and *Circle of Songs* by Kate Marks for more chant ideas. Listen to the CDs of artists such as Carolyn Hillyer, Libana and the work of the Norwich Chant Collective. Many of these chants have accompanying circle dances, which are super to teach kids and adults. You can check the melody for these in various sources, or make your own tune!

- *Fly like an eagle, souring so high, circling the universe, on wings of pure light...*
- *A circle is cast again and again and again...* (To be intoned on one note)
- *Air I am, fire I am, water, earth and spirit I am...*
- *The dawning of a new day is coming, golden light is flowing all over the earth...*
- *Power, power we are calling, power, power we are calling, come, come, come to us tonight...*
- *This little light of mine, I'm gonna let it shine...* (Oh yes, anything can be transformed into a chant!)
- *Tread gently on the earth, breathe gently of the air, lie softly in the water, touch gently to the fire...* (This is a beautiful chant by Carolyn Hillyer which we often dance a simple circle dance to. See below.)

Music and chanting are great ways of introducing different cultures and languages. But I think it is worth noting that children of whatever culture or geography should have a sense of their own traditions before we glorify others.

Connected to the power of chant is the beauty of dance. For so many of us dancing is a liberating act. Allowing our body to feel the pulse of music whether this is a favourite song, or the mad patter of raindrops in a storm, the stately pax de deux of medieval long dancing or the ecstatic pogo-ing at a rock gig, we can't help ourselves. We need to dance. The urge to match our body to rhythmic sound is utterly primal. We are hard-wired for it.

Just watch a toddler when you turn on Radio One. When the day is cold and cloudy and your kids are driving you crazy because they want to go outside but the weather prohibits it, put some music on and move and watch them laugh at you and join you. You may be amazed at how it can change the mood!

It is also one of the best forms of exercise you and your kids can get and you can do it together. Beyond its remit to be expressive, creative and of course cool, dance is ecstatically social. Most kids can move, in some capacity and therefore everyone can be moved by music. You can do it anywhere and it requires very little. It can be tailored to suit your musical tastes and your personality.

The two forms of dance Pagans enjoy and I think should be central to kids are interpretive dance and folk dancing, or what used to be called country dancing. Unlike so many classical forms of dance, which are wonderful and I would strongly encourage (especially as one of my sons has studied ballet since he was very little) folk dancing and interpretive dancing cost little and are open to all.

Circle dancing is a great example of where folk dancing and spiritual dance meets and it's an excellent form of dance for teaching spatial awareness. It is also a way to embed the circle as the model for co-operation, continuity and energy movement. I can think of so many public rituals that would have been so much better with adults who had a little knowledge of circle dance. Circle dancers are also generally very open people, welcoming to Pagan folk and kids alike. You can also learn them yourself, as they are mostly simple and easily directed.

Country dancing as it used to be called when I was at school, or folk dances are the traditional dances of your place. In the UK it is the dance traditions of England, Scotland and Wales often danced in circles, with partners. Molly dancing, broom dances, sword dances, clogging and of course Morris dancing, with its bells and sticks, are all folk dances from across the UK. Likewise in Europe and the United States there are rich and varied folk dance traditions very much alive and kicking. Although I remember us 'taking the mick' out of country-dance class when we were at school. We all got to dance every day during primary and middle school. And every year during the school summer fair, we got to show our parents how great we were.

Traditional dancing can be a way of opening up our kids to local and national stories and different traditions and cultures. Sacred circle dance does this by teaching dances from all over the world, some ancient some very much still used. Little did I know how useful it would be until I went to an Albanian wedding, where I actually knew some of the dances!

Likewise, dances are a language in many countries, they are a part of national and cultural identity, so to know the dances of your own country and those of the country you are visiting can be a way of communicating beyond words in places or spaces that may otherwise feel foreign. Dance allows us to connect with others in an open and uncomplicated way, allowing boundaries to break down and joy to creep in.

Children can dance as soon as they are in the world. My eldest boy had his first experience of communal circle dancing when I took him to the annual Pow Wow at Harvard, in celebration of the university's long-standing relationship with the First Nation peoples. Dancing a simple greeting dance, holding my baby, amongst 150 people in a shady green just five minutes from the bustle of Harvard Square was a wondrous experience. Watching Summer's awe as he felt the big drum reverberate through his body as we danced was inspiring. When he turned four and wanted a fairy party, I taught a simple circle dance to his friends, which years later they still recall as a demonstration of the 'authentic' nature of the fairy party!

Dancing teaches us the twofold consciousness of opening

ourselves to the dance and disciplining our body to move in rhythm. When we dance a Maypole, for example, we are not only opening ourselves to the vibrant forces of the fecund earth, we also have to contain it, focus it with the discipline of each step each turn of the ribbon, each under and over. As the dancers step across time and space, between youth and maturity, they connect to the ancient forces in the universe and lend their energy to the tides that move us from one season into another.

Dances to do with kids

Basic circle dance

All hold hands, form a circle, have someone start a drumbeat or a chant – rhythm is important to maintaining movement in any kind of circle dance. Start with a slow walk and then try to have everyone skip around the circle. Here is a dance that we constructed for Tread Gently on the Earth on the album *House of the Weavers* by Carolyn Hillyer:

- Take hands in the circle. Walk for eight beats to the right. *"Tread gently on the earth."*
- Stop, break hands and everyone take a slow little circle on the spot, as if doing a twirl in slow motion to the count of eight. *"Breathe gently of the air."*
- Then take hands again, and sway gently side to side for eight counts. *"Lie softly in the water."*
- Drop hands and all move into the centre of the circle for four counts and back to your original places for four counts. *"Touch gently to the fire."*
- Repeat!

Maypole Dances

There are so many wonderful dances to choose from, and we should all know how to lead one or two of these in our community. They take work and practise, many of them, but are worth doing, as the weaving ribbon they create can be kept to bless the school/community group all year! The single and the double plait, the Spider's Dance, The Barber's Pole, Gypsy's Tent, Jacob's Ladder, circling (very good for very little ones). A simple dance where the even numbered dancers travel clockwise and raise their ribbon to go over the ribbons travelling towards them and the odd numbered dancers travel anticlockwise and duck under the ribbons travelling towards them can be done by young and old dancers alike with little preamble.

Procession/Parade

A simple step together, step together (step forward with the right foot, left foot joins, left foot steps forward right foot joins) in a parade can be a wonderful way to open a ritual or to go about cleansing or blessing a place when there is a group of you. It can give an occasion a sense of ceremony and a stately air and everyone can join in.

Spiral Dance

Here the emphasis is not on the steps so much as creating a collective pattern, that can move us from one phase to another, from one season to another, from the everyday world to the space between the worlds. To do this in a group of kids can be incredibly healing and perfect to mark a transition such as the end-of-year school party, to a rite of passage for a young person. The main pointers are, whoever is dancing MUST NOT break hands with those on either side. The spiral leader must set a pace everyone can follow and must know where s/he is going:

- Holding hands in a circle, the leader breaks the left hand hold and moves on the inside of the circle, travelling to the left.
- When the spiral becomes tight and the centre becomes too

close to sustain or continue, the spiral leader simply turns direction and goes back on herself, and starts travelling.

- This way the spiral unwinds.
- When it has completely unwound you will see the end person head towards that and reform making a circle once more.

Spirituality and School

Dealing with difference in a school environment can be one of the biggest challenges we face as Pagan parents and educationalists. Many Pagan parents choose to circumnavigate the issue and homeschool kids in order to offer an education that is markedly different both in form and content. Many choose to homeschool in order to place a Pagan worldview in the centre of learning. Others choose it in order to not have their kids exposed to the difficulties of 'fitting in'.

In the UK religious education is a part of the National Curriculum and as such woven into the fabric of school life. Current legislation in British law requires all state schools to hold assemblies that include an act of collective worship. Every state school is currently required to provide a daily act of worship arranged by the head teacher and it must be wholly or mainly of a broadly Christian character. Only 51 per cent need be identifiably Christian with the remaining 49 per cent reflecting other faiths or interests over the course of a year. It is clear that whether or not we want to acknowledge it, Christian discourse is the dominant religious voice in schools across Britain.

How your child's school manages this provision varies hugely and it could be that your child goes to a school where the focus is on values and principles of good living. However, it could also be that you end up in school where the influence of Christianity is much more heavy-handed. The issues with Faith Schools and faith-based Free Schools are too numerous to mention here, but many Pagans, parents and teachers have legitimate worries regarding the faith-based admissions policies of such schools. Questions of fair access and ensuring these schools are representative of Britain as a whole society, are also under scrutiny. Surely the primary role of state-funded education is to prepare children for the world they are going into as adults? Finding the right school for your kids is a hard decision and when house prices are exorbitant in areas with good or outstanding schools, it is not surprising that many parents find themselves attending church in order to get their kids a good education.

Importantly, by law parents can withdraw children from religious education and religious assemblies. I have spoken to Pagan parents who have chosen to withdraw their children, or who have allowed their children to attend or who have little feeling one way or another. Many changed their approach dependent on the age of their kids or the emphasis of their child's teacher. You might be concerned that your kids will be the target of bullying or will feel or be left out if they are absent – often assemblies are times when school notices are handed out.

However, if you are uncomfortable with your child being present, it is the school administration's responsibility to ensure your child has access to the information they need and is not penalised by the choice to remove them. My sons are the only children who do not attend religious assembly in their school, and proudly remind their head teacher that they are not to attend. They spend that time doing extra reading or quiet work, so the time is not wasted.

For me the question is that I didn't want them to learn the mechanisms of Christian myth and practice as 'the norm'. I also knew that our head teacher was openly Christian, which helped me come to that decision, as I understood she would strongly emphasise Christian content. My greatest concern was that my children might feel polarised between home and school, that if they came home telling me all that they had heard in assembly I would spend my time making connections with our beliefs and practices or challenging what they learnt/heard in school. I didn't want them to feel placed in the middle of a complex philosophical debate with the school!

The school nativity play is a great example. Due to our experiences as homeschoolers in the USA, they had no knowledge of Jesus and the story of the nativity. When they were introduced to the Christmas story in their first year of British schooling they were uncertain as to whether they wanted to be a part of it (yes, you can ask to have your child withdrawn if you wish). I was torn between knowing that this is (unfortunately) the culmination of the school year and an opportunity for parents to watch their kids perform. They chose to be part of it, and spent their time trying to understand where the nativity took place, and why there were rabbits present and why all the angels were girls. They would attempt to explain how Jesus is another sun God, returned to us like the real sun at Yule. Sadly their questions, observation and connections fell on deaf ears. Unfortunately for them the whole story seemed a charade and lacked the mythic resonance I am sure it is meant to have. The lesson I learnt was how important it is to know the approach of your school. Ask the tough questions so that you know exactly what is taking place in assembly and in the classroom. Go into the school and ask for outlines, take it seriously.

In terms of the provision for religious education, the focus should be on learning about religious traditions, not learning how to do them, but you may find, as I have that the curriculum and approach can be skewed and interpreted in various ways. And Gods forbid Paganism is even mentioned in the context of RE in primary or middle schooling! Consider the outrage recently in the British Press when the Cornish director of education said it 'might' introduce Paganism to the teaching of Cornish history and religious belief (http://www.bbc.co.uk/news/uk-england-cornwall-17804422. Accessed 28/08/13).

If you are lucky to live in a diverse neighbourhood and your child goes to a school where many faiths are represented you have a greater chance to be involved in the curriculum. In England, the RE syllabus is locally agreed. If you can, contact your local SACRE chapter and find out if there is a Pagan voice within your area, and ask to see the Agreed Syllabus for Religious Education for your area.. NASACRE is the national body made up of SACRE chapters, Standing Advisory Councils on Religious Education who report and design schools' RE provision across an area. If your chapter does not have a Pagan representative, why not offer to get involved? If they do have a Pagan representative, ask how you can help. Having a say in such organisations can teach us how RE syllabuses are designed and implemented and although it is unlikely that you will get them to include Paganism on the curriculum, you can certainly add your view to discussion on experiential learning models, ethics and morals and the importance of interfaith. On a local level, offer to go into schools to talk about Pagan festivals. I have known many Pagans, parents or not, to go in at times of sabbat celebrations and talk about our traditions and festivities.

In a British village or town school the default is often to suggest that Christianity is the dominant religious model and all else is what "other people do". When I opened a discussion about this at my local Pagan Family Meet Up, I was struck by one father's insightful statement. "In my kids' schools," he said, "it's not just that Christianity is the main religion taught, it's the emphasis on all the other religious traditions being exactly that – others. Paganism hasn't got a chance whilst all the other major faiths are the alternative to Christianity."

In the village I live in, after I had berated the narrowness of religious perspectives covered in RE, one parent told me there wasn't much point teaching the kids about Islam, because there weren't any Muslims in the village. It is worrisome to think that we leave the content of RE so unexamined and underestimate the influence of RE in school to such an extent. Other parents have used the argument that kids don't really believe what they are taught in RE anyway, that it's a soft subject and therefore its content isn't taken seriously by kids. One of my husband's colleagues opened this line of argument regarding his kids in RE, and how it wasn't "that bad" and eventually went on to explain how he had to educate his kids that the Christian creation story wasn't actually how the world was made – that it was a story. Creationism may not be taught directly in schools, but it is a dominant story. It requires vigilance and knowledge to ensure that the emphasis is not on one faith to the exclusion or "othering" of all others.

If you feel that your spirituality is neglected in the context of school look at how the school deals with diversity and difference more generally before considering yourself maligned on the basis of your spiritual views. You may be the first and only Pagan family the school has met, so you bear the burden of representation. In all dealings with schools, open, honest and thoughtful engagement is the best policy. Educate yourself on current issues and look at organisations that are actively working to illuminate the challenges of teaching RE (see the Further Reading section at the end of this book). Then educate the school administration about Paganism, point them to national bodies such as the Pagan Federation, and to simple introductory books that may outline Paganism in a way that gives them a good overview of our beliefs rather than a 'how to be a Pagan' book.

Take time to talk openly to teachers and head teachers about your spirituality, and whilst you may not receive a warm welcome you may find that a surprising number of other parents come to talk to you about their own approach to religion and faith in school. The debates regarding faith schools in Britain open some troublesome issues. They are often high achieving schools, and as such parents find them desirable as they are state funded (an issue for a longer discussion); all self-selecting schools rank higher in national tables than open state schools.

Religion and education are clearly tied to social class and academic success, whether we want to admit it or not. The question is, what can we do to ensure that our kids are represented, included and not victims of discrimination or objects of fun? We cannot sit on the sidelines and expect that our kids will work out these discrepancies for themselves. Likewise we cannot expect our kids to keep quiet about their own beliefs. Despite the variety of paths within Paganism, despite the ways in which the Pagan community is a living representation of the diversity we so admire, we can find areas of commonality and not let others dictate the provision of religious education to our children. Get involved and let's add our voices to the mix.

Know Thyself

The keys to knowing who you are, are knowing the history of the land you are from, knowing the history of the land you are in and knowing your place in the world.
Bonnie

What does it mean to know yourself? For most of us, this is a life's work. Being in relationship with little folks adds new depth to this question. There is suddenly an imperative to know ourselves when we are faced with the charges of small ones. For our kids, allowing them to explore who they are is as crucial to their understanding of the world as breathing is. To give our children a fighting chance to change the world they must first know who they are and in order to do this it naturally follows that they must be allowed to understand where they come from and where they are.

As a Brit, married to a proud Scotsman, but having boys born and raised in America, I have worked hard to maintain a connection to the rich cultures of our homelands, whilst trying hard not to exclude them from the land they were born into.

When we lived in the USA we regularly travelled back to the UK and travelled all over; from Edinburgh in Scotland to South Wales and the West of England, and on to the East of England where my family still live. For me these journeys and the drama that accompanies any trip home was balanced in part against the need to expose my kids to the culture of their family – not just to see their family, but to give them the opportunity to 'be' in my culture of origin.

Since they were babies, I have found that telling them family stories or family histories dressed up as tall tales has been a source of wonder and amusement to them. Hearing of when mum and dad were little and the family that stands behind us has been one of the primary ways I have been able to propose large concepts; death, lineage, ancestors and the Gods. Bringing histories and family traditions to life gives us an understanding of where we come from and allows us to see the good in what may be very difficult, ambiguous or painful recollections. As guardians we get to choose how to frame such experiences. If we are parents of foster or adoptive children this can be challenging but also freeing. As we learn alongside the child about their country of origin, we have many strands of family to choose to explore.

If you come from a land or a family that has in some ways been ravaged or destroyed, this can be a hard process indeed, a painful one to expose our children to, but everyone has a pathway into their history that can show courage, triumph, humour. Start here and see what comes.

Once you have a grip on exploring your family history, you can allow your children to push this exploration to their community. To know themselves, children will enjoy learning the stories and histories of their local area. Talk to neighbours, go to local sights of interest, learn the names of the trees, the flora and the fauna that bring shade to your garden or rashes to your shins. Is there a dark mystery to the neighbourhood? Children love this form of investigative work, and many a happy day can be spent researching the supposed haunted house, or dark and shady woodland. Know what your locale is known for and allow yourself to get involved as your kids do. If they see that this is information you value, they are likely to value it too – at least until they are teens!

Once you have focused on the local area, with older children, particularly, you can facilitate knowing the nation you live in. Cultural and national identity is something of a problematic discourse at this particular historical junction. For many of us, national pride is uncomfortably mixed with notions of xenophobia and nationalism. Being English in the main, I find the binarism of xenophobic vs. apologist tiresome and reductive. It is possible to be proud of your national cultural identity whilst seeing its flaws, and part of knowing ourselves is knowing what our culture's strengths and weaknesses are, of understanding that a nation, a culture is a changing thing. The dynamics of Britain's historical colonialisation are still living today, and unfortunately we are still dealing with the consequences on a global scale. However, this is also a nation that prizes humility and rain and misery, it is a nation of nations with a rich and diverse history. I encourage you to allow your children to understand their cultural identity beyond 'celebrationism' or the politics of cultural guilt, but instead see themselves as living manifestations of agents of change.

When my husband talks about his very mainstream, comprehensive schooling in Edinburgh in the 1980s he describes an education where every academic subject was infused with an understanding of Scottish cultural identity. The education system had developed to actively make Scottish history and identity a part of educational life. Pakistani, West Indian and Celtic families were all cognisant of what being in Scotland, what being Scottish meant, in all its colours. Growing up in England I had a different experience and yet, there were glimpses of such an understanding of the importance of cultural foundations in education, such as the country dancing, the morning assembly songs we sung and the storytellers that visited on high holidays.

Such an education roots children to the identity of their geography. This is not to deny the centrality of their family origin, their cultural or religious foundations, but to allow kids to experience themselves they must be given a sense of where they live. When we replace where we are with a multicultural focus, we lose something, we risk losing the nuances and depths of all cultures within our place. 'Celebrationism' in education and wider culture more generally studies all cultures by their festivities. Consequently our understanding of Buddhism or Hinduism for example may be limited to special holidays, and certain key figures. Although an important part of our teaching cultural diversity, often the wholesome nature of such rich traditions is reduced to surface knowledge.

Anchoring children to the land they are in, rooting them to where they are, does not disavow the project of multiculturalism, which is to celebrate diversity, but embraces it as part of the rich diversity of the land we live in, of its colours, its textures, its histories and peoples. If we anchor our children to the place we are in, we begin the journey into stewardship, connection and pride for the land, and we can begin to show the responsibility we place in their hands. We can promote guardianship of a place and all who dwell within it.

What does it mean to belong? From the time my kids were born we very consciously promoted their identity as Anglo-Scots-American. I know that in part this seems a uniquely American description yet it positively locates them in family, history and place. Summer understands that this composite identity uniquely marks his 'difference' and gives us a way of exploring our family landscapes and history in meaningful ways. We have tried to foster the distinctions between these places and their cultures that go beyond the obvious of accents and foods and the likes.

270

If you are living in your hometown surrounded by your family, and the history of your family, you are uniquely placed. You are surrounded by memories, stories, celebrations. The passage of time, the transitions of family life, are held by all those around you. If, however, this is not your story then you may have to get really creative. If you are beginning this exploration with older kids or teens, this journey into 'heritage' and belonging may be a mutual exploration, and a way of connecting with your kid.

You can steer the kind of exploration towards your kid's likes and strengths. If you have a kid obsessed with war games, find out if any of your family members fought in the great wars, personalise this for them, go to the library, contact old regiments, be a detective in uncovering your family history.

Find local heroes and heroines. Living in Norfolk, England was a little too easy on this front, as stories of pioneering women such as Boudicca and Edith Cavell abound. You may be surprised at what you uncover if you give yourself the task of finding those people and events, energies that connect you to who and where you are in the world. At a time of emphasis on celebrity culture, where to be interesting and special requires money, looks and the machinery of mainstream media behind you, such explorations can give our kids another way of perceiving their unique individuality.

Landscape is inextricably linked to human communities. Where we lived in Boston there were as many Spanish speakers as English, and despite our shocking lack of Spanish language skills it was important to our understanding of this place to recognise the culture of this community in all its diversity. As is often the case in strongly Spanish speaking neighbourhoods, there was a strong Catholic community presence. Despite my personal animosity towards much in the Catholic Church, my maternal grandfather was Irish Catholic. I integrated this neighbourhood into stories about my grandfather's youth, retold now to the point of mythologizing his harsh Jesuit education. So, my kids and I frequently went into the church and chatted to the priests, (who are subsequently, no longer referred to by my kids as "the men in brown dresses"!) and appreciated the workmen's diligence as they cleaned the church façade.

And when we went into the church, I watched the grandeur and peace of the place bring them to a moment of quiet and stillness inside its cool blue walls. Just watching them transition from boisterous boys to poised quiet kids I see the value of this exposure. This is a magical part of their neighbourhood, connected through story to their dead great-grandfather, and a part of their experience of self, home and family. In such ways we show our kids that knowing themselves, knowing who they are, is interconnected to what is around and within us.

"Be Brave" – Encouraging Gallantry as the Model of Strength

Encouraging our kids to know themselves is easy when they are young, when they look to us as the font of all wisdom and constraint. When they enter the tricky territory of tween-dom or teens, when sometimes just having to talk to them can be explosive, this can be a much harder (if more necessary) activity. Often adults describe to me how their once intuitive, confident and thoughtful child becomes insecure, precocious, tired, defiant, or falls prey to one of the numerous emotional and psychic diseases that plague our young in transition. Here, ritual, meditation and rites of passage can be literally life-saving.

Visible and invisible signs of transition need to be attended to and often kids at this point want more independence, separation or alone time as they replace adult identification with peers. However, continuity, rhythm and support are crucial during these times. It is all too easy to think as a caregiver that our kids' need for more separateness means that the rhythms of our family life are outdated. The key is balance, it lies in ensuring daily family rhythms are still in place whilst acknowledging that your kid may need to redefine these.

A focal point I have found particularly useful in working with kids at transition points in their lives is to encourage them to be brave – to really contemplate upon what courage and bravery mean. In times gone by we would have sent them on a quest, a dreamtime, a vision quest. Their courage would have been outwardly tested and rewarded as a sign of their maturity and growth. Young folk would have gone inside to contact the divine within, or look to have an encounter with the Goddess or Gods of their culture through sacred exercise and devotion.

Through such encounters, the family and clan would have acknowledged their coming of age. These celebrations of biological change; first menstruation, voice breaking, maidenhood and warrior-ing, were our doorways into divine intention and adult life. But for many of our youth such physical transitions no longer resonate as authentic and defining rites of passage. Instead we have rites of passage that reference external achievements: school graduation, driving a car, legally being able to drink or make love. These are valuable and celebratory moments, but they are not rites of passage in that they commend you to a new life stage in all its fullness. These new transitions rarely have the touch of the Gods.

Coming to adulthood is a stepping up. It is marked in part by letting go of our childhood identity and coming to a place of true independence, where you recognise that you are your own person, connected and in relationship with others, but ultimately in command of yourself. This kind of stepping up means that in coming to adulthood we look ahead to a life of necessary bravery.

Taking on the mantle of true independence requires a strength of spirit and courage that deserves recognition. It also requires a letting go, an acknowledgement that not all things are within your control. Some of our future is literally in the hands of the Goddess. Am I advocating our kids to go sit in a cave without food or drink for three days in search of a vision? Well, maybe! Think back for a moment, remember what you thought it would be like to be an adult when you were a child. My kids express this daydreaming in fantastical terms; "When I am a grown up, I will eat ice cream every day", "I will go to bed when it's midnight!", "I will tell everyone else what to do!" If only adulthood were really this freeing! Often, teens on the cusp of the transition into adulthood balk at the gateway because they know it is going to be hard, they know through uncanny instinct that adulthood is not their child self's dream. Focus on what values adulthood requires:

B: **Benevolence**. Move ahead with a helpful and generous attitude. Act out of kindness.

R: **Respect**. Show thoughtfulness in your actions and appropriate deference and honour to your elders, your teachers, your friends and your Gods and Goddesses.

A: **Activism**. You need vigorous action in pursuing your goals. Speak up and act on behalf of the things you believe in.

V: **Value**. Understand your true worth, and to know what it is that you value, that you esteem and act in accordance with that.

E: **Equanimity**. Always seek balance, contentment and harmony within.

With our older kids, being brave has become synonymous with being strong, and often this is conflated with certain modes of power: aggression, persuasion, allure, wealth. Bravery is so necessary in contemporary culture as we battle some of the greatest challenges to society, global sustainability, and personal happiness. In this model of bravery, taken in part from the older notion of gallantry and chivalry, we encourage adult personal

274

behaviour that roots us to principles of stewardship. In caring for ourselves, we care for others, and likewise in caring for others we foster balance in our lives.

How can we put this into practice? Begin with the stories that inspire you. Start closest to home with the stories of family members who acted from a place of bravery, then problem solve with these foci in mind, perhaps each day discuss what you did today that fostered such bravery.

This can also be a great reminder for us as caregivers of young adults, as they can require intense amounts of bravery! What can we learn from this approach to our kids, how can these principles help us navigate our behaviour differently? Consider the exercise below as a way of touching base with your own moments of bravery as a tween or teen, and what you would want to offer yourself as a young adult today.

Exercise: Remembering Your Bravery (For Adults)

Ground yourself, deepen your breathing, take ten deep slow breaths and go into a light trance... In your mind's eye, find yourself in a corridor. Along this corridor are a series of doors that are moving you back in time, across the trajectory of your life, as you walk along the corridor look at the doors, see various life ages and stages as you pass them...

You are moving towards your teen years, and a door seems to be compelling you to open it. This door leads to a memory of a time where you felt you needed a strongly guiding hand, when you needed to be brave. Perhaps you were brave here, and it changed the direction of your family or friendship circles. Perhaps someone strongly advocated on your behalf, they were brave for you...

Walk through the door and see yourself at this life point.... What are you doing? How are you feeling? What would you want to say to yourself? What would your younger self say to you now? Be gentle with your younger self... What is it your younger self most needs at this point? Give your younger self a gift; thank them for their insight. Bless their journey onwards...

Come out of the door behind you, back into the corridor. It is time to leave now, but know you can return to this place whenever you need insight and knowledge...

Count yourself up out of trance. Allow your breathing to return to everyday breathing. Write your experiences down.

All Acts of Love and Pleasure

Transitioning into adulthood also comes with the heady knowledge of sexuality – this is the time when our adult sexual identity is blooming. Sexuality is a natural expression of selfhood. However, it can be difficult to maintain a positive and encouraging explorative attitude towards burgeoning sexuality when our youth are bombarded with contrary messages from mainstream culture.

Recent developments in child safeguarding have made discussions of child sexuality fraught. The fact that there are people grooming children online, that child pornography is frighteningly prevalent and that child abuse is finding new outlets due in part to new technologies, is something we should all be aware of. Paganism abhors all forms of child abuse. The abuse of power is unacceptable within our community and anyone who for whatever reason uses their spirituality as a mask for abuse should be reported immediately.

Much has been written and spoken about regarding the need for adults to speak openly and honestly about sexuality with kids and to try to counterbalance the kind of sexuality that mainstream culture esteems. We need to be frank with our kids from the get go about what they could be exposed to and how they can stay safe and advocate for themselves.

Knowing how to say no, how to stay safe and keeping safe sexual practice are crucial parts of your older child's education. You never know when they may need it. The key is of course openness – to foster dialogue. As a guardian you cannot possibly compete with the allure of sexual experimentation. All you can do is ensure that you stay relevant to your young ones. You don't have to prompt or promote them, but making it safe for them to talk builds trust.

Pagan sexual morals are notably different to mainstream religious teachings on the subject. For some members of the Pagan population our model of sacred sexuality, "All acts of love and pleasure are my rituals", means that sexual identity is fluid.

Many Pagans consider bisexuality the norm and queer identity is generally included and accepted. Even in the most rigid balance-based traditions of Paganism (those that see the male/female balance as crucial to worldly well-being), there is a respect for the sexual self – sexual expression is at the heart of nature's generative powers. And if nature is the model for our spirituality then it acknowledges that there are multitudinous patterns through which the world creates itself. Sexuality is not defined by the gender of a person. Fertility is at the root of a Pagan understanding of sexuality and sensuality as Druid leader and writer Emma Restall-Orr states. Paganism honours the fecund earth's generative and decaying life cycles. She writes:

> [Yet] all Pagans are attentive to everything that inspires and nurtures creativity, working to free the soul of all that blocks creative expression [...] Fertility flowing naturally upon the currents of the Gods is most powerfully achieved when there is pleasure. So does the spiritual focus move to sensuality, sexuality and the exquisite experience of deep relationship. (*Living with Honor* p.51)

Whether you practice monogamy, polyamory or celibacy, whether you are gay, lesbian, transsexual or straight, fertility as creativity and pleasure are key principles of a Pagan attitude to sexuality. I would add that reciprocity and respect are guiding principles when it comes to sexuality within Pagan spirituality. We cannot come to another person to experience pleasure if we do not know how to be respectful towards others and ourselves.

I watched with fascination when my then two-year-old youngest son discovered the pleasures of the sensual world. He loved to roll in mud, to walk barefoot in the rain. In fact when a giant rainstorm arrived, he would strip and go running in it with glee and delight. Self-pleasure comes from allowing kids freedom of experience, and it is a natural part of kids' creative expression. In a culture that seeks to associate children's nakedness as a site of anxiety – projecting onto them the fears of adult lust – we run the risk of denying our children the basic right to be themselves freely.

In the growth of identity, children need to be allowed to explore the sensual world, and to do so without shame, reprimand or guilt. The simplest way to do this is facilitating and encouraging our kids' awareness of their body's needs and appetites. Appetites, our desires, our appreciation and needs are significant in helping kids come to a grounded sense of the power and reverence of their whole identity. This starts when they are babies, intricately connected to the mother's body: baby wearing, nursing, wearing natural fibres, and allowing our children time to be naked. By expressing and fostering affection – whether your children as they get older find it embarrassing (most probably) or annoying (definitely) – we teach them that affection is a natural part of forming and bonding relationships.

Self-pleasuring is an instinctive urge in children and is one of the greatest sources of comforts the Goddess has bestowed upon us. Self-pleasuring starts in infancy and is our introduction to our uniquely personal sexuality. It can bring great comfort, healing, energy, rest and eroticism. It is both natural and necessary if we want to learn our body's likes and dislikes. Whilst I am not suggesting you make masturbation a part of mealtime discussion, acknowledge that this is a natural, personal activity, a normal and healthy expression.

The hetero-normativity of 20th-century culture is slowly eroding, as more and more people deny the restrictive labels of sexual identity. Sexuality is slowly becoming less about gender and more about love and desire. Our sexuality can rarely be directed by our mind; Eros is rarely tamed by logos. Desire comes in many forms, and at times our sexual expression reflects the shifting patterns of our desire.

Our older kids may find that all kinds of people are the objects of their desire and it need not 'define' their sexuality. Your 15-year-old son may 'crush' on his gym teacher, or if you stumble upon your 12-year-old daughter and her best friend making out, do you put this down to them being gay or dismiss it as experimentation? Perhaps we can see these as all natural extensions of children coming into their acknowledgement of their sexuality and the force of their desire. To whom it is aimed is important, but their gender less so.

Allow for the spirit of Eros to freely range and encourage choices based on their desire to share themselves, rather than desire for acceptance into a secret club or to show prowess.

Children and young adults have drives towards the essentially sensual nature of being in their own skin, in seeing beauty in the rawness of nature. As Starhawk so famously describes in her polemic on sex, magic and power *Dreaming the Dark:*

> [...] through our sexuality we can again connect to the realm of deep feeling we touched as children through our mothers. So the deep forces of life and death, which manifest in mothering and in our development of a sense of ourselves as separate, autonomous beings, also manifests in sexuality. (p. 138)

To allow our children to live in the sensual world for as long as possible ensures their spirits are enlivened to the force of raw nature. In homes where physical affection and the joy of the body are restrained or, conversely, without appropriate boundaries, children's relationship with their desire and their own physical nature doesn't thrive. These kids are those likely to struggle later with body dimorphisms, affection problems within relationships or their own sexual identity.

If you are part of a non-traditional family in our culture, you may feel that the expression of the erotic is more heavily policed than it may be within normative hetero families. Look to nature. It is necessary for all of us to recognise that no singular model of relationship is correct. Just as the natural world presents us with different matrices of love, so do our cherished human communities. Above all else, love the body you are in and encourage your kids to accept and love their own.

Exercise: Blessing the Body's Sacred Sexuality (Transitions)

In traditional Wiccan ritual, the five-fold blessing is given to a priestess or priest as they are honoured as the vessel or embodiment (dependent on tradition) of the God and Goddess. Five points of the body are sanctified and affirmed as holy. This is a beautiful and intimate ritual in itself, to be used for adults or older teens in initiations, coming of age rites, conception rites and many others. You can use this to bless a newly pregnant friend or spouse, during a coming of age ritual or an end of life rite.

Although traditionally done by priestess to priest, or priest to priestess, I have found that irrespective of gender, this is a powerful blessing, and below is a version appropriate to use with your (uninitiated) charges during coming of age ceremonies. After each spoken blessing you can anoint the area or place your hands flat on or above that part of the body. The core is the lower abdomen or dan tien. By anointing we affirm, you are the divine, you are part of the flow of life. It is a powerful ritual, to show that the divine dwells not outside us, but within us.

Blessed be your feet, that walk the ancient ways...
Blessed be your knees, that kneel only in honour...
Blessed is your core, from which creation springs forth...
Blessed is your chest, formed in strength and beauty...
Blessed are your lips, which utter words of power...

Bestowing Blessings – The Art of Making Sacred Wishes.

Teaching our kids how to bless is such a beautiful and empowering skill. When Pagans bless something, we amplify its spirit; we illuminate its inherent connection to the generative force of the universe. The act of giving blessing transforms it from mundane to sacred. "Bless you," we say, meaning, "May you be well, may things go well for you". Sometimes we say, "Blessed be," a phrase in Pagan circles which communicates, be sacred, be aware of how you are sacred. I am a big believer in daily blessings. Unlike other forms of sanctifying (consecrations or purifications for example) blessing is a way of allowing our children a particular agency, a sense of their own sacred power. It is akin to the magic they see on TV or in fairy tales; it is a wand-waving sort of magic! Give them the language of blessings and you will find it weaving into much of their play and their daily life. My kids have loved giving blessings, watching them move to a place of solemn calm before the pronouncement of a blessing, but also creating crazy spontaneous blessings is a great source of pleasure to me as a parent! Blessing a garden before planting, or for my youngest, blessing an ant accidentally squashed with the pushchair, there are hundreds of opportunities every day. Remind our kids of the blessings we do in our culture – singing "Happy Birthday" is a blessing we all know!

A close cousin to blessing is, of course, prayer and as a spiritual practice, prayer, much like meditation or visualisation, can be a calming and comforting discipline. Some Pagans have a problem with the notion of prayer, as the language of it is so founded upon the monotheistic, Abrahamic conception of universal power and the hierarchy of intercession. In all these rich and glorious spiritualities, prayer is a means to talk to God, it can be a petition ("Please God, if I say a hundred Hail Mary's really well, make Sarah love me"), or entreaty ("Please, please, please make Sarah love me!!"), or recognition of submission ("Oh God I am lowly and an unworthy worm, but please could you make it possible for Sarah to just simply look at my shameful visage today?")

We can reclaim the powerful practice of prayer. In order to do so we need to be clear about how we can harness this ancient art. Think about prayer as a means of building a very personal relationship to the divine. If your spiritual worldview does not include a deity, are you left with the possibility of praying to graven images? Prayer is natural magic, akin to invocations. It is a way of calling in or attuning ourselves to the great turning of the world, a means by which we can clear our minds and state our desires.

Would it help if we changed the word from prayer to invocation? Witches invoke and incant, yes, and incantation is the repetitive chanting of words to bring about a desired effect – incantations are the weaving of a spell. Much like prayer we can use invocation to petition a specific Goddess to help or aid us. Or we can simply ask the elements – elemental prayers are wonderful experiences. They are simple and yet tangible to children of all ages.

Here are four very different forms of prayers and invocations, which all closely resemble spells in part. They are written in different tones, from the very formal to the informal. Try some out, use these as a template, or invite your older kids to write their own.

Prayer for Strength (Earth)

Build a stone tower, using found stones, or construct one out of Lego, or wooden blocks. As you build imagine it tall and strong.

Say: *"Like this tower may I be filled with the strength of earth, firmly rooted, solidly built, sturdy in every way."*

Prayer for Healing (All Elements/Deity of Your Choice)

Place a bowl of clean cold water before you, hum a quiet tune, reminding the water of the sea it came from, of the rain it has once been. Into your humming consider what needs to be healed, bring the person or place, or object to mind. Continue to look into the water, hum, visualise and, when you are ready, in your own words ask the water to take your wish out into the world. Place it back into some form of running water – stream, toilet, garden...

Invocation for Forgiveness (Goddess of Water – Isis/Yemaya/Ran)

Say: *"To the Mother of water, gentle rain that falls, to the fierce storm that rolls, to the mist that rises I grieve at my wrong doing* [state here what it was that has caused you to need forgiveness – hurting a friend, dishonesty, cheating etc.]. *I ask you to hear my apology, my heartfelt sadness at my behaviour, and I ask you soothe my soreness with your cleansing nature. Spirit of water, force of nature, grant me forgiveness. Blessed* Be."

Invocation for Wisdom (Earth Element)

At night go outside and sit on the ground. Take with you bread and salt. If this isn't possible, remain inside and find a crystal of your choice, to hold or place in front of you.

Close your eyes and state: *"Guardians of the watchtowers of the North, great powers of Earth, all those that dwell in the dark and warm places, gnomes, dwarves, spirits of trees, those who are as old and knowing as the rocks and mountains. I call to you, and ask that you bestow upon me a taste of your aged wisdom, that I may* [fill in specific request here]. *I offer you bread to nourish you, and salt to preserve and keep you always. Guardians of earth I thank you. Hail and farewell!"*

Place the bread and salt somewhere discreet, under a tree or upon a stone.

Prayer for Success (Sun God/dess – Lugh/Freyr/Ra/Sol or Sol/Sunna)

Go find a sunny playground, or a place where you can stand in the sun and where there is either pavement, concrete or sand you can draw on. Take something you can make a mark with – chalk, salt, a stick to make shapes in the sand or soil.

Slowly draw the picture of the sun, and place your name, or initials within it, and some symbol of your project or desire for success. Once completed, walk around it 12 times, imagining the sun's light and warmth bringing success to your endeavour.

Leave it and do not return.

Prayer for Inspiration (Air)

Go and find a set of swings. Swing on them for as long as you can, and as you swing focus on your breath. Allow your mind to be lifted with ideas, and thoughts. I often used to do this whilst listening to my favourite music on my headphones, but singing is also great whilst swinging. Whether you like it or not, this is a fantastic way to unlock your inspiration and be in air!

As you may have guessed from some of the examples given above, it also helps if we consider prayer not as verbal or word bound, but as dance, song, a garden or a flower arrangement, a playground exploration.

If calling up the Gods or elements is hard, then try praying to your ancestors. We honour our ancestors every Samhain, but can in fact use their love and wisdom to guide us throughout the year! A prayer to a granny, or a dead pet, or simply to our beloved ancestors connects children to a sense of their family, their place and their own inherited knowledge.

Prayer to the Ancestors

Say: *"To my* [insert details of ancestor] *who once breathed the air I breathe, who once walked the earth as I walk, who once felt love and sorrow as I do, I ask for your guidance now as I* [insert details of what you need guidance for]. *I am your daughter/son, I am your kin and walk in your memory. Your blood runs in my blood. I remember and honour your life. Blessed Be."*

If you are a deist or your child is very drawn to a pantheon or the Goddesses then craft prayers that directly petition that deity. This gives you an opportunity to really consider the powers associated with the Gods/Goddesses dear to you, and enables your kids to embody a personal relationship with the energy s/he radiates. If, however, you want to call in general terms for the God and Goddess, you can use a more generic form of address such as Lord and Lady, or Mother and Father, or Mother Earth or Wise One.

Invocation to Pan (Great for Rambunctious Small Kids!)

Go out and howl at the sky, run wild around the garden or park. When you are completely out of breath, lie down on the ground and call Pan's name three times. In very simple words, if you have to use any at all, ask for his blessing!

Prayer to Aphrodite (Adaptation/Ruination of Sappho's The Hymn to Aphrodite)

Say: *"Immortal Aphrodite, beautiful daughter of Zeus, weaver of wiles, I pray thee don't break my spirit with anguish and distress, O Queen, but come. If ever you listened and heard my voice, if ever you left your father's golden house and made the fair fleet sparrows flap their fast wings around the dark earth, from heaven through mid sky to help me, come again now! If ever you asked me 'What beauty do you need? Who wrongs you?' hear me again now. Come, I pray, now too, and release*

me from cruel cares and all that my heart desires to accomplish, come,
be my ally."

...Are my rituals...

The structure of most Pagan celebrations and the general form created by which we touch the divine and honour the elements, the Gods and Goddesses and the turning cycles of the earth and the heavens, is the quartered circle. All of our rituals are conducted, in the main, in this sacred shape, enabling us to embody harmony and balance and recognise the eternal nature of all we do.

In encouraging kids to partake in ritual and perhaps create ritual for themselves we can start by familiarising them with this shape and its correspondences. In the North of the circle we honour earth, in the East, air, in the South is fire and water in the West. Above we welcome the Gods, and beneath our feet the soul of nature, Mother Earth.

We have already talked about casting circles and establishing children's relationship with energy work. Ritual is a set of actions that take place in a prescribed order with a degree of solemnity, either in purpose or tone, with a desired result. Ritual punctuates our every day. When we talk about spiritual rituals we are attempting to create symbolic order in our actions as a means of bringing ourselves to new modes of awareness.

Pagans love ritual, and we often have the most creative and joyous rituals. Being a relatively new spirituality that has had to recreate meaningful rituals from the shreds of the past, we approach ritual with a real knowledge of what it can bring to us, with an air of spontaneity. Here are the building blocks of Pagan rituals, which you can use to establish ritual form with your young folk:

- Sanctify a space: Cleanse/bless/consecrate a circle space. Often we use incense and salt water. Travel in an anti-clockwise direction (widdershins) if you are cleansing or ridding the place of negative energy, or travel in a clockwise (deosil) direction if you are imbuing the space with new energy.

- Cast the circle: Using the energy of dance, song, chant or visualisation, create an energetic circle around and about all those participating. Focus on the energy moving clockwise. You can use formal words or silence.

- Invite the energies you wish to be present: Usually this involves invoking the elements earth, air, fire and water, calling in the Gods and Goddess, and any other spirit, genius loci, fairies, ancestors etc. (Sometimes this part takes place before the circle is cast.)

- Statement of purpose: This is made to bond everyone's focus and to state intention in the "place between the worlds".

- Raise energy: This is done to bring the purpose about. Or conduct a ritual play in order to being our focus more deeply to the time at hand.

- Undo everything that has been done: Leave everything as you found it. Give thanks to all those present or "dismiss" them. Open the circle by moving or focus on the energy dissipating widdershins, and feast before departure.

These are the building blocks of ritual and you can apply them to every great sabbat or esbat celebration should you wish, although it's not necessary with young children to expose them to the nature of formal ritual until you feel they are ready for it and can sustain attention and interest. At times your children may not see or feel the order of ritual, but slowly they will recognise it takes on a rhythm of its own. What I want to outline are the types of ritual tailored to family life.

Ritual Play – Midsummer – The Death of the Oak King and the Rise of the Holly King

I have been a part of this ritual play since I was a teen growing in a pagan family. Now we do this with my own kids and join with another family. Close friends of ours loved to celebrate the solstice but had no tradition of their own so when we told them our tale of the Oak and Holly Kings we decided to create a ritual play based on those of my youth that we could all enjoy.

It begins with our boys and their dads dressing up and deciding whether they would be the old King Holly about to rise again to welcome and bring the waning half of the year or the new Oak King. Headbands with the respective tree leaves were worn and usually created with much hilarity. Dressing up and setting the scene is important and we would make sure a feast was prepared for afterwards full of summer fruits and a huge salad.

My friend's daughter would solemnly lead us in procession, telling us about Midsummer as we went – she was sometimes a Queen of Fairies, sometimes Mother Earth and sometimes both – you never know with five-year-olds. Sprinkling fairy dust as she went she led us to the place where the battle would commence.

Upon her command the boys and dads would battle most dramatically with sticks and swords, as the rest of us cheered. The Oak King fell, and we would all crouch round and honour his passing. The Holly King would then bow before the Queen of Summer to be blessed with her fairy dust and the balance of the world once more restored, we would go in to eat.

Requiem For a Loved Pet – Returning to Earth

The death of a pet in a family is a very sad and difficult time. To give them a solemn and heartfelt requiem is fitting to their status within our family. The gravitas of such a ritual expresses a lot to our kids about the nature of death and death rituals. Adapt if it is a school pet that has passed.

You need:

Clay and paints
Incense
A small potted rosemary plant

Wrap your pet's body tenderly in a blanket and choose a place to bury it (if you are having your pet cremated then adapt the rite to suit). When you are ready and able to, take a lump of clay and fashion it into a semblance of your beloved pet. Allow your hands to imbue the love and feelings you had towards this special animal. Each family member will make their own version, and no two will be alike. As you do this recall the times you spent and the relationship you had with this blessed beast.

Once these are complete, dried and decorated as you see fit, place the body of your beloved pet next to the site for their burial, gather in a circle around and take hands. Slowly let the circle form around you and quietly call in the elements and the other spirits or Gods you wish present. Light the incense.

Say: *"Blessed Earth Mother, we are here to bring to you the body of our precious* [insert name of pet]. *Their spirit has already returned to you, and we hope to see them in the earth's turning once again. Today though we are here to mourn and remember their beautiful earthy form and return it to you."*

Going round the circle, all present should each speak a memory or something that they hold dear to them about this pet. When you are ready, place the body of your pet into the earth and give everyone time to sit. Place the clay figures upon the body of the pet, and say any words of blessing: *"May your spirit return in the form of your choosing,"* or, *"We hope you are happily chasing butterflies in the Summerland."*

When everyone has had the chance to say goodbye, bury your beloved pet and plant the rosemary to mark the grave. *"We plant Rosemary for remembrance – you will always be in our hearts. So mote it be."*

All respond.

Add the name of your beloved pet to your Samhain beloved dead rollcall, to be read out next Samhain.

Rite of Passage – Leaving Home

(This is a ritual adapted from one given to me by a friend who used something similar with her son when he left to go to university.)

Your kid has turned the tide, and they are ready to leave home. Hopefully this is with your blessing under good circumstances, but however it happens, it can be really valuable to all the family to mark the occasion.

You will need a white candle in each room, something from when your child was very young – a baby blanket say – and something from their middle years, a school book or a drawing, and something representing their recent time at home.

Place a candle in a holder in each room in the house. Open all the doors in the house. Take your child's hands and lead them through each room, and in each room pause, light the candle saying, "*You travel now from us, into the world. Your path takes you from your family home. Carry us with you and may everything you have learnt here with us illuminate your journey.*"

When you finally reach the front door pause, take hands and embrace. Say: "*The door here is always open to you. You leave us but you are free to return.*"

Ask him/her to step over the threshold – and turn back to you where you show him/her the items from his/her past. Place them in his hands and both of you can recollect when they were made.

Say: "*These are pieces of your past here. I carry their memory and your history goes with you. Be blessed.*"

Close the door – even if it is only symbolically. Go into the house and if they want to come back, they should knock on the door and be welcomed by you.

Ritual for Honouring the Moon – Making Moon Flags.

Fly the flag for the beautiful moon, mother of the night, great inspiration for poets and singers, magicians and witches alike.

You will need:

Some plain calico cloth or other soft cotton squares. You can even use plain white dishcloths or tea towels.

A length of twine or yarn.

Fabric pens or, if you would rather, paints and decorations.

Make a sacred circle by sitting as a family, and start a gentle hum whilst holding hands. Welcome all the elements, ancestors and Gods/Goddesses you wish to have present, and particularly the lady of the moon.

Chant together, *"Mother Moon shine down on me, I am you and you are me, and we are part of everything, we are part of everything."*

Each person should choose which moon phase they wish to represent – New/First crescent, Full, Dark, Waxing or Waning. If you have a smaller family or fewer people doing this then you may choose more than one. Going round everybody present, embody the moon phase you represent. *"I am the full moon, round and bright, I help sailors through the night,"* or, *"I am the waxing moon, watch me grow, from the first sliver of light like Artemis' bow to the gibbous moon with my beautiful glow."*

Now everybody should make their flag. Decorate the moon with signs, symbols words, drawings, anything that you are inspired by, and then attach them to your yarn with glue. In this way they resemble Tibetan prayer flags or bunting. Open the circle and take your moon flags outside, attach them to your home, or hang them from a tree in your garden under the moon's light.

Let them flutter outside for a complete lunar phase. Watch as they wave in the breeze and let the weather change them. When a full 28-day moon cycle has past, bring them in and use them again at family celebrations where you need the moon's qualities of light and beauty, or you need the energy of a specific phase.

You can expand this project by talking about the flags we have

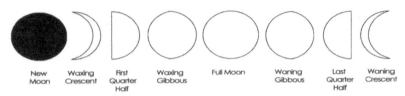

| New Moon | Waxing Crescent | First Quarter Half | Waxing Gibbous | Full Moon | Waning Gibbous | Last Quarter Half | Waning Crescent |

put on the moon, or finding the flags of nation states that have a moon shape upon them…

The Moon's Phases

Like all of Pagan spirituality, ritual should respond to a real need. At its best it is born of a creative impulse to make a change. Ritual should never be staid or dull, without energy. This is one reason why children can make wonderful partners in Pagan spiritual practice, as they can bring an authentic wild energy and openness to the energy of ritual.

I will finish by telling you about a Summer Solstice ritual I did with my family a couple of years ago. In the back garden of our apartment, the four of us stood. We had laid out the four directions and in each quarter placed an elemental representative chosen by my boys. We gathered together for a simple acknowledgement and honouring of the solstice energy – a thanks to the Sun. Boo, took my hand as Summer started the circle chant. Suddenly he let out a gasp: "MUM! DAD! I just saw a fairy. REALLY I did. A spark from the candle went right up – and it was a – what's it called?"

"A Sprite!" his brother yelled, jumping with excitement at the thought.

"It was right there!"

We all stopped to see if another sprite emerged from the candle, and when it didn't Boo said quietly to himself: "It was taking our thanks to the Sun. Only I saw him."

Some years on, this ritual has solidified in his mind and it is why, despite being the most boyish boy you will ever know, he is adamant that fairies do exist. "I saw one, at the Solstice," he tells his cool kid friends. And again, we feel lifted by the knowledge that he will remember this moment of enchantment seen with his own eyes, framed by the ritual for Litha in our back garden.

I wish for you many moments when the children you know and care for experience the divine in nature through their own lived experience of it. Whether it is in ritual or play let yourself be lifted by need and the spirit of gratitude and blessings will find you. And remember, there is no end to the circle, no end...

Spirit Activities

Write a prayer or blessing

Practise circle casting

Make a dowsing pendulum and use it

Listen to the earth

Sit in silence and breath...

Create your own Zener cards

Sing to the moon

Dress a candle with oil

Walk in a forest

Bake bread

Incant to the Goddess

Learn a spiral dance

Further Reading

These are a few of the books that inspired my own thinking, and the titles I have referred to throughout this book. Many of these authors have written other excellent titles and I hope that each one opens a doorway to a myriad of other resources.

Paganism and Related Titles

Aburrow, Yvonne. *Many Names*. lulu.com, 2012. (A book of prayers written from a pagan perspective.)

Adler, Margot. *Drawing Down the Moon: Witches, Druids, Goddess-Worshippers, and Other Pagans in America*. USA: Penguin Books Revised edition, 2006.

Ceanadach, Siusaidh. *Let's Talk about Pagan Festivals*. New Arlesford: Moon Books, 2012. (A great workbook for Pagans with young children.)

Crowley, Vivianne. *Wicca: The Old Religion in the New Age*. Aquarian Press, 1989.

Farrar, Janet and Stewart. *Spells and How They Work*. Washington: Phoenix Publishing, 1990.

Greywolf. *The Sign of the Rose*. Audio CD. A CD of songs, spells and incantations from BDO Chief Phillip Shallcrass. From www.druidry.co.uk.

Harrow, Judy. *Spiritual Mentoring: A Pagan Guide*. ECW Press, 2002.

Hutton, Ronald. *The Triumph of the Moon: A History of Modern Pagan Witchcraft* Oxford: Oxford Paperbacks, 1995.

Jackson, Ellen. *The Winter Solstice*. Minneapolis: Millbrook Press Reprint edition, 1997.

Jackson, Ellen. *The Summer Solstice*. Minneapolis: Millbrook Press, 2001.

Jackson, Ellen. *The Spring Equinox: Celebrating the Greening of the Earth*. Minneapolis: Millbrook Press, 2003.

Johnson, Cait and Shaw, Maura. *Celebrating the Great Mother: A Handbook of Earth-Honoring Activities for Parents and Children.* Vermont: Destiny Books: 1995.

Kindred, Glennie. *Sacred Celebrations: A Sourcebook.* Glastonbury: Gothic Image, 2001.

Kindred, Glennie. *Earth Wisdom: A Heartwarming Mixture of the Spiritual, the Practical and the Provocative.* London: Hay House UK; Reprint edition, 2011.

Leek, Sybil. *The Complete Art of Witchcraft.* New York: New American Library, Reissue Edition, 1991.

Madden, Kristin. *Pagan Parenting: Spiritual Magical and Emotional Development of the Child.* St Paul: Llewellyn Publications, U.S., 2000.

Restall Orr, Emma. *Living Druidry: Magical Spirituality for the Wild Soul.* Piatkus, 2004.

Restall Orr, Emma. *Living with Honour: A Pagan Ethics.* O Books, 2008.

Shan. *Circlework: A DIY Handbook of Practical Ritual.* House of the Goddess Publications, 1994. (This is currently out of print, so if you find a copy treasure it!)

Starhawk. *The Pagan Book of Living and Dying: Practical Rituals, Prayers, Blessings and Meditations on Crossing Over.* San Francisco: Harper San Francisco, 1998.

Starhawk. *Dreaming the Dark: Magic, Sex and Politics.* Boston: Beacon Press, 1993.

Starhawk, Baker, Diane and Hill, Anne. *Circle Round: Raising Children in Goddess Traditions.* New York: Bantam Books, Reprint edition, 2000.

Valiente, Doreen. *An ABC of Witchcraft Past and Present.* London: Robert Hale, 1994.

Valiente, Doreen. *Charge of the Goddess: The Mother of Modern Witchcraft.* Hexagon Publications, UK, 2000.

Spiritual Development

Carson, Anne. ed. *Spiritual Parenting in the New Age*. Crossing Press, U.S., 1989.

Cles, Robert. *The Spiritual Life of Children*. Boston: Houghton Mifflin, 1990.

Cunningham, Scott. *The Complete Book of Incenses Oils and Brews*. St Pauls: Llewellyn Publications, 2nd Edition 1989.

Fincham, Johnny. *The Spellbinding Power of Palmistry*. Green Magic Press, 2005.

Harrison, Calesta. *Earth Mother Yoga: Reclaiming out Feminine Divinity through Mind Body and Spirit*. Lulu.com, 2012.

Heller, David, *Talking to Your Child About God: A Book for Families of all Faiths*. US: Bantam Books, 1988.

Jennings, Pete and Sawyer, Pete. *Pathworking*. Somerset: Capall Bann Publishing, 1993.

Marks, Kate. *Circle of Songs: Songs, Chants and Dances for Ritual and Celebration*. Full Circle Press, US. 1994.

Napthali, Sarah. *Buddhism for Mothers: A Calm Approach to Caring for Yourself and Your Children*. Sydney: Allen and Unwin, 2011.

Napthali, Sarah. *Buddhism for Mothers of School Children*. London: Orion, 2009.

Prana Chants Prana, c/o Faith, Brithdir Mawr, Newport, Pembs, SA42 0QJ, UK. (Prana Chants has some great recordings as well as this lovely booklet of chants.)

Rinpoche, Sogyal. *The Tibetan Books of Living and Dying: A Spiritual Classic from One of the Foremost Interpreters of Tibetan Buddhism to the West*. Surrey: Rider Press, 2008.

Sinetar, Marsha, *Spiritual Intelligence: What we can learn from the early awakening child*, New York: Orbis Books, 2000.

Soule, Amanda Blake with Stephen Soule, *The Rhythm of Family: Discovering a Sense of Wonders Through the Seasons*. Trumpeter Books, 2011. Amanda's blog soulemama.typepad.com is also a great resource for everyday activities for earth- focused families.

Education and Child Development

Armstrong, Alison and Casement, Charles. *The Child and the Machine: How Computers Put our Children's Education at Risk.* Brighton: Roundhouse Publishing Ltd, 2000.

Bandura, Albert. *Social Learning Theory.* New Jersey: Prentice Hall, 1977.

Etherington, Natasha. *Gardening for Children with Autism Spectrum Disorders and Special Educational Needs.* Jessica Kingsley Publishers, 2012.

Holt, John. *Learning all the Time.* Cambridge, MA: DeCapo Press, 1990.

Holt, John. *How Children Learn.* London: Penguin Press, 1991.

Hughes, Fergus P. *Children, Play and Development.* Sage Publications, 4th Edition, 2009.

Linn, Susan. *The Case for Make Believe.* New York: The New Press, 2009.

Louv, Richard. *Last Child in the Woods: Saving our Children from Nature Deficit Disorder.* London: Atlantic Books, 2010.

Louv, Richard. *The Nature Principle.* New York: Algonquin Books, 2012.

Montessori, Maria. *The Secret of Childhood.* New York: Ballantine Books, 1982.

Montessori, Maria. *The Discovery of the Child.* New York: Ballantine Books, 1994.

Montessori, Maria. *The Absorbent Mind.* New York: Holt Paperbacks; Reprint edition 1995.

Panksepp, J. "Can Play Diminish ADHD and Facilitate the Construction of the Social Brain". In *Current Directions in Psychological Science.* 7, 91-98, 1999.

Robinson, Ken. *Out of Our Minds: Learning to be Creative.* Chichester UK: Capstone Press, 2011.

Rodman, Robert and Winnicott, D.W. *Playing and Reality.* London: Routledge, 2nd Edition, 2005.

Sutton-Smith, Brian. *The Ambiguity of Play.* Harvard University

Press, 2001.

Winnicott, D.W. *The Family and Individual Development*. London: Routledge New Edition, 2006.

Child Raising/Parenting

Biddulph, Steve. *Raising Boys: Why Boys are Different and How to Help Them Become Happy and Well Balanced Men*. Harper Thorsons, 2010.

Biddulph, Steve. *Raising Girls: Helping your Daughter to Grow Up Wise, Warm and Strong*. Harper, 2013.

England, Pam and Horowitz, Rob. *Birthing From Within*. London: Souvenir Press Ltd; Rev Ed edition, 2007.

England, Pam. *Labyrinth of Birth: Creating a Map, Meditations and Rituals for Your Childbearing Year*. Birthing from Within Books, 2010.

Gaskin, Ina May. *Ina May's Guide to Childbirth*. Vermillion Books, 2008.

Hayes, Shannon. *Radical Homemakers: Reclaiming Domesticity from a Consumer Culture*. USA: Left to Write Press, 2010.

Howard, Judy. *Growing up with Bach Flower Remedies*. C.W. Daniel Co., 1994.

Jarvis, Pam. "Rough and Tumble Play: Lessons in Life", *Evolutional Psychology*, 4, 330-346. http://www.epjournal.net/wp-content/uploads/ep043303462.pdf.

Kabat-Zinn, Myla and Jon. *Everyday Blessings: The Inner Work of Mindful Parenting*. New York: Hyperion, 2008. (A great book on Zen parenting).

Mongan, Marie. *Hypnobirthing: The Mongan Method: A Natural Approach to a Safe, Easier, More Comfortable Birthing*. Florida: Health Communications, 2008.

Murray, Lorraine. *Calm Kids: Help Children Relax with Mindful Activities*. Edinburgh: Floris Books, 2012.

Odent, Michel. *Birth Reborn: What Childbirth Should Be*. Souvenir Press Ltd, New edition, 1994.

Palmer, Sue. *Toxic Childhood: How the Modern World is Damaging our Children and What We Can Do About It.* London: Orion Press, 2007.

Palmer, Sue. *Detoxing Childhood: What Parents Need to Know to Raise Bright, Balanced Children.* London: Orion Press, 2008.

Satter, Ellyn. *Child of Mine, Feeding with Love and Good Sense.* Bull Publishing Company, 2001. (The best book around on food and feeding issues with babies and children.)

Tisserand, Maggie. *Aromatherapy for Women: A Practical Guide to Essential Oils for Health and Beauty.* Healing Arts Press, Revised Edition, 1996.

Uvnas Moberg, Kerstin forward by Odent, Michel. *The Oxytocin Factor: Tapping the Hormone of Calm, Love and Healing.* London: Pinter & Martin Ltd.; 2nd edition, 2011.

Weed, Susan. *Wisewoman Herbal for the Childbearing Year.* Georgia: New Leaf Distribution Company, 1986.

Useful Organisations

Hejohnston.com – My own blog with musings on music magic and raising kids.

wildhunt.org. – An intelligent and informative news/issues blog on Pagan related issues founded by Jason Pitzl-Waters.

The Pagan Federation is UK's oldest Pagan organisation, promoting awareness and acceptance of Paganism across the UK and Europe. paganfed.org

www.paganpride.org.uk – Raising awareness and acceptance for British Pagans.

The Witches Voice is the oldest online news and networking site for Pagan folk across the US. www.witchvox.

British Druid Order – www.druidry.co.uk. Rekindling the sacred fires of Druidry as a living, breathing, Earth-honouring, life-affirming spirituality for the 21st century.

The Druid Network – druidnetwork.org – aims to inform, inspire and facilitate Druidry as a religion.

Patheos.com – Patheos is a blog gateway covering a spectrum of spiritual religious discussion. Have a look at www.patheos .com/blogs/paganfamilies

http://www.paganparenting.com is an online support and resource for Pagan parents in the US.

The Police Pagan Association, policepaganassociation.org is a UK-based organisation supporting Pagan officers and forging links between the police force and the Pagan community.

www.ukpagancouncil.org. The UK Pagan Council is a free membership organisation promoting support and information sharing within the Broad UK Pagan community.

There are few Pagan Homeschool resource sites in the UK but numerous US-based sites. See http://groups.yahoo.com/neo /groups/Paganhomeschool/info.

For inspiring "Pagan Mum" blogs see Lily Shahar Kunning's in Ohio USA for lots of great ideas and laughter. parentingbythe-lightofthemoon.blogspot.co.uk. Another good one is by American witch and mom Joni Rae. http://jonirae.com

For organisations that support women's birth choices see the National Childbirth Trust www.nct.org.uk and Birthing Without Fear – birthingwithoutfearblog.com

paulgarrigan.com – A personal blog on spirituality and addiction recovery.

Norwich Chant Collective – A resource for Pagan chants. See https://www.facebook.com/pages/Norwich-Chant-Collective-with-Gina-Dunn

Society of Elder Faiths – elderfaiths.org is incorporated as a church in the USA. This group sponsors open and friendly sabbat festivals that are family-friendly and classes for teen and tweens on Paganism.

liferites.org.uk – providing resources help and practical assistance for rites of passage.

reclaiming.org – founded by witch and activist Starhawk, Reclaiming is a global community of people working to unify spirit and politics through magic and activism.

www.Pantheism.net is a site detailing the pantheist world view. Useful for anyone seeking more information on living a spiritual life without deity.

youngminds.org.uk – an excellent resource, a charity that looks to help young people in Britain with emotional and mental health challenges. Use research to help influence policy and practices in Britain.

The National Association of Standing Advisory councils on Religious Education in the UK has local SACRE groups, which include members from recognised faiths. Get involved in yours. http://www.nasacre.org.uk

The Bumblebee conservation trust – bumblebeeconseration.org.

Woodcraft Folk, http://woodcraft.org.uk, is a progressive educational movement dedicated to bringing young people into better community each other, society with nature. There are groups all across the UK and if they aren't near you, then you can start one!

British Red Cross – www.redcross.org.uk – has some great information for preparing for emergencies and disasters.

The Royal Society for the Prevention of Accidents, www.rospa.com, has important home safety information. Also see www.homesafetygame.com for how to ensure your home is safe.

If you are in the US www.ready.gov has all the information you need to make a disaster preparedness plan for any eventuality.

http://outsidemom.com – a nice blog written by an environmental educator and parent on survivalist techniques for kids, and the joys of being outside.

MOON
BOOKS

Moon Books invites you to begin or deepen your encounter with Paganism, in all its rich, creative, flourishing forms.